facades

beauty . utility . performance

ORO Editions
Publishers of Architecture, Art, and Design
Gordon Goff: Publisher

www.oroeditions.com
info@oroeditions.com

Published by ORO Editions

FOLLOW ONLINE
smithgill.com
smithgill.blog
Facebook @smithgillarch
Instagram @asggarch
Twitter @smithgillarch

10 9 8 7 6 5 4 3 2 1 First Edition

ISBN: 978-1-954081-38-3

Color Separations and Printing: ORO Group Inc.
Printed in China

ORO Editions makes a continuous effort to minimize the overall carbon footprint of its publications. As part of this goal, ORO Editions, in association with Global ReLeaf, arranges to plant trees to replace those used in the manufacturing of the paper produced for its books. Global ReLeaf is an international campaign run by American Forests, one of the world's oldest nonprofit conservation organizations. Global ReLeaf is American Forests' education and action program that helps individuals, organizations, agencies, and corporations improve the local and global environment by planting and caring for trees.

contents

introduction

Facades: Beauty Utility Performance illustrates the depth and breadth of the many innovative exterior wall facades that were designed from 2007-2020 at Adrian Smith + Gordon Gill Architecture (AS+GG).

The featured projects, both built and unbuilt, are explored through photographs, renderings, model images, detail drawings, narratives, and illustrations. Each project addresses a series of environmental concerns, offering site-specific, performative solutions and innovative techniques that harvest resources and maximize efficiencies.

Performance is at the core of what we do at AS+GG. We approach design problems systematically and seek to provide our clients with buildings that are both beautiful and high performing. Our buildings are designed to become an intrinsic part of their community with facades that work as interactive systems, symbiotically with the local environment. When we explore free and available natural resources to generate power, capture daylight, or harness wind, the architectural response to these concepts can manifest in many ways, expressing the design in different aesthetic compositions with a similar purpose.

We approach facade design as an opportunity to solve specific problems, therefore we are forced to think outside the box to design systems that serve multiple functions. With increasingly stringent energy codes, and the need to protect our natural resources, standard glass walls systems do not provide effective solutions to meet these new goals.

Our facade designs are holistic, effective systems that can increase thermal performance and visual interest by incorporating new layers and materials. The exterior walls that we design impact the user's relationship to the building and, in special cases, provide users with the opportunity to see or participate in how the building is responding to the environment. This is the basis of our approach; we find solutions driven by performance and transform their basic expression into envelopes that are beautiful, functional, and unique.

methodology

The performance of a building can be improved through the integration of intelligent systems into their facade. These attributes are accompanied by the below symbols throughout the book to highlight the concepts where they are applied.

Solar Control

Ventilated

Intelligent

Daylight

Wind Power

Luminous

Solar Power

Thermal Mass

Modular

Solar Control

Facades that control interior or exterior direct sunlight through geometry. Solar control is a proven strategy that regulates the internal temperature of a space. Appropriate design can help keep spaces cool in the summer and warm in the winter. To employ this design technique the designer must understand the sun's trajectory and local climate conditions. This data informs designers of the sun's movement throughout the year and predicts the amount of radiant energy control to improve occupant comfort. One of the main goals of solar control is to optimize head gain or heat loss in the building without compromising access to natural light.

Daylight

Daylight specific facades use the sun as their most important resource to capture light. Adequate levels of light are required to complete daily tasks efficiently and safely. Although we have access to artificial forms of light, extending useful daylight hours through design provides a free alternative for lighting. Daylight helps us reduce our dependence on electric lights, improves the quality and even distribution of light into a space, and enhances the connection of the building users to the exterior environment. Facades that increase daylight typically are designed to bring light further into the space, while simultaneously reducing glare. Daylight modeling is used through computer software to test the designs and optimize the impact of daylighting strategies in the interior environment.

Solar Power

Facades that utilize solar harnessing technologies, such as photovoltaic panels, to generate electricity for buildings. A tower's small footprint may prohibit the inclusion of solar panels on the roof but the large vertical planes that form the exterior wall are an opportunity, where appropriate, to harness the sun's energy. The facade integration of photovoltaic panels takes advantage of otherwise underutilized areas of the building, such as light shelves or spandrel panels, and provides pedestrians a glimpse of how the building works. Software is available to evaluate how much sunlight a specific surface can efficiently harness based on geographic location, proximity to other buildings, and angle of the facade. We use these tools to help optimize yield when integrating PV panels by understanding the levels of incident radiation of the proposed locations and testing parametric iterations to find optimal solutions.

Thermal Mass

Thermal mass uses building elements to absorb, store, and release heat energy as temperatures fluctuate. Specific materials, such as stone, ceramic tile, and concrete, are excellent at this and therefore are considered to have high thermal mass. This strategy can be used effectively in places with high temperature fluctuations throughout the day. Thermal mass is used in exterior walls, roofs, floors, and interior walls, where the sunlight can be absorbed easily by direct contact throughout the day. The heat is then released back into the space at night when temperatures drops, helping maintain a comfortable interior environment. In heat intensive climates, high thermal mass surfaces can absorb heat during the day and prevent it from entering the conditioned space. At night, this heat is radiated back into the atmosphere, maintaining a comfortable interior microclimate.

Ventilated

Facades that incorporate operable components to introduce natural ventilation into the space. Natural ventilation, when unsupervised, can have adverse impacts in a building including affecting interior temperatures against desired setpoints, negatively affecting humidity levels, introducing poor air quality in locations where smog is present, and triggering unwanted stack effect issues in tall buildings. Therefore, integrated strategies for natural ventilation in tall buildings are typically automated and connected to the building management systems. This guarantees that the introduction of outside air is helping, not harming, the interior air quality of a space. Positive impacts of introducing fresh air into a building include the reduction of dependency in HVAC systems when the outdoor temperature is comfortable and the elimination of odors and improved air quality provided by constant airflow. When designing an exterior wall the air coming into a building and how we use building facades to channel the wind direction to generate energy and shed ice and snow, must be analyzed.

Wind Power

Facades that harness wind power into electricity through building integrated wind turbines. Wind is a readily available, natural resource. However, for wind power to be successful, the turbines need to be strategically placed and the building geometry must be designed to direct the wind and increase its velocity to activate the turbines. The study of Computational Fluid Dynamics (CFD) is a useful tool to understand how wind behaves around a building and how wind yield from can be maximized through design. Wind flow around or through buildings can also be used to create negative pressures to ventilate, or exhaust, interior spaces.

Intelligent

Facades that are designed to be modified through communications with a BMS. These facades can change their base responses to react to changing weather or other predefined forms of stimulations. Through the integration of sensors around the building, the BMS analyzes current conditions and adjusts its facade to achieve maximum efficiency of the building's systems. Examples of this include measuring radiant heat/glare and controlling shades accordingly; measuring air temperature, speed, and humidity levels to control natural ventilation openings; measuring light levels and dimming electric light, while maintaining a desired luminance in a space; and measuring occupancy in a space to determine HVAC and light levels. Another form of intelligent response is the programming of facade elements to respond to building occupants in an interactive way for information or entertainment purposes.

Luminous

Facades that incorporate light or projection fixtures as an integral part of their design. Luminous facades are dynamic, providing interest and can be programmed to respond to exterior conditions, programmatic concerns, or interactions with users. Luminaires add a level of variability that cannot be obtained from more conventional materials and include facades that change color, convey messages, and perform as glowing beacons at night.

Modular

Facades with complex geometries that can simplify the number of different panels or parts in the system. Modular facades can refine concepts into constructible modules that minimize the number of unique pieces. In other cases, large open spans optimize the building's structure, maintain safety standards, and increase flexibility. Computational tools are used in the initial design intent to simplify a building's geometries. This aids in resource conservation, and in constructability, which can affect construction time, cost, and the embodied carbon of a building.

case studies

01 ACTIVE FACADE

Project: FKI Headquarters Competition

Location: Seoul, The Republic of Korea

Climate Zone: DWA - Continental, Dry Winter, Hot Summer

Program: Office

Status: Concept

Client: Federation of Korean Industries

Date: 2009

Strategies: Solar Control, Daylight, Solar Power, Ventilated, Intelligent, Luminous

AS+GG was invited to a competition to design the new Federation of Korean Industries Headquarters in Seoul, Korea in 2009. The entered scheme features a double-skin wall that is high-performing and adds interest to the rectangle form that was required by the competition brief. The facade responds to the local climate and functional needs of a modern, energy-efficient office tower.

The inner wall consists of insulated Low-E glass units set within an aluminum mullion system and a stainless-steel spandrel area. The inner wall houses the integrated Building Maintenance Unit (BMU) track, which responds to exterior facade preservation activities like window washing, panel replacement, and panel repair. Automated sunshades are also contained within the cavity of the double wall.

The outer layer of the facade is laminated, tempered low-iron vision glass that is point supported on a stainless-steel system with integrated LED lights and 20mm tension support rods. This 800mm span establishes space for maintenance workers, while improving air circulation, by creating a "thermos effect," which preheats air in the winter and blocks or expels hot air in the summer. The columns and spandrel panels are clad with a stainless-steel insulated panel designed to minimize temperature loss during the winter season. As a result, the heating systems have a smaller energy footprint and a lower the capacity cost for a building of a comparable size. Studies show that the temperature differential in the cavity creates enough natural connections that the cavity can ventilate itself and create a balanced thermal envelope.

The design of the exterior wall prioritizes natural light and dramatic views by making them accessible from most workstations. The double wall features light shelves that help direct sunlight into the interior of the tower, brightening interior spaces throughout the daytime. As a result, interior electrical light can be dimmed in accordance with available light levels.

Photovoltaic panels are located on the roof and are integrated into the light shelves on all floors, further improving the performance of the building. Solar analysis calculates that the panels, along with favorable feed-in tariffs in Seoul, may allow for an over 50% operational energy cost reduction.

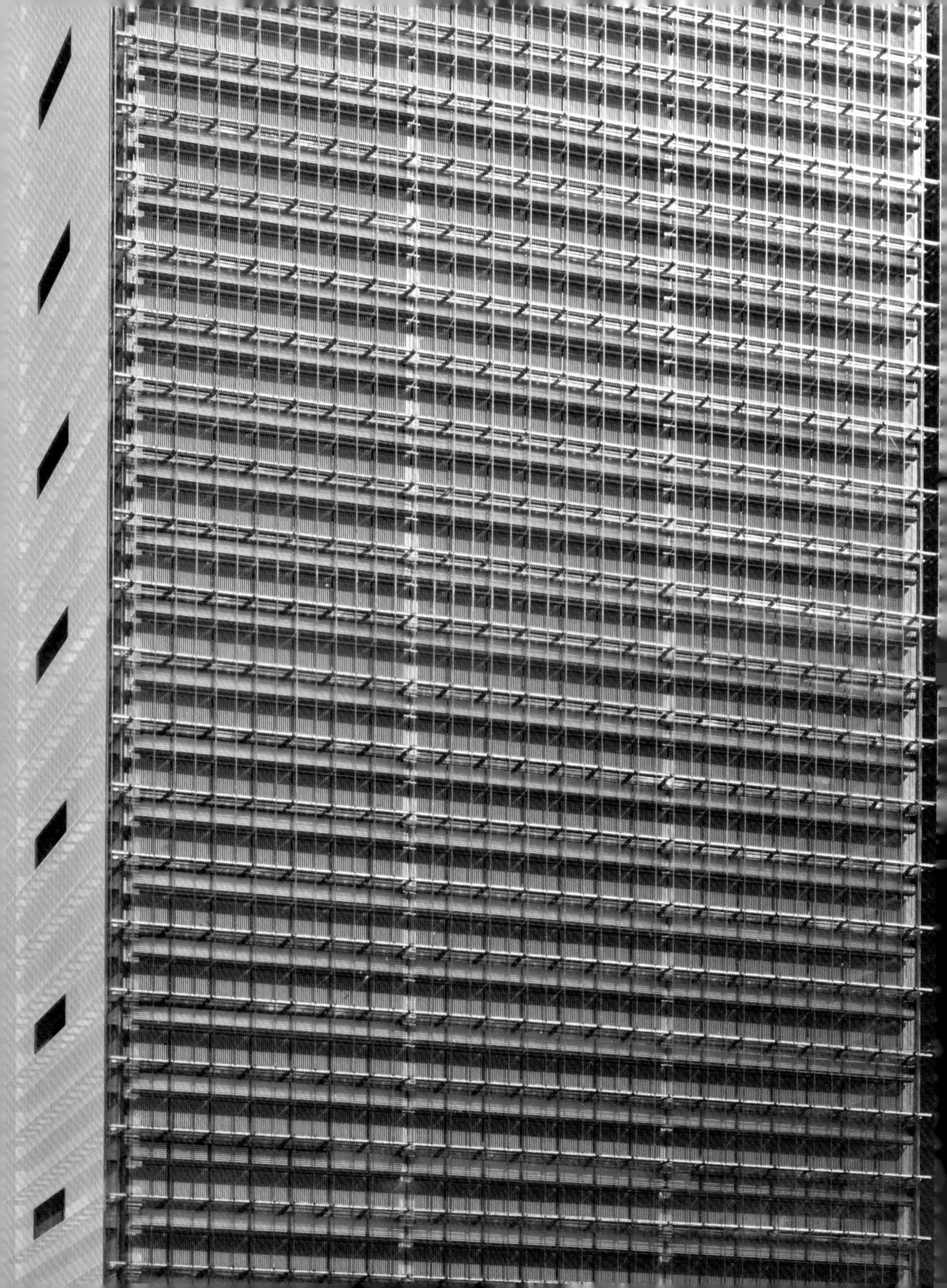

Double Skin Facade Daylighting Concept

Increasing daylighting can lead to operational energy savings that exceed 20%, as well as increased productivity and tenant satisfaction. An open plan interior layout is an efficient solution to the deep-lease spans necessary for a high-efficiency floor layout. This type of configuration receives natural daylight that is sufficient to offset artificial lighting, which is further increased when vision glazing with a higher visible transmittance is combined with cavity integrated operable shading and a light redirecting shelf.

BIPV

BIPV (Building Integrated Photo Voltaic) panels are made from laminated tempered glass that is embedded with monocrystalline silicon cells. Seoul's feed-in tariffs for renewable energy generation are more than seven-times the wholesale cost of electricity, therefore adding sustainable technologies, like the BIPV, is highly economical. In the FKI Headquarters competition design, the light shelves already redirect light, thereby serving as a logical location for photovoltaic integration.

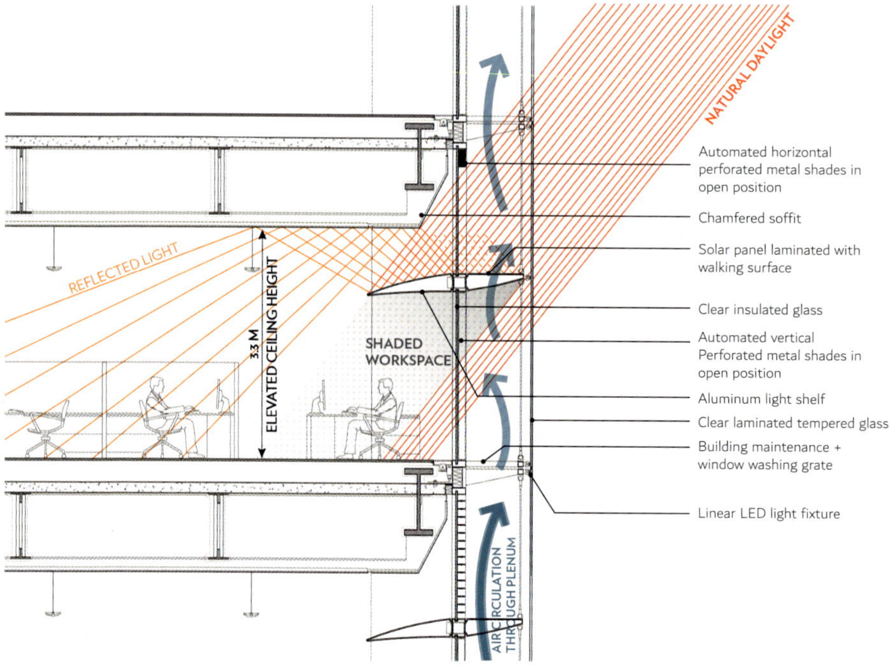

SOLAR CONTROL CONCEPT - HIGH SUN

FACADE CONCEPT RENDERING

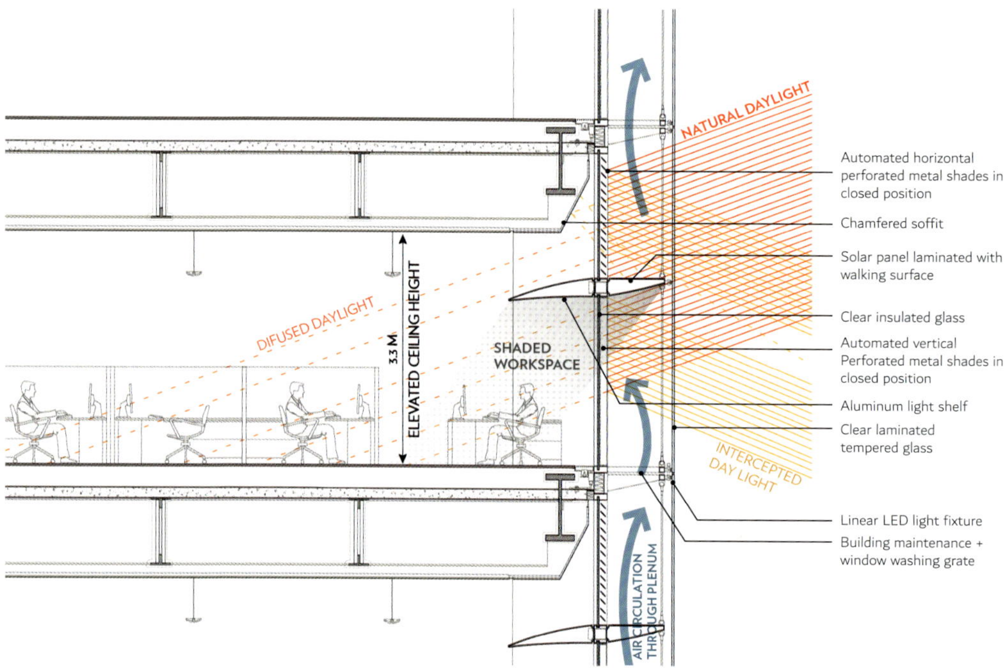

SOLAR CONTROL CONCEPT - LOW SUN

Double Skin Facade Thermal Concept

During winter operation, solar energy is collected within the cavity on the southern facing facades over a three-floor height, or alternately floor-by-floor. What could possibly translate into a cooling load for the internal office space is instead converted into a resource by moving this air to the cooler north side of the building. The result is a neutralization of temperatures across the building surface and dramatic reductions on conductive losses and perimeter heat requirements.

Similarly, during summer operation, solar energy is collected within the cavity and removed before it has an opportunity to enter the space, resulting in a cooling load. As the heat is no longer necessary on the northern sides of the building, a combination of the thermal buoyancy of the warmed air and winds incident on the building passively exhaust the heat to the outside.

Energy Savings

It is estimated that this high-performance facade will achieve an overall reduction in energy use of 17.5%. These reductions are mostly attributed to the double wall as a thermal barrier, compared to a conventional wall. Aside from reducing the load on equipment, other technologies are provided that contribute further to energy and cost savings. These include power generation using BIPVs (-5.5%), daylight harvesting (-12.5%), underfloor air distribution (-2%), and LED lighting (-3%). Adding these provisions contribute to a 40% savings over a conventional code-compliant building.

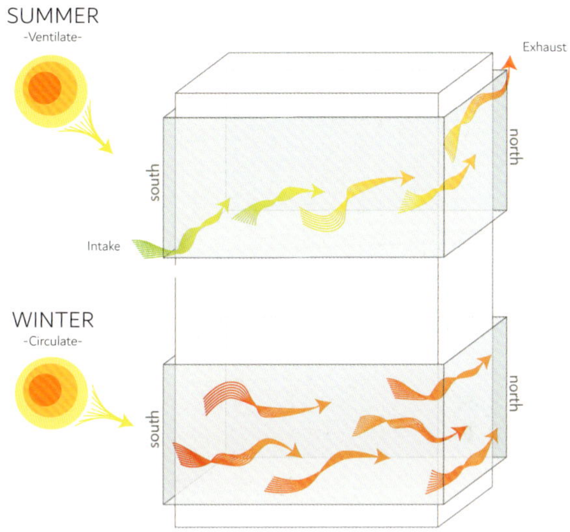

AIR FLOW WITHIN THE CAVITY

In the summer, the cavity is ventilated to prevent overheating. In the winter, direct heat gain warms the cavity air which circulates evenly due to natural buoyancy forces. In the winter, direct heat gain warms the cavity air which circulates evenly due to natural buoyancy forces.

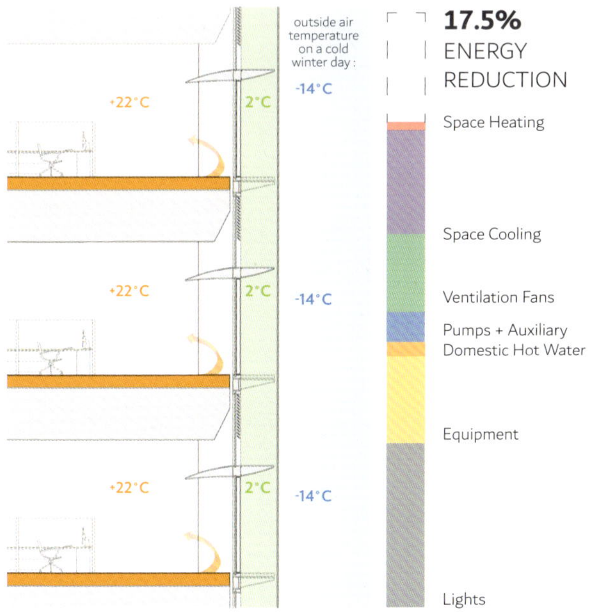

CONVENTIONAL SKIN VS. HIGH PERFORMANCE SKIN

Unlike the conventional single-skin facade, the double-skin facade acts as an insulating barrier to the outside air temperature, thus reducing the mechanical heat load and energy costs. In the summer, the cavity is ventilated to prevent overheating.

FACADE CAVITY CONCEPT RENDERING

02 LUMINOUS FACADE

Project:	Energy Hall
Location:	Nur-Sultan, Kazakhstan
Climate Zone:	DFB - Continental, Without Dry Season, Warm Summer
Program:	Cultural
Status:	Built
Client:	Expo2017
Date:	2013-2017
Strategies:	Intelligent, Luminous, Modular

Energy Hall is one of 26 buildings AS+GG designed for the 2017 International Exposition in Nur-Sultan (formerly Astana), Kazakhstan. Located directly across from the Kazakhstan Pavilion sphere, the theater is at the heart of the exposition site. The design ambition was to create a cultural hub that remained active, regardless of its programming and daily movements. The 1000-seat auditorium is a "theater within a theater," contained behind two tiers of exterior wall. The first layer is floor-to-ceiling, clear glass walls that are part exterior facade and part interior facade, enclosing a pre-function lobby space. The form geometrically engages with the covered street roof that extends to the adjacent buildings, framing the arrival.

The exterior enclosure is a unitized thermally broken painted aluminum fixed window wall with vision panels of high-performance triple glazing and solid frit insulated glass spandrel panels. The window wall, which is oriented to the interior covered mall, has vision panels of high-performance double glazing and solid frit insulated glass spandrel panels. The roof is an insulated low-slope system designed have building integrated monocrystalline photovoltaic cell roof panels, although the panels were ultimately not included in the final structure.

The second layer, which contains the actual auditorium space, is a digitally programmable light wall that is visible from the outside promenade, helping the theater stand out among the other expo buildings. The multi-functional wall can act as a billboard for the theater, drawing interest from visitors that will anticipate a change in the skin. This "digital canvas" envelops the interior pre-function areas as an immersive experience, guiding visitors in up a flight of stairs to the balcony-level lobby. The first layer exterior glass wall wraps the canvas, protecting and revealing it, 24-hours a day.

Design Process

Several initial design concepts were analyzed including different configurations and installation methods, and various densities, sizes, and configurations. Early studies rotated the tiles in different directions and varied their densities to improve buildability and function.

Through analysis, a functional prototype was developed. Uniformity proved to be the best strategy to make the system most constructible and had the desired design effect on the wall. The final design features glass LED-lit cells that are double-sided and can be viewed from both the outer lobby and in the smaller inner lobbies.

A vertical mounting system forms an organizing grid that holds the necessary electrical components, along with a six-sided tile that is stretched for a greater horizontality than a typical hexagon and to reinforce the overall design and flow of the space. Once the design was determined, several mock-ups were tested to determine the most successful ways to mount the light tiles and how to program the lights to create different patterns and colors.

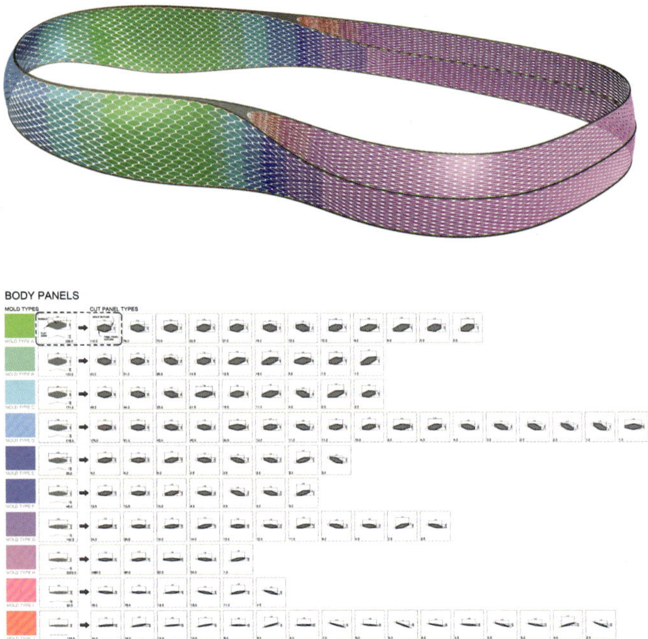

MOLD TYPES FOR PANEL MANUFACTURE

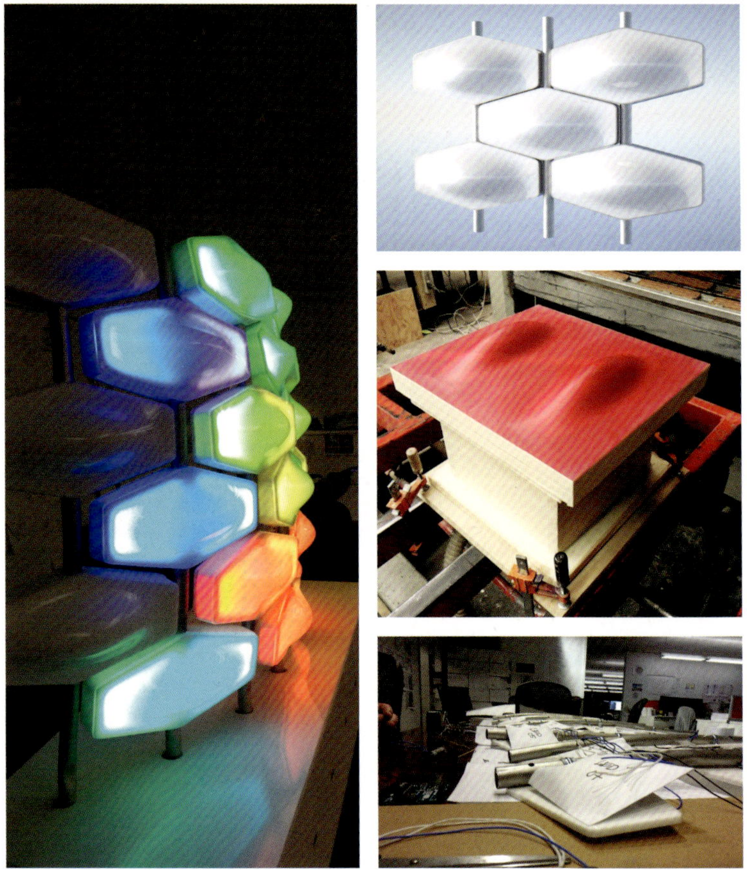

PANEL FABRICATION STUDIES

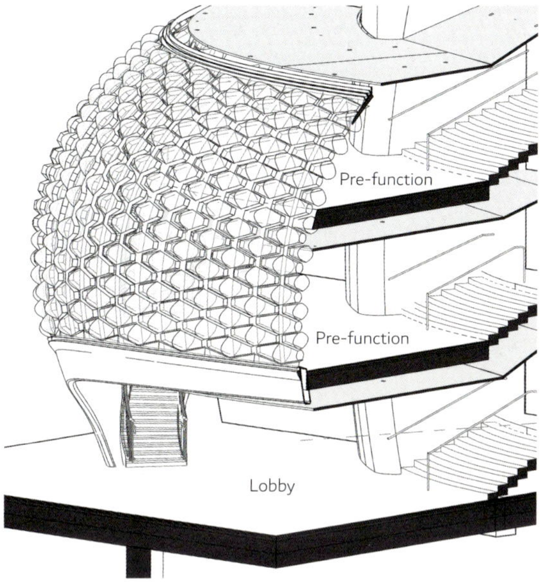

BIM MODEL

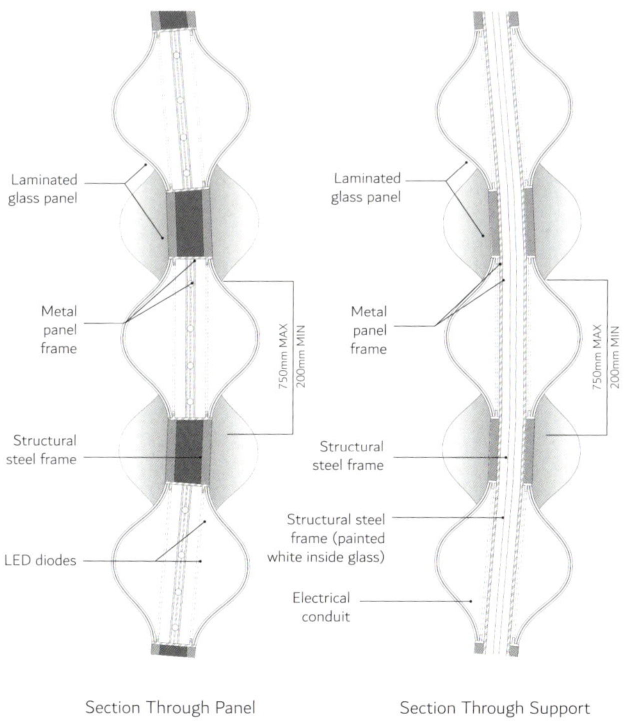

WALL DETAIL SECTIONS

GLASS LED-LIT CELLS

03 SHELL FACADE

Project:	KAPSARC Competition
Location:	Riyadh, Saudi Arabia
Climate Zone:	BWH - Arid, Desert, Hot
Program:	Mixed-Use
Status:	Concept
Client:	Saudi Aramco
Date:	2009
Strategies:	Solar Control, Daylight, Solar Power, Intelligent, Modular

AS+GG's KAPSARC (King Abdullah Petroleum Studies and Research Center) competition entry was designed to engage the intense climatic conditions of its desert setting. The form merges vernacular design strategies into sleek, cutting-edge architectural and engineering systems. The design approach seeks to apply and incorporate technology that achieves several goals including becoming a "net-generator" of energy and a carbon offset mechanism; maximizing occupant satisfaction, comfort, and air quality; promoting responsible water consumption; and committing to a low- to no-waste construction and operation.

The goals are achievable through a series of strategies including site orientation and selection of materials. As designed, the building generates more energy than it uses on an annual basis, making it a "positive energy" building. AS+GG investigated every aspect and element of the building's design to reveal opportunities to develop complementary solutions.

The dune-like shape maintains a predominantly north-south aspect ratio, allowing for enhanced control of daylight and views—an effect reinforced by the gentle inward slope of the southern facade. The building's form also acts as a protective canopy, drawing on building strategies that have been used in the region for centuries. Taking cues from regional, traditional Bedouin tents, the building's skin serves as a modern interpretation of the form by creating a shaded microclimate.

The building's skin, which uses a high-performance, lightweight polymer ethylene tetrafluoroethylene (ETFE), was designed to have high corrosion resistance and strength over a wide range of temperatures. The cladding is also designed to intelligently respond to solar radiation and wind. The lower floors engage the inward-sloping skin, so tenants will have access to direct views with minimal thermal penalty. The upper floors disengage from the skin, allowing for a climatic buffer and the integration of a photovoltaic energy field to enhance buoyancy-driven wind-flow.

ETFE System

KAPSARC's exterior "shell" is not just an iconic form that makes the facility instantly recognizable, it is also a purposely designed, highly sustainable positive-energy solution that applies several layers of technology to help it achieve its goals. The structure is an independent clear span consisting of prefabricated steel truss elements spaced at three meters on center. The outer layer is a series of prefabricated sunshades. These louvers utilize a Teflon coated translucent fabric, which is stretched over a lightweight stainless-steel frame and incorporates solar thermal or PV solar panels where feasible.

The inner layer is a pneumatic ethylene tetrafluoroethylene (ETFE) foil membrane system, which is a fluorine-based plastic that is typically used in the building industry to replace glass in appropriate applications. It is both transparent and lightweight and has effective thermal insulation properties, while maintaining its translucency. It is also self-cleaning and recyclable. Varying combinations of opacity were studied, including transparent, translucent, fritted, and Nanogel filled membranes that allow the modulation of natural daylight, thermal properties, and solar heat gain coefficients. The ETFE system can also be prefabricated and then erected onsite, providing enclosure to the site while under construction and saving on construction costs associated with onsite debris.

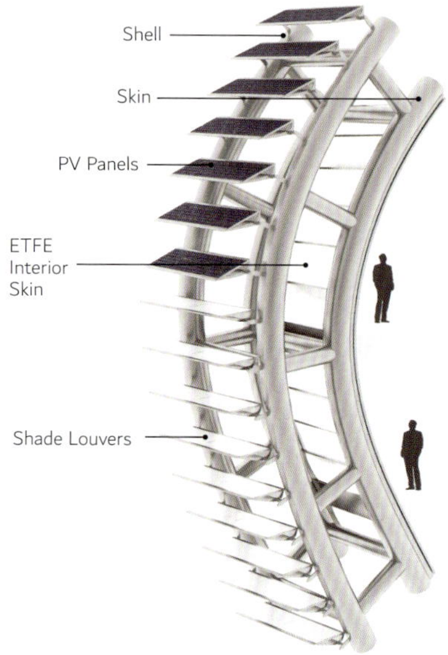

FACADE VIGNETTE
Exterior View

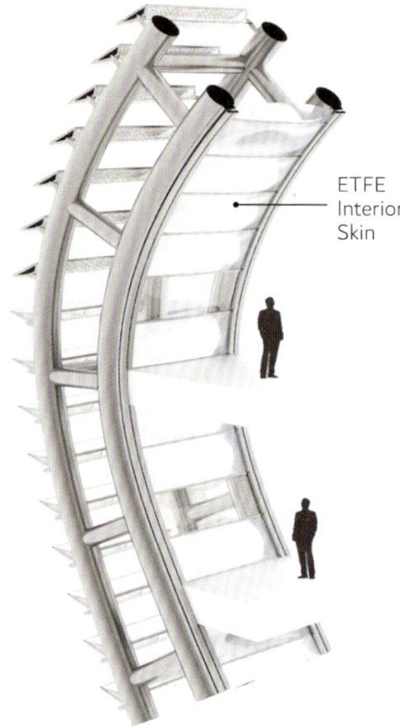

FACADE VIGNETTE
Interior View

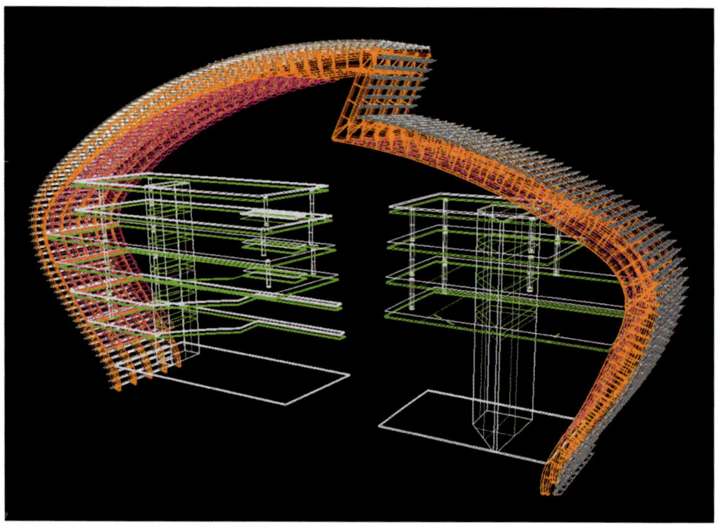

STRUCTURAL MODEL SECTION

The structure of the shell is an independent clear span consisting of prefabricated built up steel truss elements spaced at 3 meters on center.

PHYSICAL MODEL

A detailed physical model was built to illustrate the facade and structural layers and depict the dynamic open spaces under the shell.

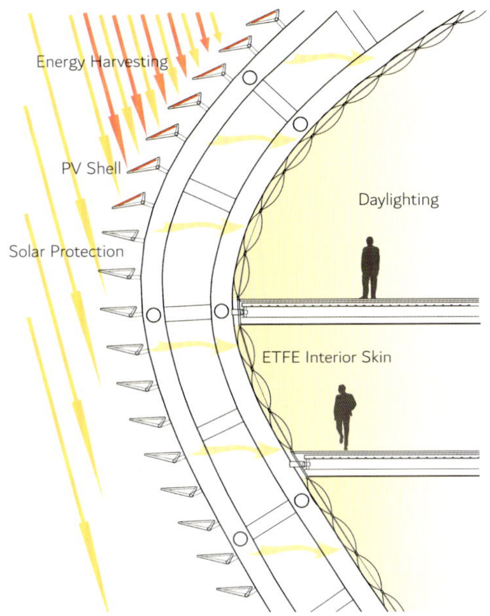

ILLUSTRATIVE DETAIL SECTION

PV Sun Shades

Sun in this region of Saudi Arabia can be severe. Therefore, the amount of energy that can be absorbed through solar harvesting, while shading the interior, can be immense and can help the building achieve positive energy. The building's power is primarily supported by solar energy, achieved through 38,246 m^2 of PV panels with a maximum output of 7,388 kWH/yr. PV solar collectors integrated into the exterior louvered sunshades produce 106% of the building's electrical power usage on a yearly basis. Solar thermal collectors provide 100% of the domestic hot water needs of the facility. At night, hydrocarbon-based power is offset by the BIPV system during the day on an annual basis.

Additional passive technologies, adaptations, and responses were utilized to attain maximum power generation including orientating the building to a north/south aspect ratio to minimize the exposure to low-angle morning and evening solar gains; further minimizing solar gains by shaping the building's shell in section with more densely occupied portions sloping inward; and orientating and rotating the sunshade louvers at the top of the building's shell to maximize the potential extent of BIPV solar collectors.

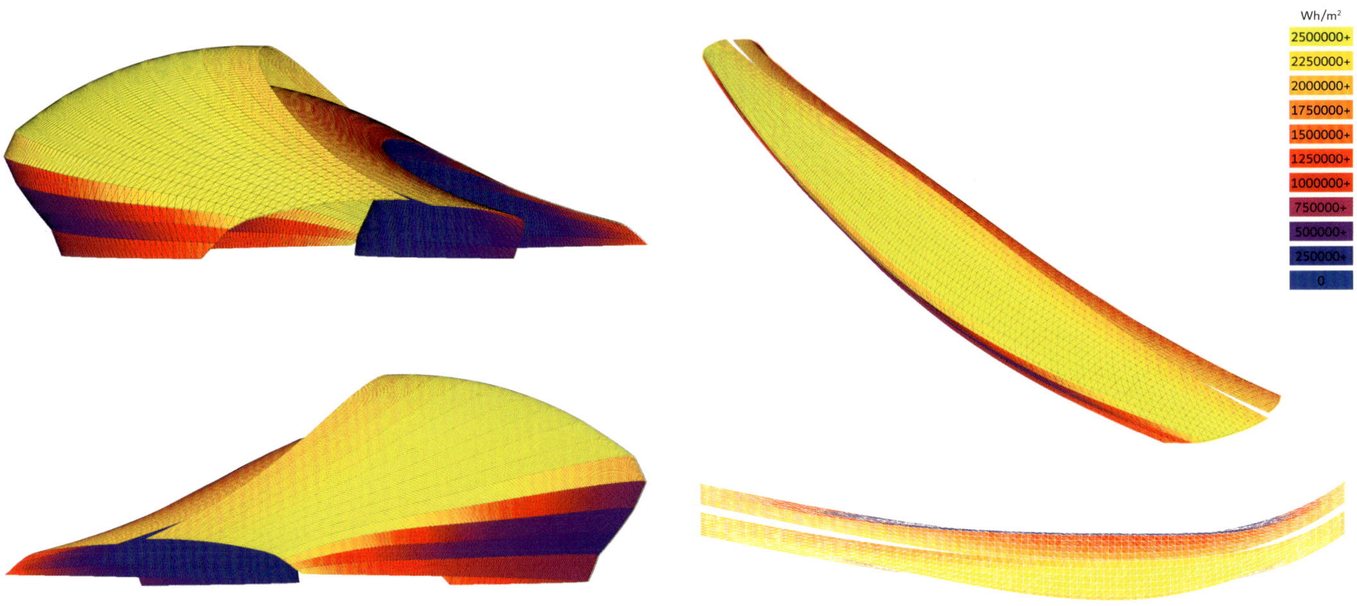

INCIDENT RADIATION ANALYSIS
(Annual Total Radiation)

04 SHINGLED VENTILATED FACADE

Project: Dancing Dragons

Location: Seoul, The Republic of Korea

Climate Zone: DWA - Continental, Dry Winter, Hot Summer

Program: Mixed-Use

Status: Concept

Client: Dreamhub Project Financing Vehicle Co.

Date: 2011-2013

Strategies: Solar Control, Daylighting, Solar Power, Ventilated, Intelligent, Modular

Dancing Dragons is a pair of landmark supertall mixed-use towers designed for the Yongsan International Business District in Seoul, Korea. The buildings, which include residential, "officetel," and retail elements, consist of two slender, sharply angled mini towers that are cantilevered around a central core. The mini towers feature a dramatic series of diagonal massing cuts, carving out living spaces that float beyond the structure. The forms are contextual, recalling the eaves of traditional Korean pagodas that are echoed in the geometry of the buildings' skin and jutting canopies at the tower's base.

Although patterned after traditional roof tiles, the facade also suggests the scales of fish or Korean mythical dragons "dancing" around the core, further supporting the concept and inspiring the project's name. The name of the overall development is also fitting for the site's geometry; Yongsan means "Dragon Hill" in Korean. The unique scale-like skin is both visually appealing and performative; panels are oriented diagonally on the cantilevered pods of the building, creating a strong texture. Air circulates through gaps between the overlapping panels that feature operable 600mm vents, making the gill-like skin "breathable," further referencing the design concept.

The central mass, or building core, has a smooth curtain wall, which enhances the contrast between the volumes. In both buildings, cuts to the mini towers are clad in glass at both ends, creating dramatic ceilings with skylights in the highest-level units and transparent floors in the units at the lowest levels.

The rhombus panels of the tower are constructed as unitized parts that are installed side-by-side to form shingles. The glazed portion consists of triple-glazed panels that enhance the thermal performance of the building. The overhanging portion is double glazed with an interlayer of BIPV in certain elevations. The interior pane of glass stops at the diagonal mullion to provide a continuous seal to the thermal break between the exterior and the structure.

Natural Ventilation

The climate in Seoul is temperate during the spring and fall, so use of an active facade system can save significant amounts of energy that would otherwise be spent on artificial ventilation. To further increase the energy value, the facade is designed to be operated automatically by the Building Management System (BMS). It is estimated that as much as 10% of the building's overall energy can be saved by using natural ventilation instead of air conditioning.

The system positions glazed, shingled panels to draw in air from the outside at their bottom and push exhaust air out at the ceiling. The shingles also act as shields for the vents to remain open, even during rainy periods. In between the shingles, a 250mm sloped operable extrusion pulls fresh air into the building.

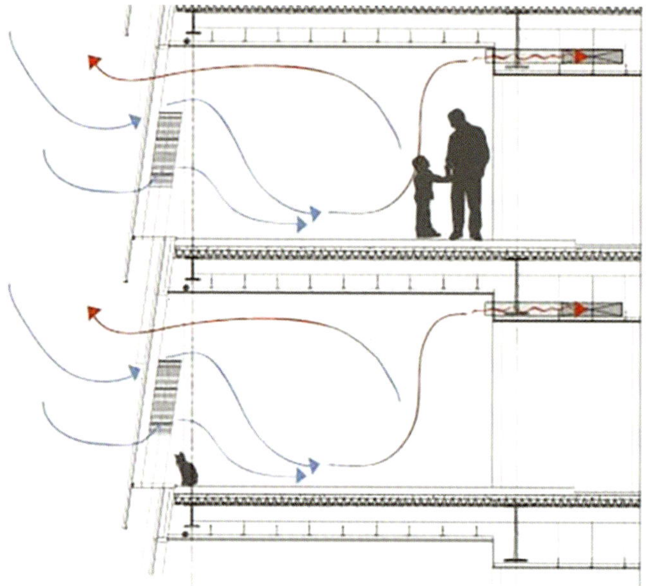

SECTION DIAGRAM

Exhaust Air Duct
Fresh Air Intake

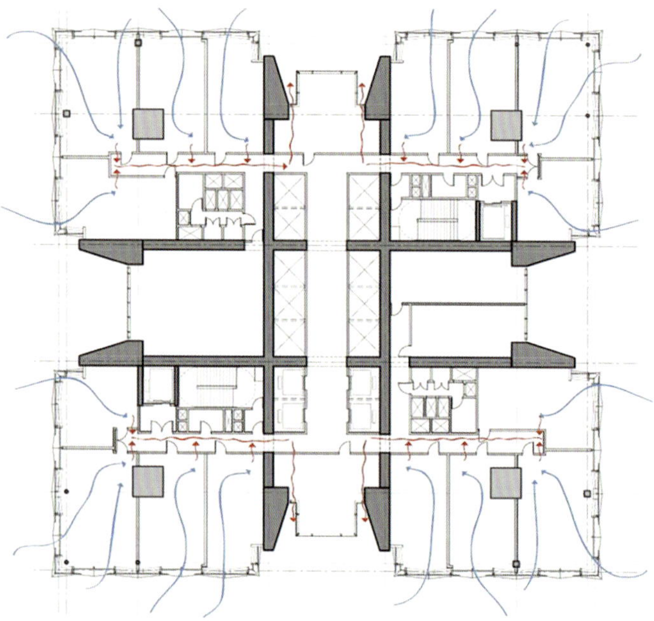

PLAN DIAGRAM

Exhaust Air Duct
Fresh Air Intake

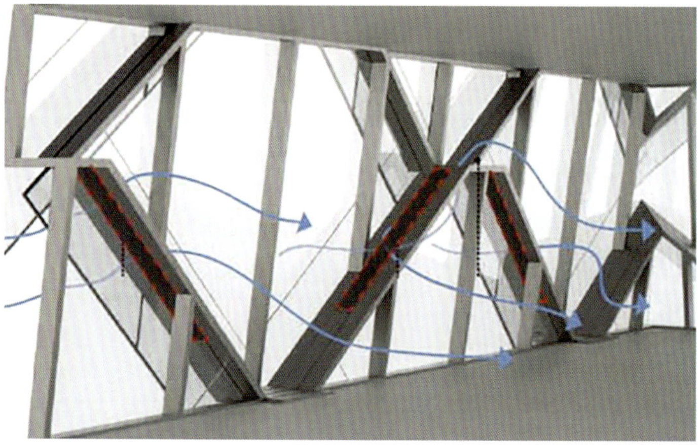

INTERIOR AIR DIAGRAM

Ventilated Mullion
Fresh Air Intake

Wall Panelization

The exterior wall is patterned after traditional roof tiles, emphasizing texture to create a unique experience from within the units. The design is fully modular, repetitive, and dynamic. A three-dimensional shingle with an overlapping glazed area offers a 0.5m deep operable panel, which can be opened to ventilate the units without excessive noise or wind velocity, and naturally shades against rain. The chevron shape formed by the mullion pattern also offers a variety of views from the inside.

The chevron shape is 4.5m at the widest point and is broken down into 1.5m wide mullion spacing. Each panel has a vertical division of modules with a mullion at the center and includes a shadow-box panel at the slab level. The shingles of the panels overlap to help control the natural ventilation and this condition would be an important consideration during installation.

TYPE A1 SECTION

1. Insulated Laminated Low-E Ceramic Frit Glass
2. Window Shade
3. Vision Glass
4. Vent Unit

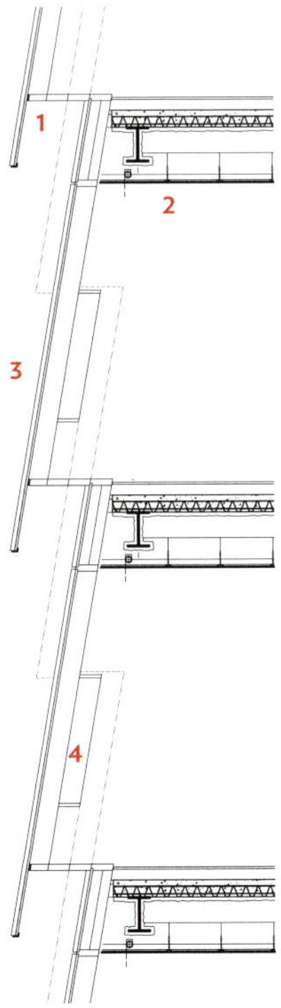

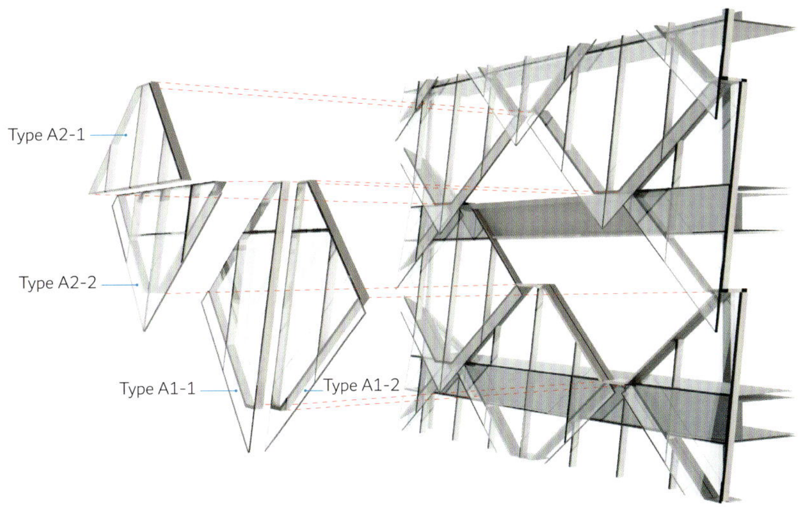

PANELIZATION STUDY

05 PASSIVE ARMORED FACADE

Project: Xi'an Greenland Tower

Location: Xi'an, China

Climate Zone: CFA - Temperate, Without Dry Season, Hot Summer

Program: Mixed-Use

Status: Concept

Client: Shanghai Greenland Group

Date: 2017

Strategies: Solar Control, Daylight, Thermal Mass

Xian's rich history is represented by several ancient artifacts, including the ornate armors worn by Qin Dynasty warriors, the world-renowned terracotta soldiers, and Xian's great city wall. These protective elements have ensured the remembrance of a great civilization. The idea of "protection" was a conceptual driver in the design of Xi'an Greenland Tower. The team sourced historical cues to create a unique architectural language; one that connects the history of Xian, while performing as a physical protector from the environment.

The character of the exterior wall is based on the armor worn by the Qin Dynasty warriors and is highly responsive to the environment. Instead of a formal fully glazed curtain-wall system, a punched window system changes in density and depth depending on the facade's orientation and exposure to the sun. By tuning the facade to protect each side of the building, it dramatically reduces the building's energy consumption, creating a synergy between the look of the building and how it performs.

The primary exterior materials—metal and terracotta—were chosen to further connect the building to the history of Xian. The metal panels recall traditional Chinese armor made from Lamellar iron plates and the glazed terracotta tiles continue to be an important historical building material in the region. The tiles are used to frame windows and sunshades to shield the glass from direct sun. The large-glazed portions, staggered and spanning two floors, are a play on scale, breaking the conventional floor-to-floor horizontality and bringing the scale closer to that of a soldier's armor.

The mixed-use tower has 101 stories with office space occupying the first 75 floors and hotel functions on the upper floors. The subtle taper of the tower and the changes to the core as elevators drop off form an ideal floor plate for functions at their respective locations in the tower.

Parametric Modeling

The exterior facade shading elements can reduce the incident annual solar radiation by 25%. A parametric design process determined the best way to block direct sun and maintain views by defining different shading depths in the four orientations. High-performance glazing and a highly insulated wall assembly minimizes the heat transfer through the envelope, reducing the cooling and heating demand of the building. If renewable energy technology is employed, such as BIPV, it can provide 25% or more of the building's electrical needs, further reducing the net-energy use of the building. The total energy savings goal versus a baseline building is a 75% reduction.

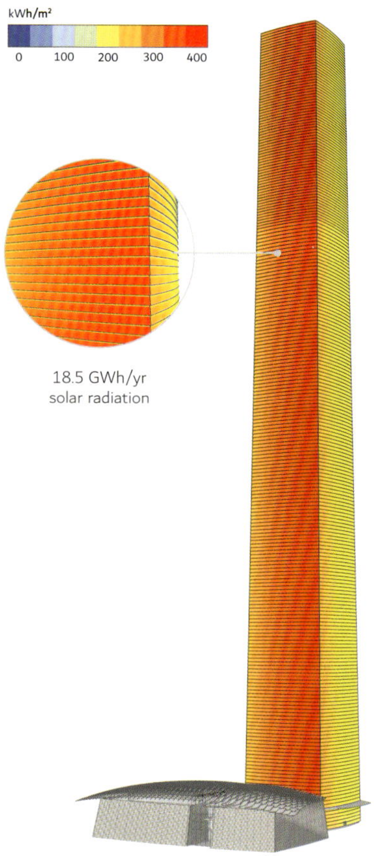

SOLAR ANALYSIS ON BASE MASSING

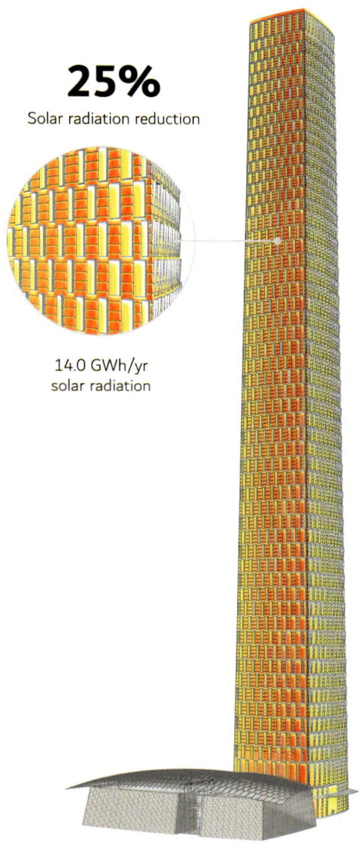

SOLAR ANALYSIS ON IMPROVED FACADE

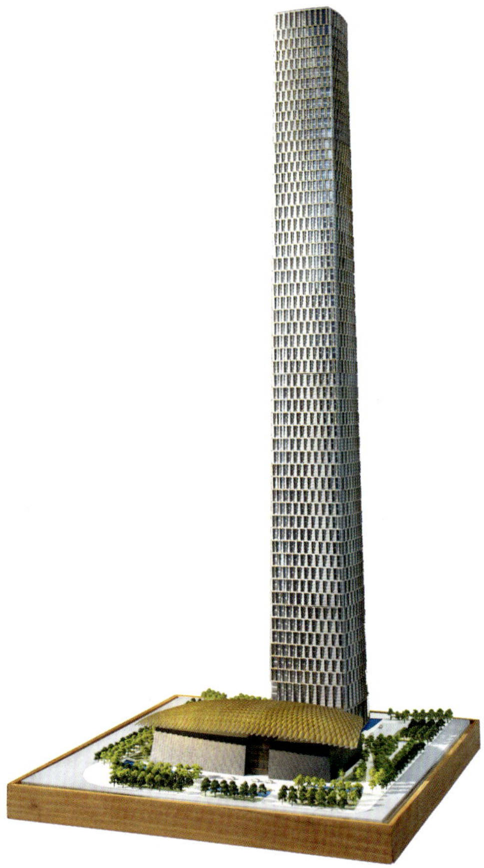

PHYSICAL MODEL

NORTH WEST FACADE

SOUTH EAST FACADE

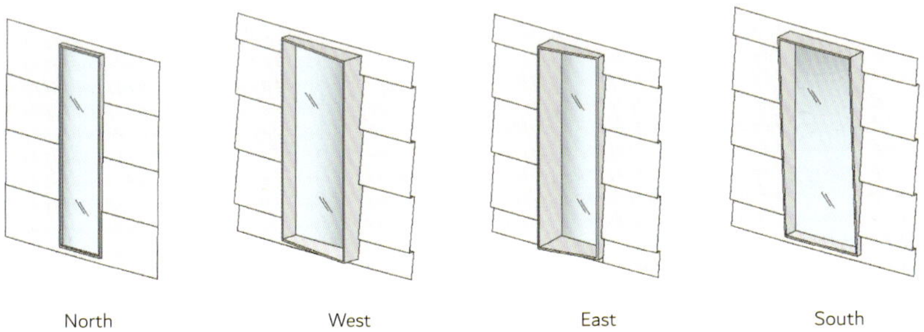

WINDOW CONFIGURATIONS PER ORIENTATION

Solar Control

The building's window-to-wall ratio is an average of 60%. The largest solid panel is 1.5 meters wide, so sizeable levels of daylighting are maintained. Shading elements and glazed areas are optimized for each side of the tower, depending on the orientation and incident solar radiation to reduce heat gain and unwanted glare, while maximizing diffuse light to achieve comfortable levels of natural daylight. The shading elements are designed to be the deepest on the east and west facades, maximizing protection and self-shading. Conversely, those on the north facade are shallower to maximize diffused daylight.

06 SELF-SHADING FACADE

Project:	Tianjin Vantone Tower
Location:	Tianjin, China
Climate Zone:	DWA - Continental, Dry Winter, Hot Summer
Program:	Office
Status:	Built
Client:	Vantone Real Estate
Date:	2010-2017
Strategies:	Solar Control, Daylight, Thermal Mass, Ventilated

Vantone Center features an elegantly twisting, faceted form and an undulating pattern of cladding on the north and south facades, evoking the rippling surface of the Haihe River and the region's tradition of bamboo weaving. The 64,000 m^2 building features Class-A office and high-end retail space, with an additional 30,000 m^2 of below-grade retail and parking. The building also has a soaring 27-meter-tall private club for building tenants at the building's pinnacle.

The tower's sustainability features include a high-performance veneer system that has alternating aluminum and inward-angled glass panels, which block solar heat gain. The east and west facades use vertical aluminum fins that balance solar heat blocking, optimize shading for the low-angled morning and afternoon sun, and improve the availability of views of the park to the south.

The south facade uses self-shading and daylight harvesting to lower the energy use of the building, while providing stunning views of the Tianjin business district's central park. Passive and active sustainable strategies helped the tower acquire LEED Gold certification in 2017.

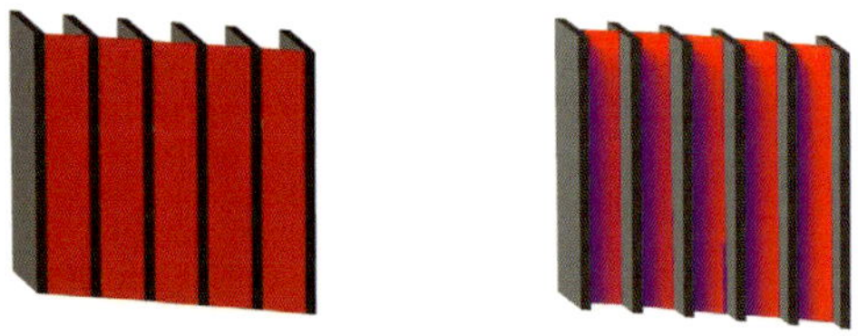

37%
Average Radiation Reduction

Baseline Daily Radiation
896 Wh/m^2

Optimum Fin Daily Radiation
565 Wh/m^2

EAST FACADE STUDY

44%
Average Radiation Reduction

Baseline Daily Radiation
2019 Wh/m^2

Optimum Fin Daily Radiation
1131 Wh/m^2

WEST FACADE STUDY

Solar Control

A preliminary solar incidence study was undertaken to determine the optimum facade fin arrangement on the east and west sides of the building. The key assumption was that an optimum facade maximizes solar radiation incidence on glazing during the six coldest months (winter) and minimizes solar radiation incidence on glazing during the six warmest months (summer).

The facade analysis began with creating a baseline energy model. Once the baseline was calculated, proposed window-to-wall ratios, self-shading devices, and high-efficiency glazing were simulated to establish a constant for other facade studies. The optimum design arrangement is configured with north-facing fins on the east and south-facing fins on the west. With the optimum facade determined from the previous facade/fin optimization, a macro-level solar incidence study was performed to determine solar availability in a contextual setting. As with the previous incidence study, both summer and winter months were analyzed.

To achieve the optimum conservation of energy, a series of iterations were run, testing different fin angles on the east and west facade that maximize solar heat gain in the winter and minimize it in the summer. The energy analysis of the facade concluded that the west fins facing south, with the east fins facing north, resulted in the highest energy savings, a 17% reduction from the ASHRAE baseline.

SOUTH FACADE STUDY

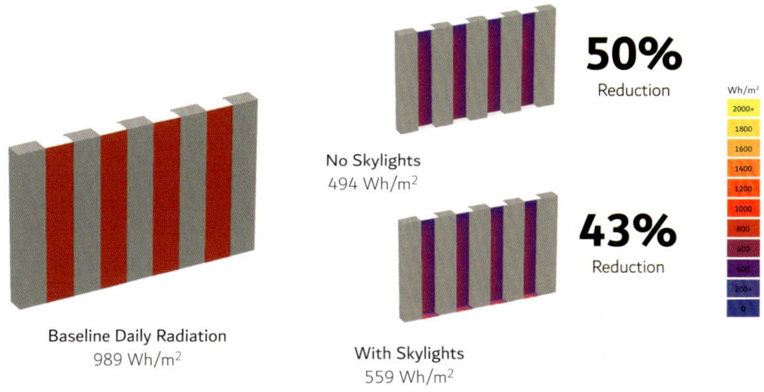

NORTH FACADE STUDY

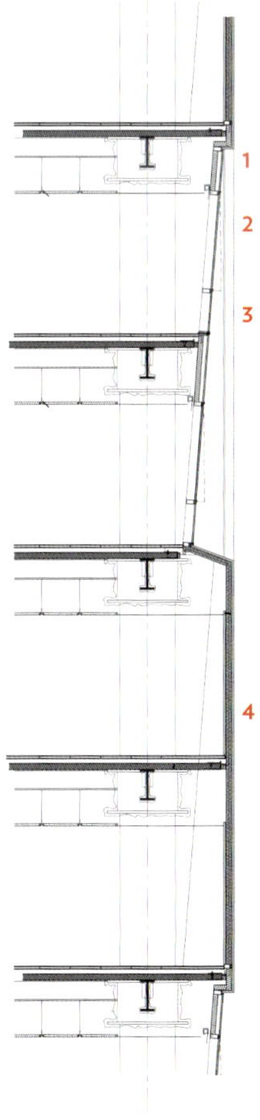

PARTIAL SOUTH SECTION

1. Shadow Box
2. Operable Vision Glass
3. Vision Glass
4. Metal Panel

07 BRISE SOLEIL FACADE

Project:	Zhongzhou Holdings Financial Center
Location:	Shenzhen, China
Climate Zone:	CWA - Temperate, Dry Winter, Hot Summer
Program:	Mixed-Use
Status:	Built
Client:	Shenzhen Centralcon Real Estate Co. Ltd.
Date:	2009-2014
Strategies:	Solar Control, Daylight

Shenzhen's Zhongzhou Holdings Finance Center's simple form and fluid skin presents a dynamic image for the district and Shenzhen at large. The mixed-use complex is located in Shenzhen's Nanshan Culture District and consists of a multi-purpose podium, a 300-meter-tall office and hotel tower, and a related 160-meter-tall residential tower. The client's objective was to construct a building that achieves balance and harmony for the building's tenants, inhabitants, and users.

The design demonstrates a refined collection of multi-purpose, performance-based solutions and coincidental aesthetic discoveries that were built, and can be maintained, on a modest budget. The design is an intersection between performance and function. It expresses an understanding of local environmental conditions through the intense refinement of passive technologies to create a timeless architectural expression.

The building's facade was strategically designed to work within the site's dense urban environment and its unique form helped the building achieve a LEED Gold certification. The glazed facade is protected from the sun with horizontal louvers made of perforated metal panel. Throughout the development, the density of the louvers changes according to program type. For example, the residential and hotel units have the lowest density of louvers, while the podium has the highest density. Insulated Low-E glass has been used extensively and by placing multi-layered horizontal shading panels in crucial areas, diffused light is introduced into the interior, thereby reducing lighting energy consumption. Patterned colored glazing in portions of the facade also lowers glare while increasing shading performance.

Performative Design

Early in the design process, solar studies were completed to establish the performance of the design as a base-case scenario to improve energy performance and user comfort levels. These studies included incident (direct) solar heat gain analysis, diffuse (indirect) solar heat gain analysis, daylighting analysis, radiance analysis, wind pressure mapping, view analysis, and social and program mapping.

The resulting shape is a gently curving facade that evenly distributes light throughout the interior, increasing daylighting while minimizing solar gain. The bowed facade is more effective at distributing daylight than a standard flat facade. A vertical notch is added to the corners as a visual break between facades in each orientation. The notches also add an experiential bonus to corner offices and units, differentiating these spaces from the rest of the floor space.

Sunshades

To further optimize daylighting and visual comfort for users, horizontal louvers are positioned to redirect light into the interior spaces to help further reduce excessive light levels near the glass. The louver is deepest near the center of the facade where the contrasts are greatest. The louver tapers to a minimal dimension toward the corners where daylighting needs, and contrast mitigation, are lowest.

The louvers also significantly shade the exterior walls. A frit is introduced to the non-vision glass panels to compensate where the louvers taper toward the corners. The tapered horizontal louvers also reduce view obstructions in the corners.

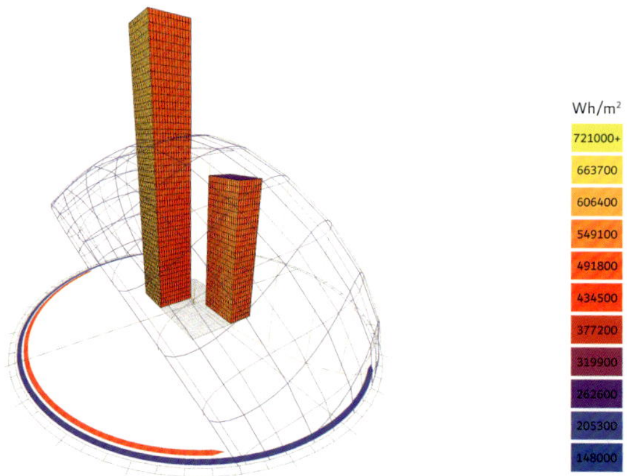

OVERALL ANNUAL SOLAR RADIATION 8AM-6PM

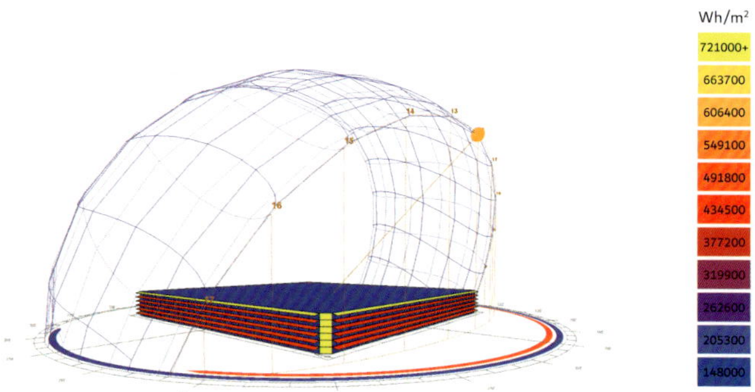

SOLAR RADIATION WITH HORIZONTAL LOUVERS AT 15°

EXTERIOR WALL

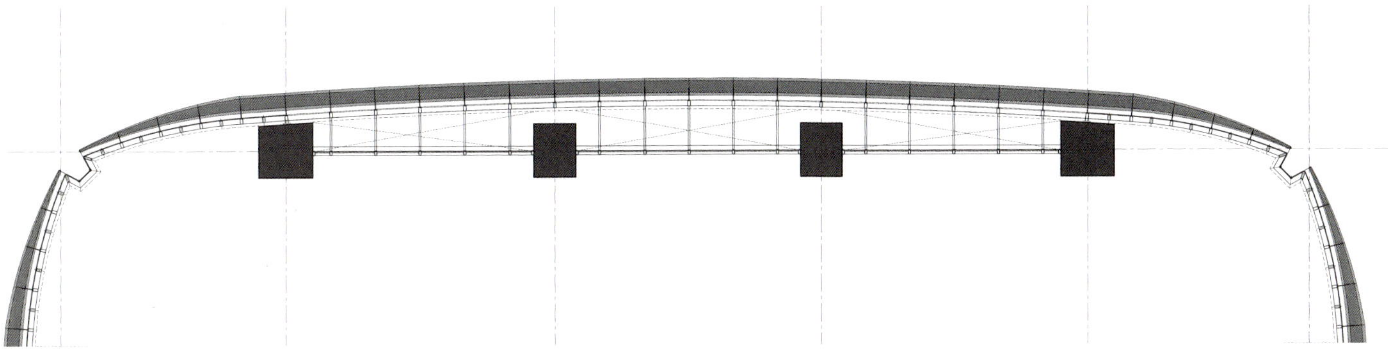

EXTERIOR WALL PLAN

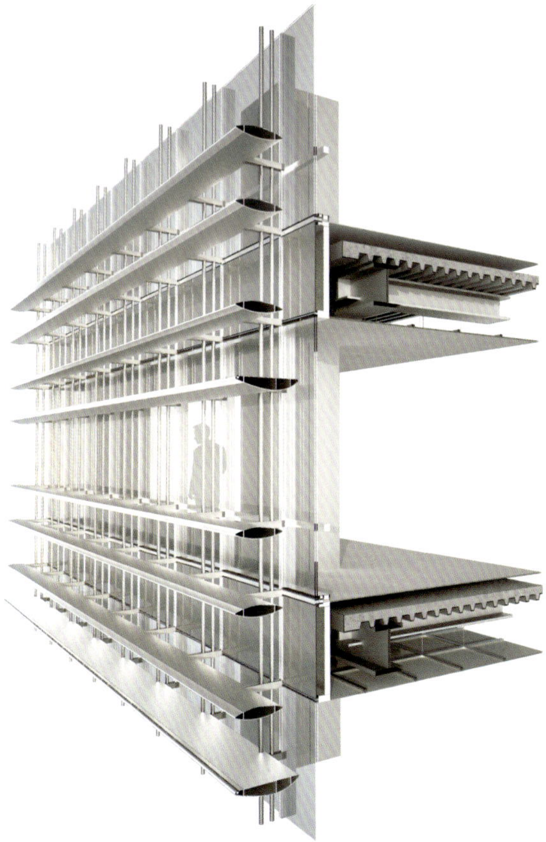

EXTERIOR WALL VIGNETTE

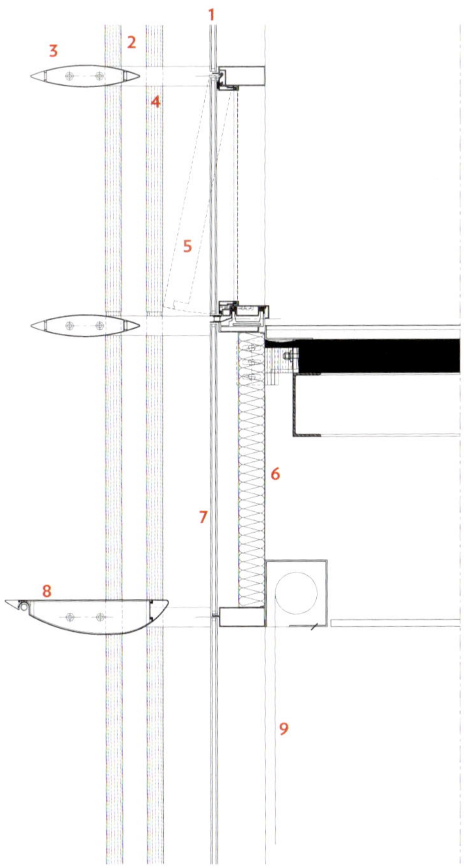

1. Vision Glass
2. Metal Rod
3. Metal Sunshade
4. Metal Edge Trim
5. Operable Window
6. Insulation
7. Spandrel Glass
8. Metal Light Shelf
9. Window Shade

TYPICAL SECTION DETAIL AT SLAB - OFFICE

08 SAIL SCREEN FACADE

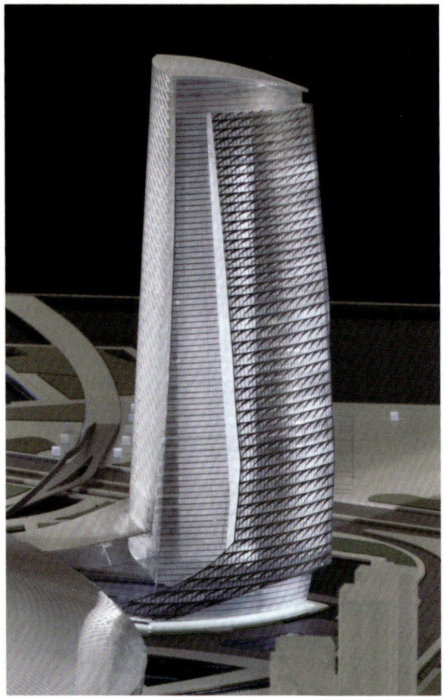

Project: Yixing Dongjiu Far East Development

Location: Yixing, China

Climate Zone: CFA - Temperate, Without Dry Season, Hot Summer

Program: Mixed-Use

Status: Concept

Client: Yixing Far East

Date: 2009

Strategies: Solar Control, Daylighting, Thermal Mass, Intelligent, Luminous

Yixing Far East Development consists of two towers and a retail podium, surrounded by a series of interconnected waterways that provide additional site access. The elegant landscape references the canals that run through Yixing, which are located directly east of the site. The shape of the development emphasizes the fluidity of the plan, creating compelling interactions between the buildings and the water.

The taller tower is mixed-use with office and hotel functions. An innovative glass skin is protected by a textured exterior screen made from Polyurethane Coated Lycra. This resilient fabric creates an overall seamless design that adds to the tower's sustainability by providing natural shade and improving the quality of the interior natural light. From an aesthetic perspective, the shape of the shades continues the language of curvature found throughout the development. The form provides optimum shade to the vision glazing during summer months, while allowing maximum solar incidence on the daylight glazing throughout the year.

The materials used throughout the complex have significant cultural and aesthetic meanings. Clay and ceramic materials are incorporated within the retail facade, inspired by the purple clay teapots that are manufactured in the region. The podium wall consists of frosted glass that is activated as a media platform at night using thousands of integrated LED lights. The media wall can be programmed with digital art and information, creating a dynamic, visually engaging feature.

Shading Screen Wall

Vertical surfaces require comprehensive self-shading or external shading mechanisms to control solar gains and glare issues that are inherent on east and west orientations with low solar incidence angles. Incident solar radiation studies illustrate this effect over an annual performance cycle that shows significantly higher reduction in incident radiation during the summer months than the winter months to maintain an almost uniform annual incidence.

The shading configuration is designed specifically for the southwest face of the hotel/office tower based on site analysis. A shadow study illustrates that the north face receives direct solar radiation during early mornings and late evenings during the summer months. For rest of the year, due to its orientation, the facade is shaded from direct sun and only receives global diffused radiation. The screen wall is optimized to shade the glass in the summer and still allow light to penetrate in the winter months. The southeast face integrates an exactly mirrored design, replicating the shading effect.

The adjacent residential tower features a series of alternating balconies that offer outdoor spaces and views, while creating another richly textured exterior facade. The shape, arrangement, and interplay of the balconies, evoke the shape of lily petals, which is an influence that can be found throughout the development.

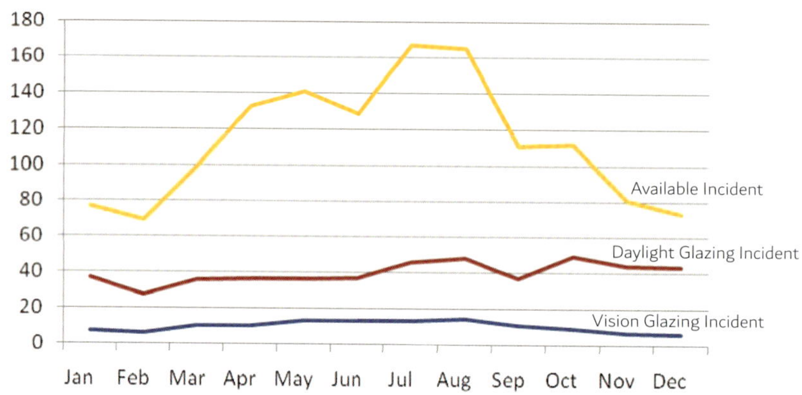

CUMULATIVE FULL HOURLY INCIDENT SOLAR RADIATION WH/M2

EXTERIOR WALL SHADING STUDY

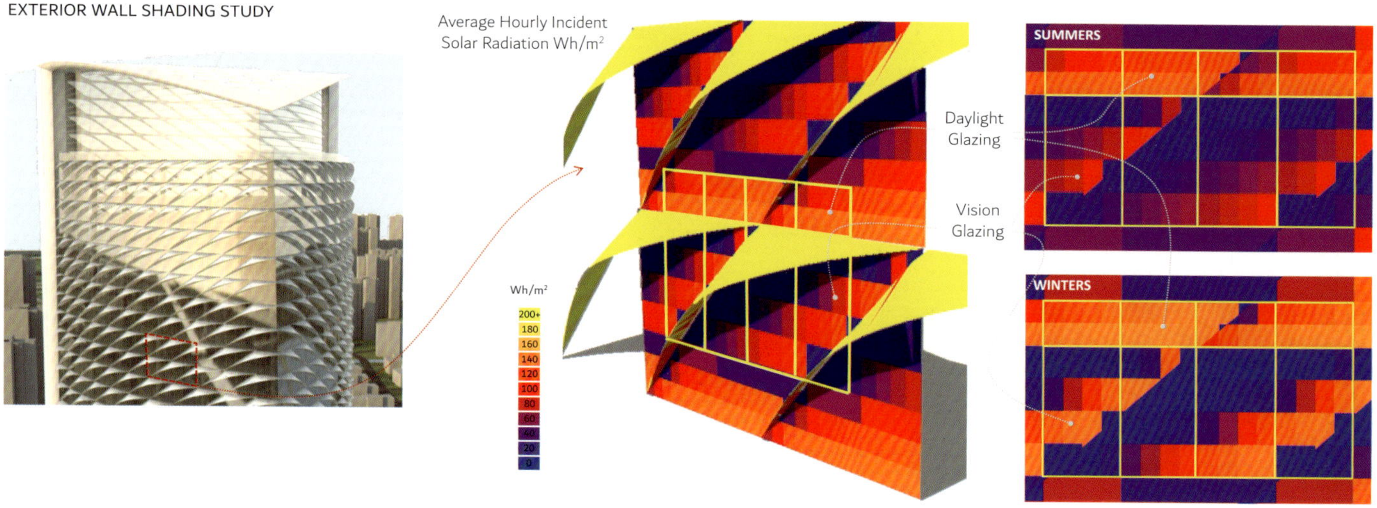

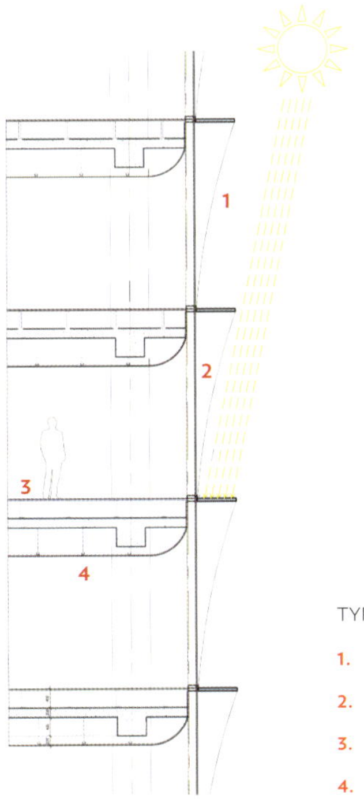

TYPICAL SECTION

1. Fabric Shading
2. Insulated Glazing
3. Raised Floor
4. Integrated Ceiling

EXTERIOR WALL RENDERING

09 CLEAN-TECH FACADE

Project:	Clean Technology Tower
Location:	Chicago, United States
Climate Zone:	DFA - Continental, Without Dry Winter, Hot Summer
Program:	Office
Status:	Concept
Client:	N/A
Date:	2007
Strategies:	Solar Control, Daylight, Solar Power, Ventilated, Wind Power, Intelligent

Building on the principles of aerodynamics, the Clean Technology Tower applies advanced technologies and climate appropriate building systems to create a symbiotic relationship with the local environment. The tower harnesses the power of the natural forces present at its site, refining the conventional methods of capturing natural forces to significantly increase energy efficiency.

The 1.8-million-square-foot tower features office, hotel, and retail functions. The tower showcases its expression of clean technology by visually displaying the building integrated wind turbines as part of the distinct architecture, forming a symbol of the next generation of building technology.

Due to its aerodynamic form, the tower is more structurally efficient, requiring less structural materials than a standard building of similar size and scale, and thereby reducing the embodied carbon. The smooth form and domed top reduce wind loads that act on the tower, decreasing the amount of embodied energy used while simultaneously utilizing negative pressure to ventilate the sky garden space at the top of the tower. A fritted glass pattern embedded into the exterior wall mediates the light reaching the interior spaces, where it is most needed, while providing shade to the glass near the top and bottom of the tower, where heat gain is highest.

The facade was designed as a double-skinned wall with an eight-inch cavity spaced between the layers and is finished by a high-performance Low-E coating. Although less common in the US, double wall facades are widely used throughout Europe because of more stringent energy codes. Chicago is a cold intensive climate; therefore, the double wall's empty space between each surface delivers a "thermos" effect that acts as an additional barrier to the extreme weather conditions. The facade also has integrated shading devices installed between the double wall.

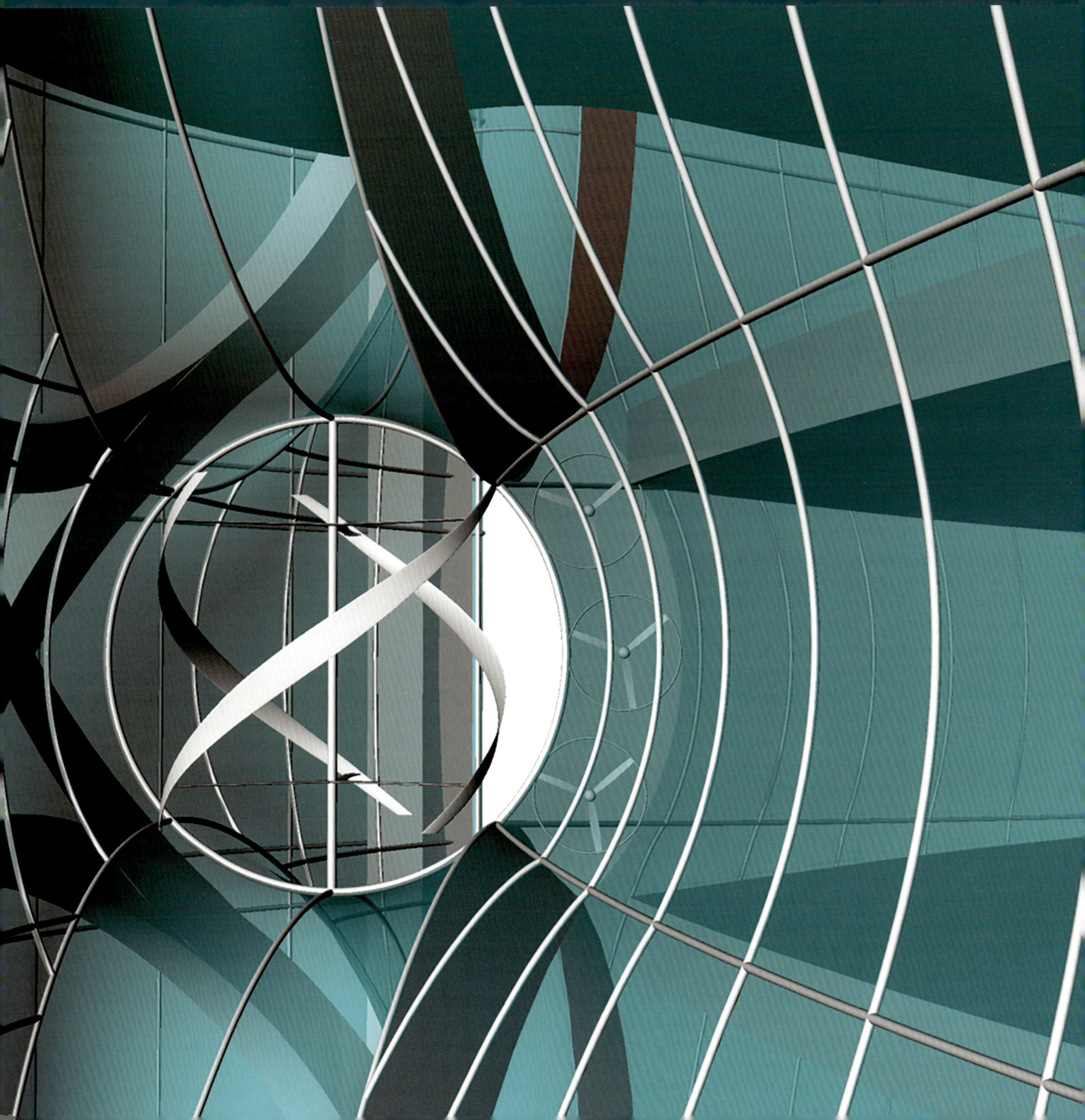

Corner Turbines

Wind turbines are integrated into the corners of the building to capture wind at its fastest speed as it accelerates around the tower. The use of compressor shields direct the acceleration of the wind though the turbine. The turbines become increasingly dense as the tower ascends and wind speed increases.

Tower Top Turbines

At the tower's apex, where wind speeds are at a maximum, a domed double-roof cavity captures air, creating a "wind farm" that uses negative pressures to ventilate the interior spaces. The dome itself is shaded by photovoltaic cells that capture the southern sun's energy. The systems provides both user comfort and usable energy to the space.

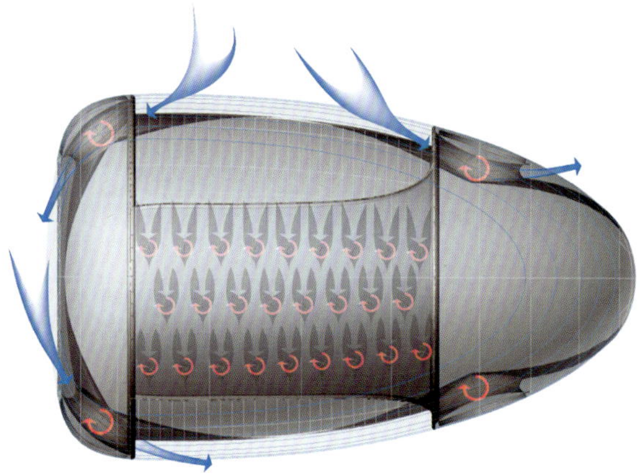

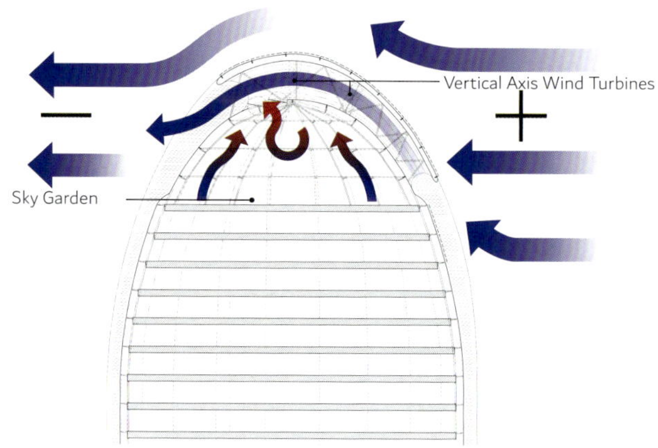

WIND FLOW DIAGRAMS

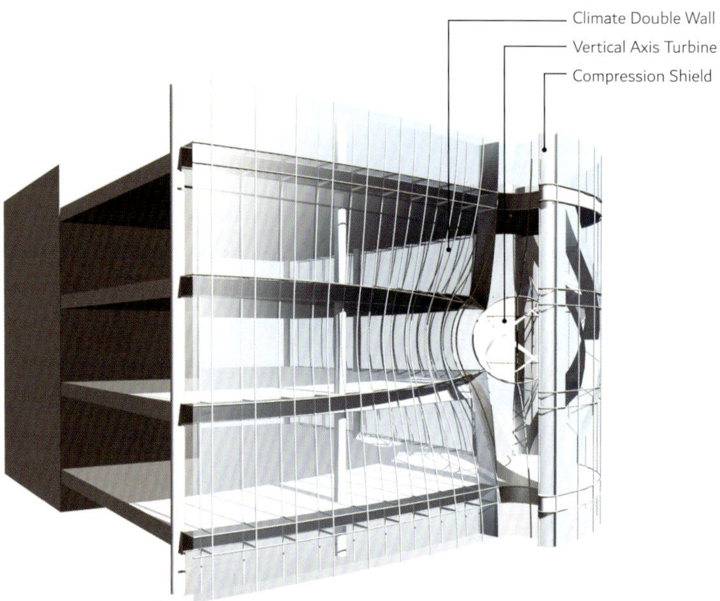

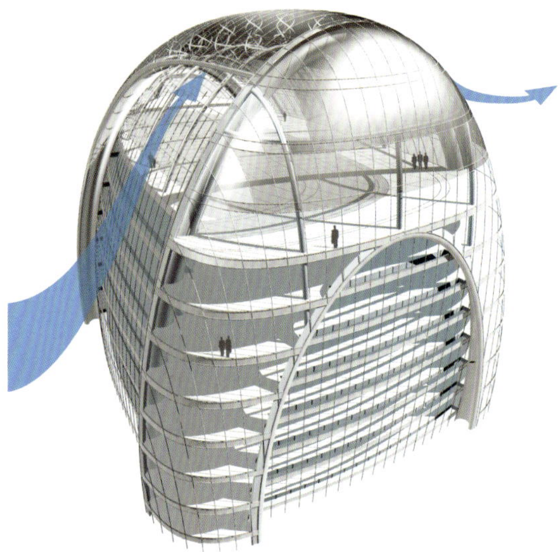

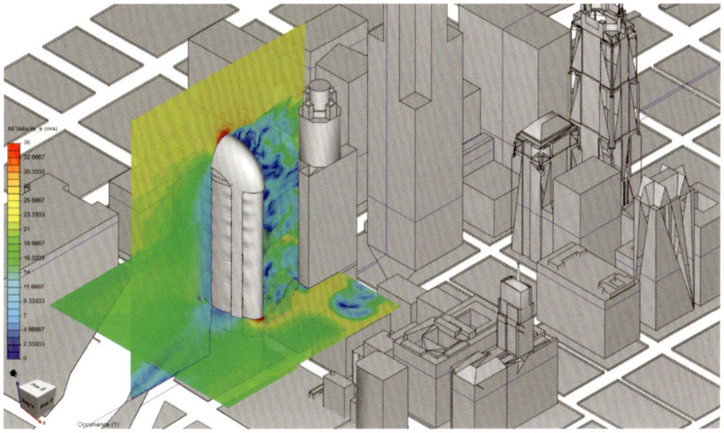

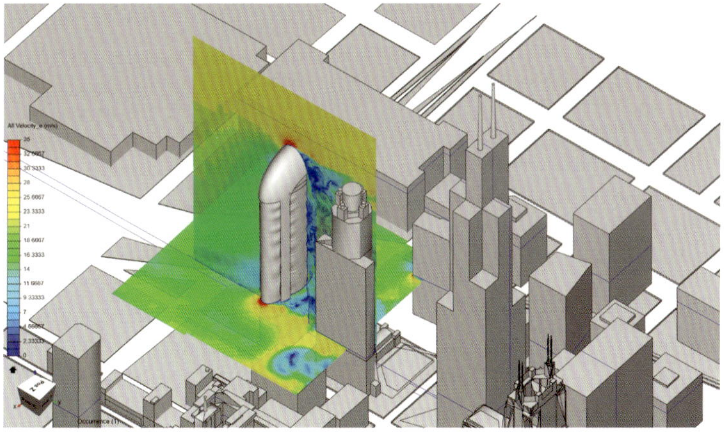

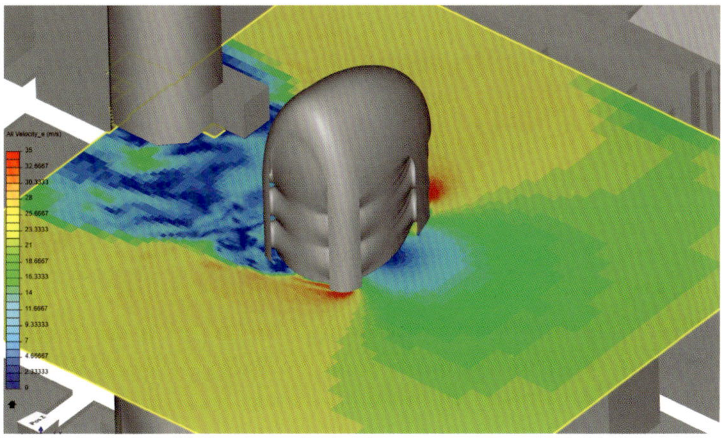

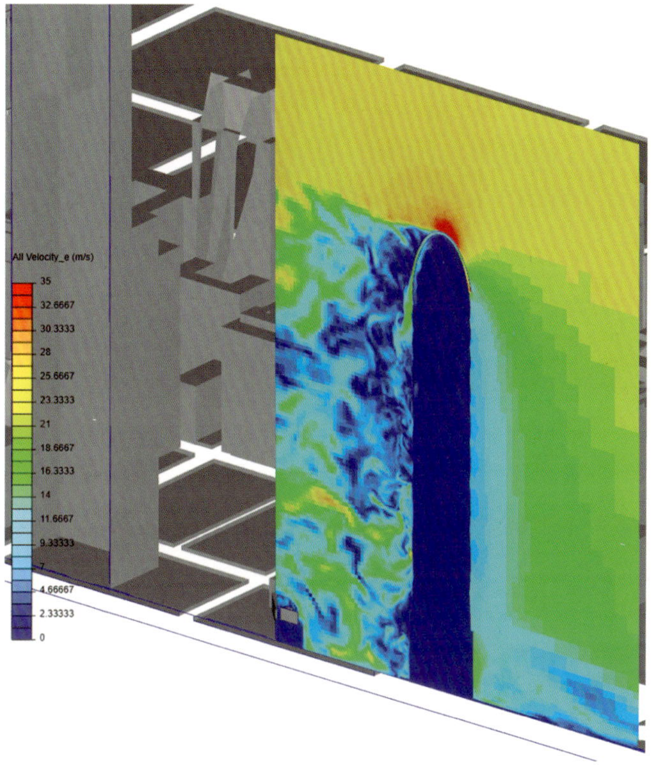

CFD Analysis

Computational fluid dynamics (CFD), which utilizes numerical methods to simulate the interaction of fluids and gases within complex systems, was used to determine the most efficient orientation of the building and the location of the tower's integrated wind turbines. FloVENT software was used to predict 3D airflow, heat transfer, and contamination distribution in and around building. While advances in CFD analysis in recent years has led to extremely accurate building modeling, additional wind-tunnel testing is recommended because of the use of wind tunnels scale models, which are better at measuring turbulence and tiny particles.

10 ENERGY FACADE

Project:	Expo 2020 Mobility Theme Pavilion
Location:	Dubai, United Arab Emirates
Climate Zone:	BWH - Arid, Desert, Hot
Program:	Cultural
Status:	Concept
Client:	Dubai Expo 2020 LLC
Date:	2013
Strategies:	Solar Control, Daylight, Solar Power, Thermal Mass, Ventilated, Intelligent, Luminous, Modular

The Global Mobility Center was a design competition for one of the Expo2020 Dubai pavilions. AS+GG's entry featured a 15,000 m^2 exhibition space in a simple shell form with a structural grid that is easy to erect. The building is fully clad in ceramic tile, a highly efficient material that is indigenous to the region. The downward sloping exterior facade creates self-shaded glass that reduces unwanted solar radiation through the glazing and achieves high levels of daylighting. The carved space below offers shaded exterior spaces that visitors can walk and gather under. Insulated Glazing Units (IGUs) are important for the Dubai climate, targeting a low solar heat gain coefficient (SHGC) while controlling glare and visible light. Exterior horizontal shading fins further reduce unwanted solar radiation.

The exterior wall has an integrated water misting system to cool the area for potential outdoor programming and overflow queuing. Sculpted soffit surfaces are designed to increase the natural wind flow to enhance comfort levels for the user. Active LED light fixtures, speakers, and flag poles with large banners add a festive and inviting atmosphere during the day and night. An LED system is integrated into the roof, creating a lively fifth elevation.

The structural grid shell performs extra functions such as renewable energy generation, daylight mediation, natural ventilation, physical movement, and a surface for a digital information display. The structure is designed to be modified or infilled in the future as floor area needs and uses evolve.

Designed as a node within a larger network of exposition buildings, the design is easily recognizable as contemporary, compact, and adaptable. The open space concept of the exhibition and museum program focuses on sharing information as "living data" that is projected onto the ceiling and across the floor. Open spaces span four floors in height, allowing information to be shared between groups throughout the building.

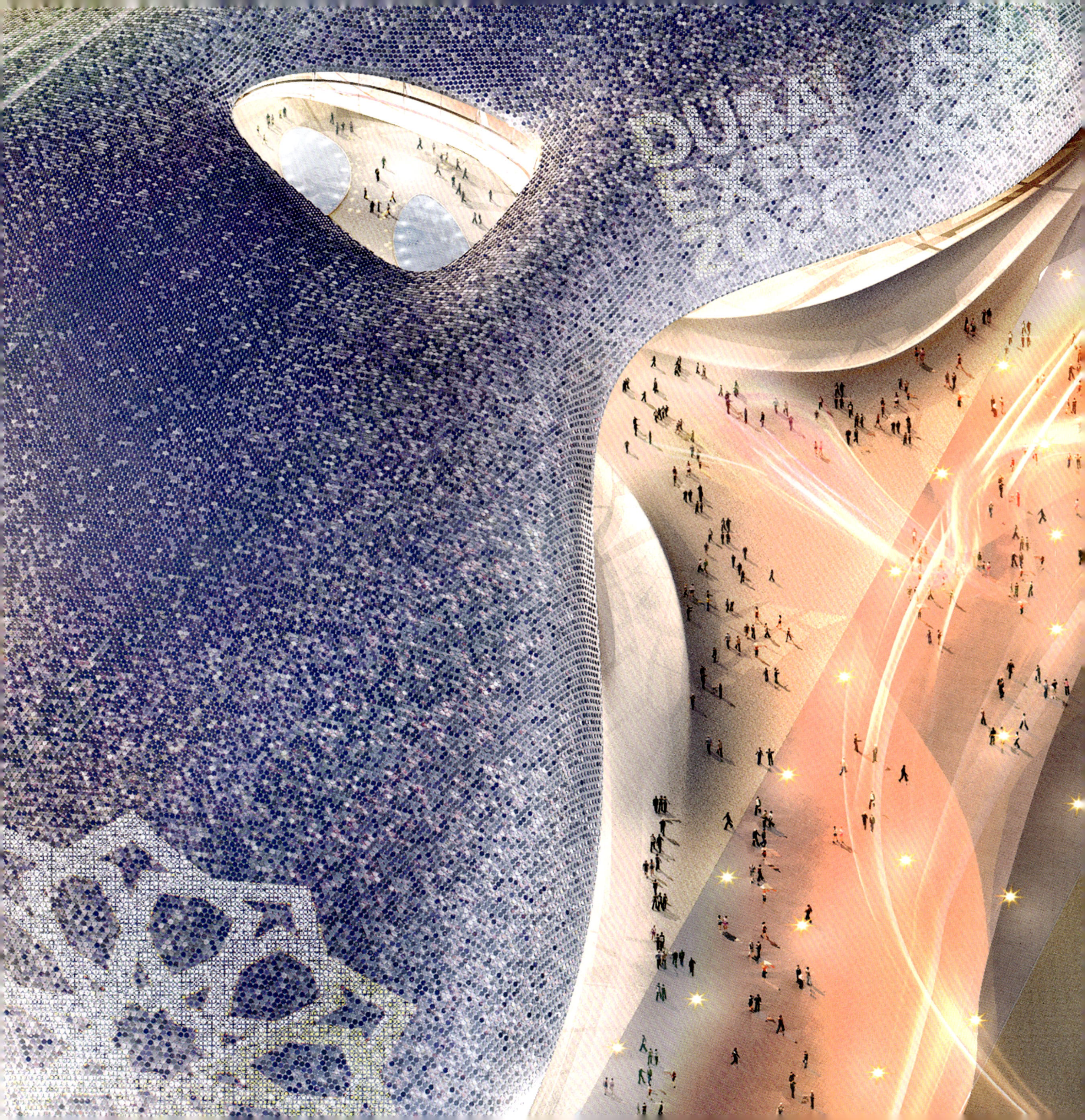

Energy Performance

The design goals for the Global Mobility Center adopt proven, best-in-class technologies that deliver an exceptional visitor experience. The space offers an increased value to the owner through ongoing operational and maintenance savings, and by relieving pressure on infrastructure through onsite reclamation and generation technologies.

The project exemplifies the incorporation of new Dubai Municipality Green Building Regulation and Specification requirements and LEED Platinum building requirements. With a highly efficient building form and systems in place, the challenge of achieving a 25% energy generation onsite is minimized through roof integrated photovoltaic panels. There is an overall 39% savings through energy efficiency and 36% onsite energy generation.

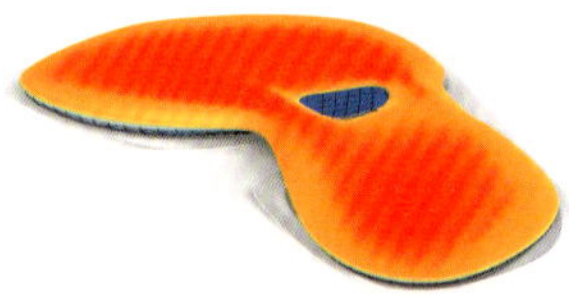

ENERGY PERFORMANCE

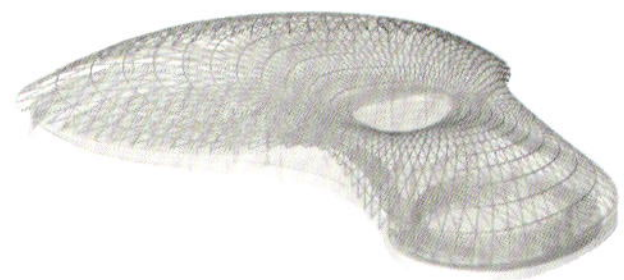

LOW EMBODIED CARBON MATERIALS

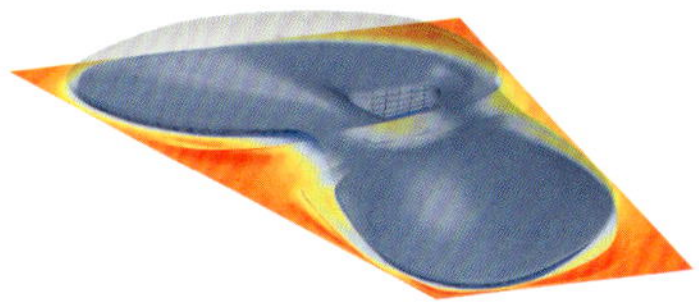

THERMAL COMFORT

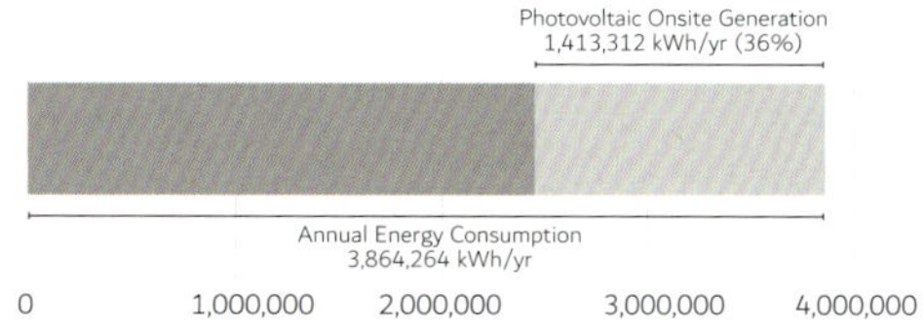

TOTAL ANNUAL ENERGY CONSUMPTION (kWh/yr)

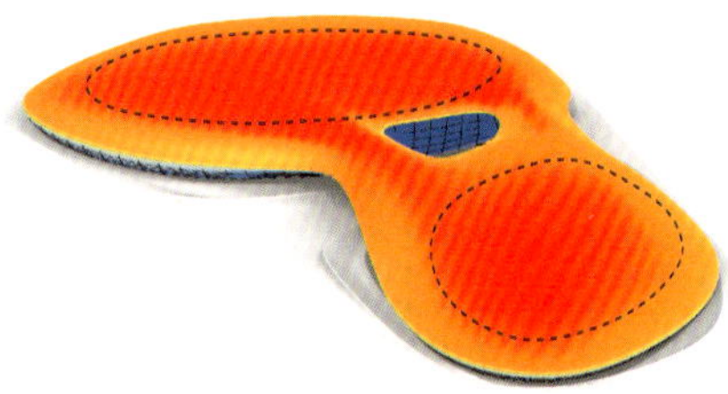

PHOTOVOLTAIC GENERATION

SUSTAINABILITY SECTION

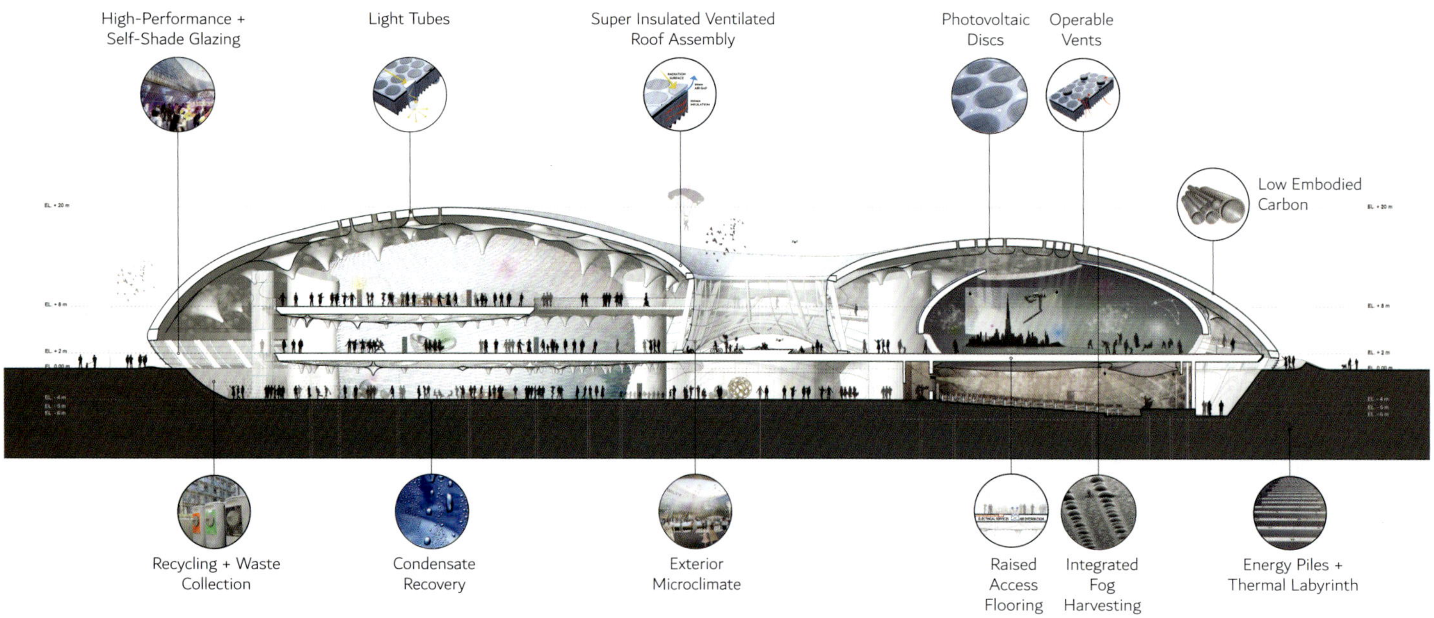

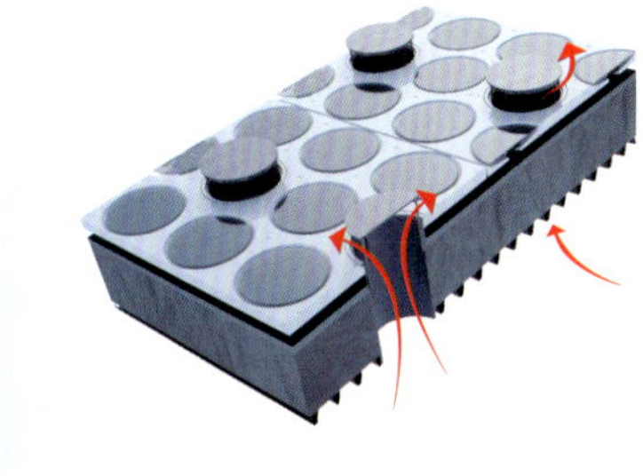

OPERABLE VENT VIGNETTE

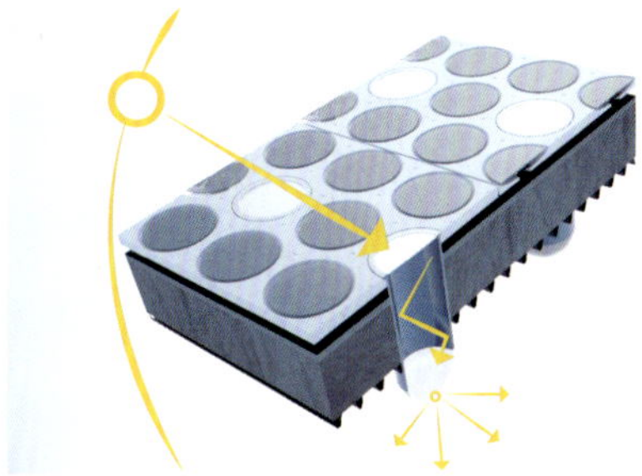

SOLAR TUBES VIGNETTE

SUPER-INSULATION VIGNETTE

Flexibility

BIPV works with the ceramic tile to achieve the 25% renewable energy requirement stated in the brief. 350mm PV discs clip into the prefabricated unitized tile roof panels. Air cools the PV by circulating behind and through the prefab panels via a void behind the disc within the panel. This void also allows for drainage. The system integrates sun tubes that bring diffused daylight into the center of the internal spaces. This interior illumination is diffused and controlled by actuated fabric cones, offering a dynamic and textural lighting. Speed to market is critical for all exposition projects, therefore the structure was designed as a simple shell that is efficient to construct, easily installed, and readily available. The structure was also designed to be flexible for future uses. Should the client need more space in the future, the system can accommodate infill areas that increase the floor plate size. As part of the submission, test fit plans were done to show how the space is easily adaptable.

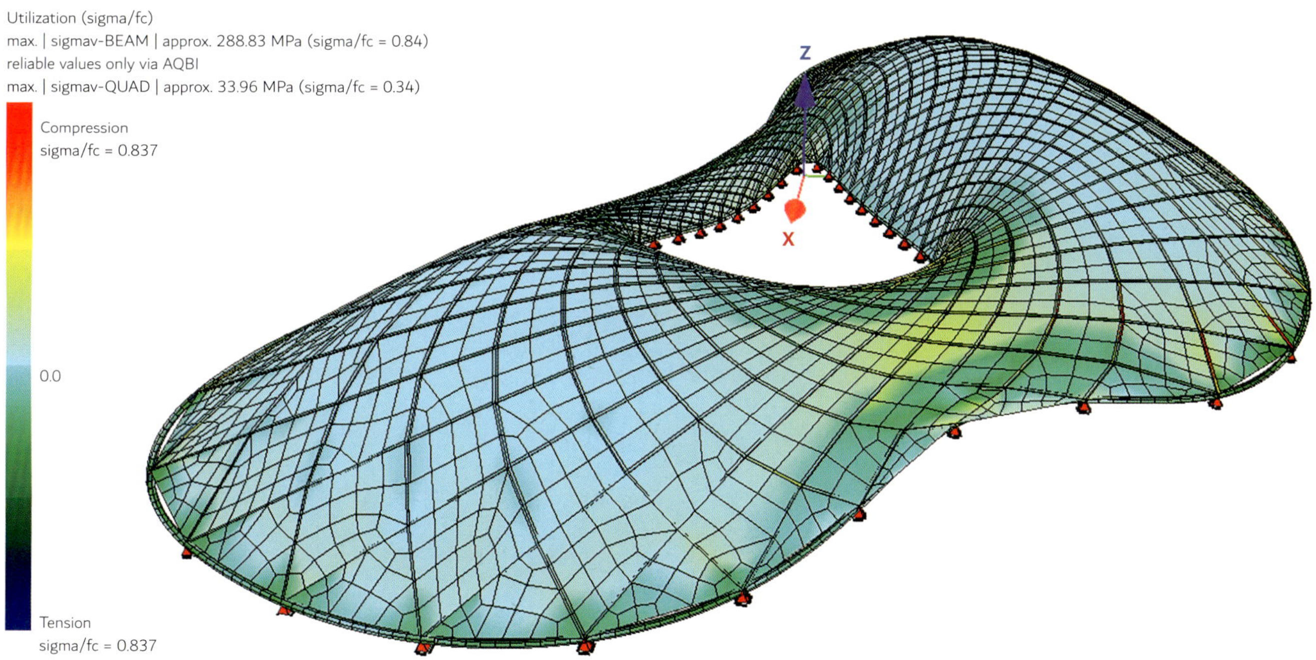

11 DIAGRID FACADE

Project: 1 Dubai

Location: Dubai, United Arab Emirates

Climate Zone: BWH - Arid, Desert, Hot

Program: Mixed-Use

Status: Concept

Client: Meraas Development

Date: 2008

Strategies: Solar Control, Daylight, Ventilated

1 Dubai combines simple geometric principles with new and emerging technologies. Designed to the highest environmental and performance standards, the complex creates three of the world's tallest buildings. The conjoined structures rise above a canal that forms an oasis at the center of its tripodal base. Between the towers, an atrium-like space transforms into one of the world's most unique event and performance spaces.

As a composition, the towers are designed to have optimized solar orientation so that the taller tower shades the adjacent shorter towers. The facade consists of two layers: an exterior diagrid layer and an interior concrete wall. Solar studies were performed to optimize the amount of solid area versus glazed area on each facade. In prototyping the exterior layer, various patterns in the diagonal panels were studied based on their solar gain.

Some openings were left unglazed for ventilation and fitted with stainless steel mesh for security and protection from bird collisions. The interior wall, or concrete tube, has punched window openings and is clad with metal panels. Window openings are infilled with insulated glazing units and are also operable.

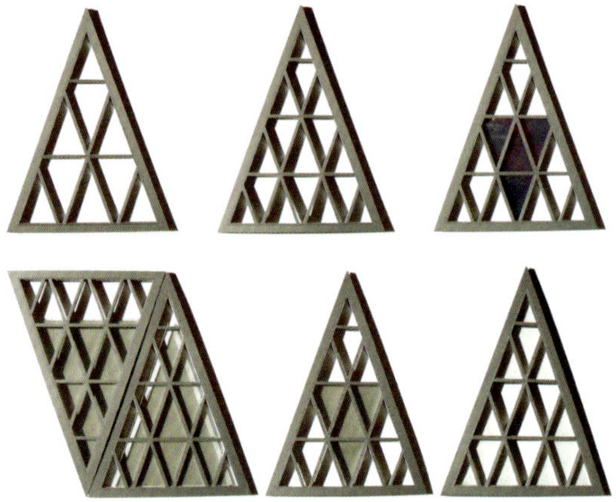

PANEL OPTION STUDY

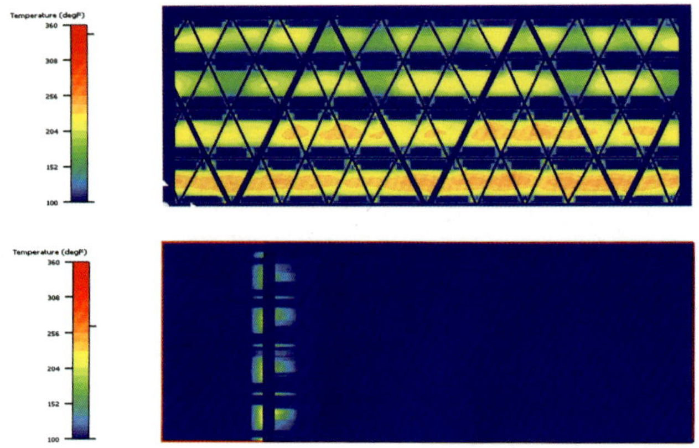

CFD STUDIES EXTERIOR WALL 20% OPENING

Layered Facade

The diagrid facade was designed as a system that works efficiently with the tapering geometry of the towers. The layered wall features a 1.5m zone that is an interior solarium or an exterior balcony that controls heat gain and helps regulate natural ventilation. The structure of the tower, which is located at the back of the 1.5m zone, is a concrete tube with punched window openings.

Several different module configurations of the diagrid were analyzed. To let in the appropriate amount of natural light and to control heat gain, the number of solid panels versus glazing was optimized based on the orientation of each wall. The panels are made of extruded aluminum, with a high-performance paint finish, and are designed to be flat, erected in a faceted manner to conform to the building's cylindrical shape.

The proposed triangular panels range from approximately 4m on each side at ground level, to 4m x 4m x 1.8m near the top of the tower. Glazing is divided into 9-16 smaller triangles, which can be infilled with glass, shading devices, and other solid materials. To avoid the use of triangular glass, monolithic pieces are panelized into trapezoids and divisions are made by metal screen pieces on top.

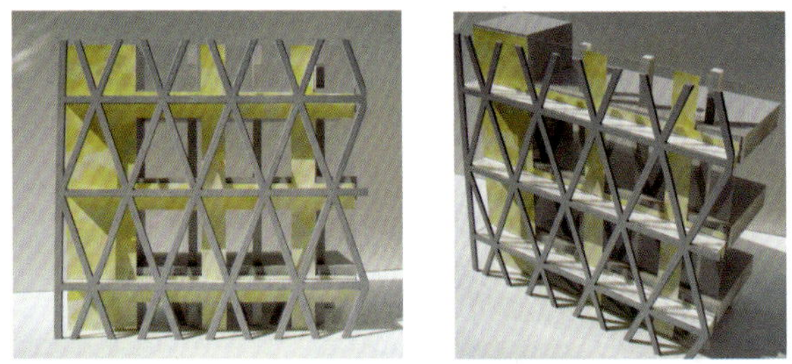

EXTERIOR WALL OPEN SCHEME

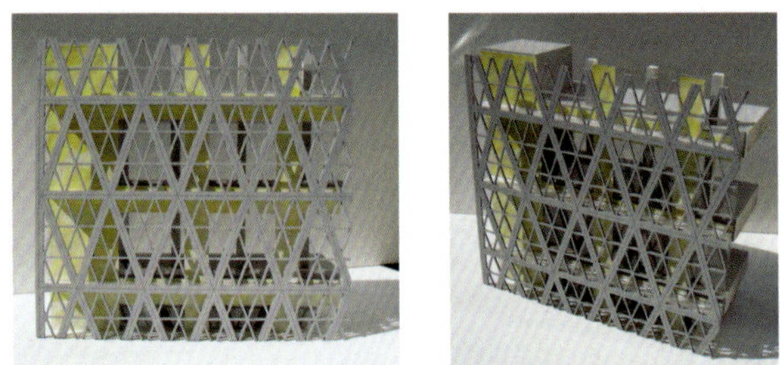

EXTERIOR WALL 9 PANEL SCHEME

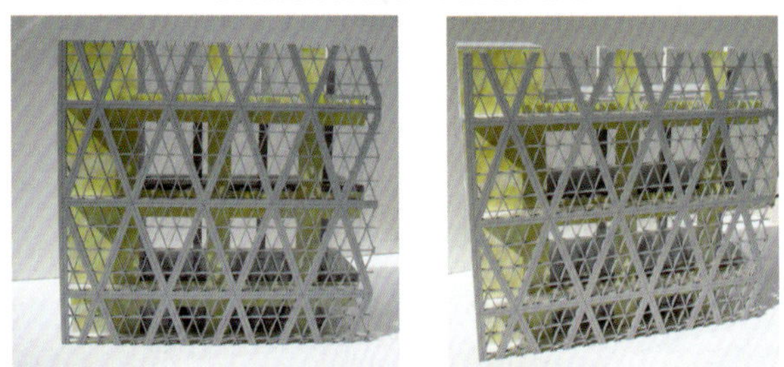

EXTERIOR WALL 16 PANEL SCHEME

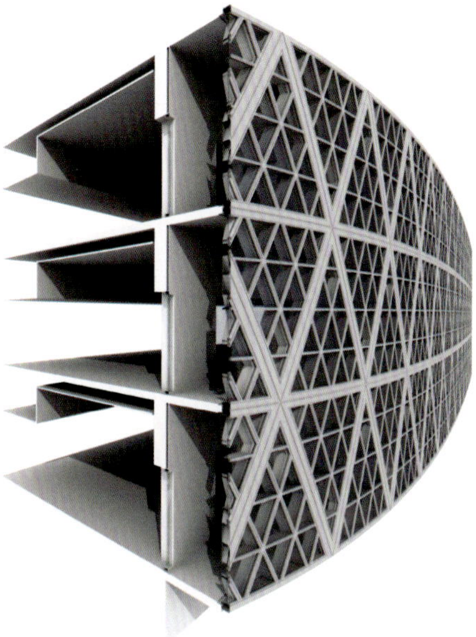

EXTERIOR WALL UNITIZED DIAGRID SECTION PERSPECTIVE

EXTERIOR WALL UNITIZED DIAGRID MODEL PHOTO

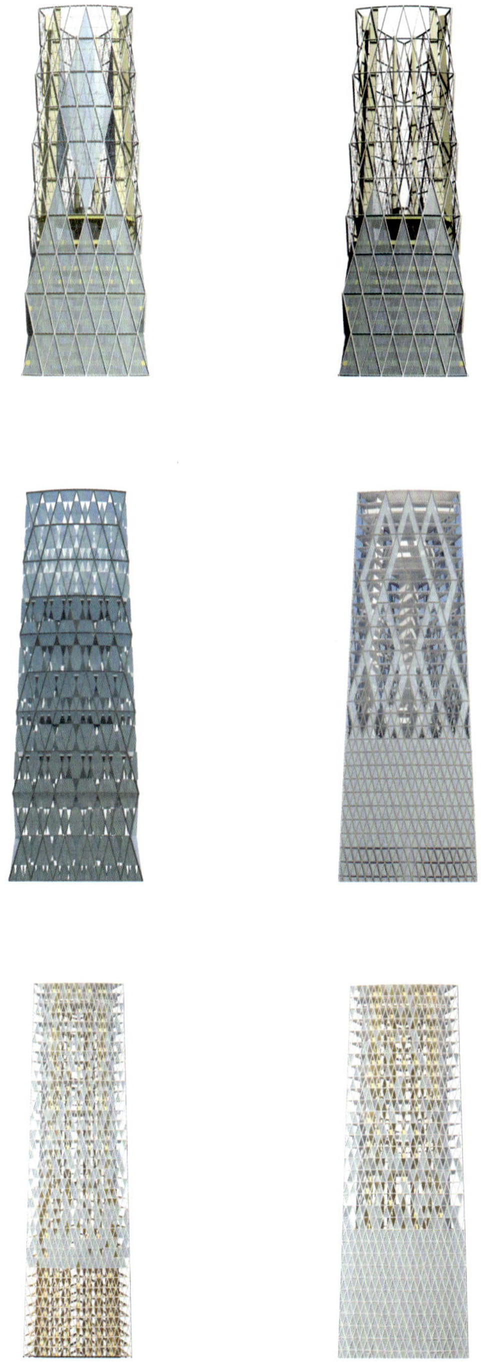

TOWER SKIN DEMATERIALIZATION STUDIES

12 AERODYNAMIC FACADE

Project:	Masdar Headquarters
Location:	Abu Dhabi, United Arab Emirates
Climate Zone:	BWH - Arid, Desert, Hot
Program:	Mixed-Use
Status:	Concept
Client:	Abu Dhabi Future Energy Company PJSC
Date:	2008-2010
Strategies:	Solar Control, Daylight, Solar Power, Ventilated

Masdar Headquarters was designed as the world's first mixed-use, positive-energy building by using sustainable design strategies and systems to produce more energy than it consumes. The project was designed as the centerpiece of Masdar City, a zero-waste, carbon-neutral development outside Abu Dhabi in the United Arab Emirates. As a source of research and development, the building is an urban lab for conducting research on energy and the environment.

The seven-story, 134,662 m^2 structure, which includes landscaped areas, accommodates commercial, retail, and cultural uses. The building's form is sculpted in response to extensive environmental analysis and adapts the ancient science of Arabic wind towers, screens, and other vernacular architecture that emphasizes natural ventilation, sun shading, high thermal mass, courtyards, and vegetation.

Thermal technology, in the form of earth ducts, draws cooler air from the underground levels to reduce the temperature of the outside air within the interior chamber. The building volumes are perforated by a series of large wind cones that bring exterior light and can both exhaust and admit wind into the depths of the courtyard spaces. The cones rise through a large roof canopy that covers, and shades, an expansive green roof. The canopy is designed to be lined with a photovoltaic and solar-panel array that simultaneously harvests solar energy while solar thermal collectors provide energy for cooling.

The building harbors a thriving natural environment. As a positive-energy building, it uses the environment to its advantage, protecting itself and its occupants from the harsh natural conditions of the region. The building uses ground cooling, shade, and site breezes to create a unique interior microclimate.

Wind Cones

Masdar Headquarters' signature architectural feature is a collection of eleven wind cones that provide natural ventilation and cooling by drawing cool air from the basement levels and warm air from the ground. Through natural buoyancy and by creating a negative pressure across the top of the cone, the warm air is pulled upward. This process forms oasis-like interior courtyards and flexible spaces, each with its own character, at ground level. The cones also provide diffused daylighting for the building's interiors.

To ensure that the natural ventilation system functions appropriately, CFD Analysis software was used to model the building's geometry and surrounding wind patterns. By doing such a model, areas of air intake and airflow are pinpointed at the base of the cone. The effects of repositioning the intake from the base of the cone to the corners was analyzed and it was found that by positioning the intake, air swirls inside the cone, providing more uniform ventilation. Follow-up testing was then performed in wind-tunnel facilities. The aperture and form of the cones were also designed to minimize the impact of solar gain on the inside surface of the cone.

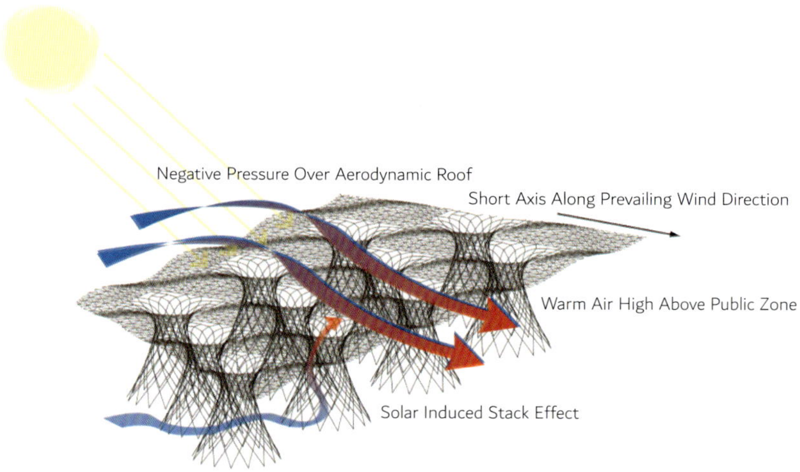

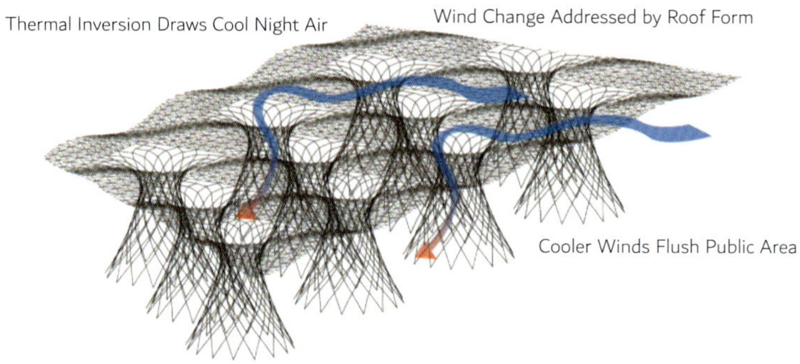

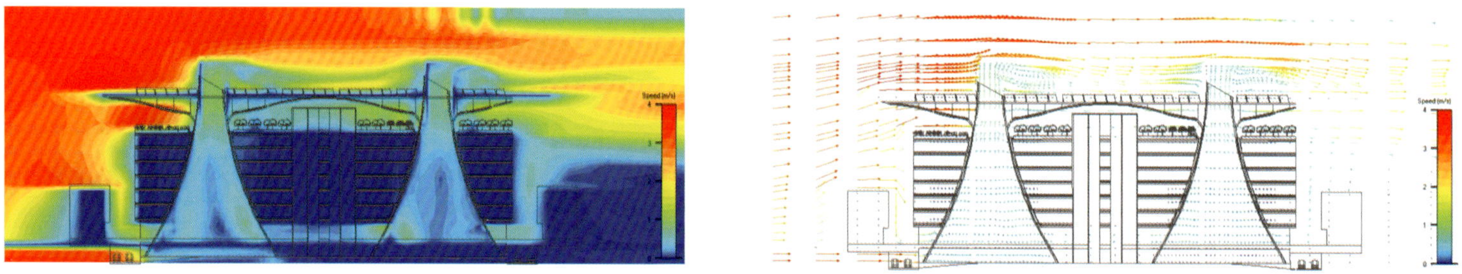

COMPUTATIONAL FLUID DYNAMICS MODEL

Hot Wind: Prevailing winds blow from the southeast, over the stack, pulling hot, old air out of the atrium

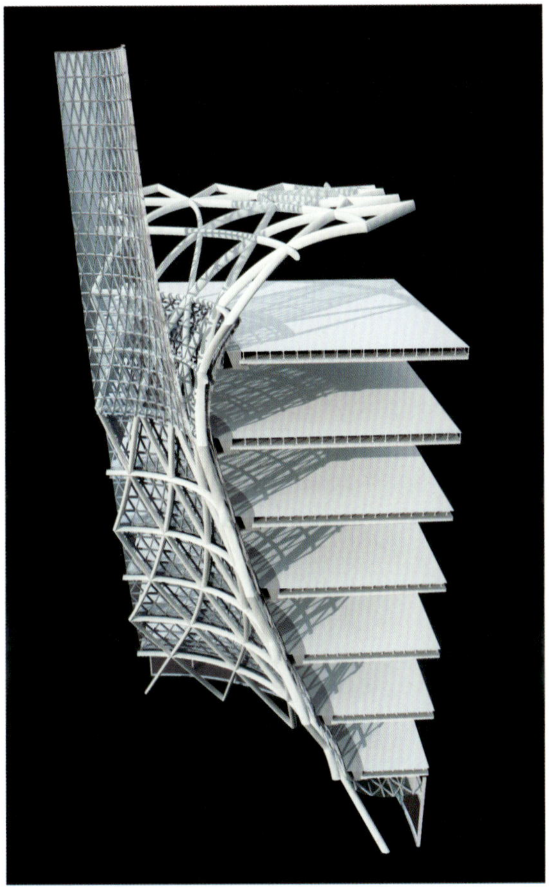

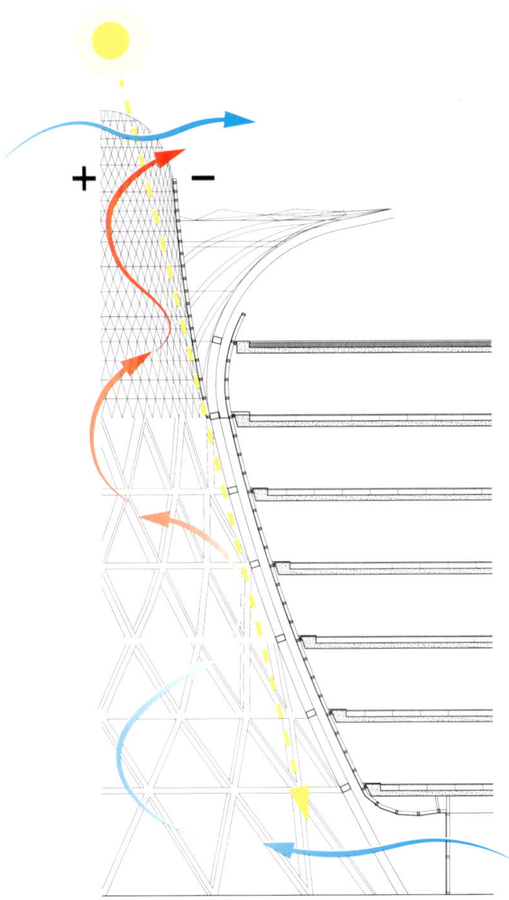

WIND CONE SECTION

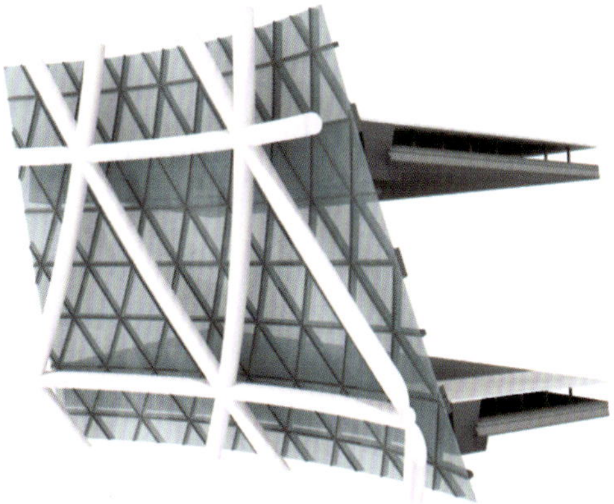

EXTERIOR WALL CONCEPT DETAIL

Wind Cone Effect

A slanted stack rising above the sunscreen allows the cone to function as an intake and exhaust, depending on prevailing wind conditions. Hot winds traveling at high velocities around and over the cone openings create low pressure areas, inducing airflow out of the cones. The geometry of the cone works to capture cool air moving in the opposite direction and to channel this air into the cone.

The wind cone's internal walls consist of custom diagrid insulated panels and a powder coated aluminum mullion system with Low-E coatings. The glazing is double curved to match the form of the cones and creates a laminar surface for air flow around, up, and out of the top of the cone.

13 SAWTOOTH FACADE

Project:	Masdar Headquarters
Location:	Abu Dhabi, United Arab Emirates
Climate Zone:	BWH - Arid, Desert, Hot
Program:	Mixed-Use
Status:	Concept
Client:	Abu Dhabi Future Energy Company PJSC
Date:	2008-2010
Strategies:	Solar Control, Daylight, Solar Power, Thermal Mass, Ventilated, Modular

Masdar Headquarters was designed to be the world's greenest mixed-use building, yielding zero-carbon emissions and zero waste (both liquid and solid) and a sustainable measure beyond LEED platinum certification. It was designed to consume 70% less water than typical mixed-use buildings of the same size and to be the lowest energy consumer per square meter for a modern Class-A office building in a hot/humid climate.

As the headquarters for the Abu Dhabi Future Energy Company, the building was also designed as the main offices of the secretariat of the International Renewable Energy Agency (IRENA), an international organization promoting the global use of energy from renewable sources.

In addition to the innovative facades in the previous section, Masdar Headquarters incorporates another pioneering, high-performance option. A secondary exterior wall incorporates a "sawtooth" design, which helps define the wall with a plan that provides correct passive solar protection and breaks down the building's long facade into human-scale modules.

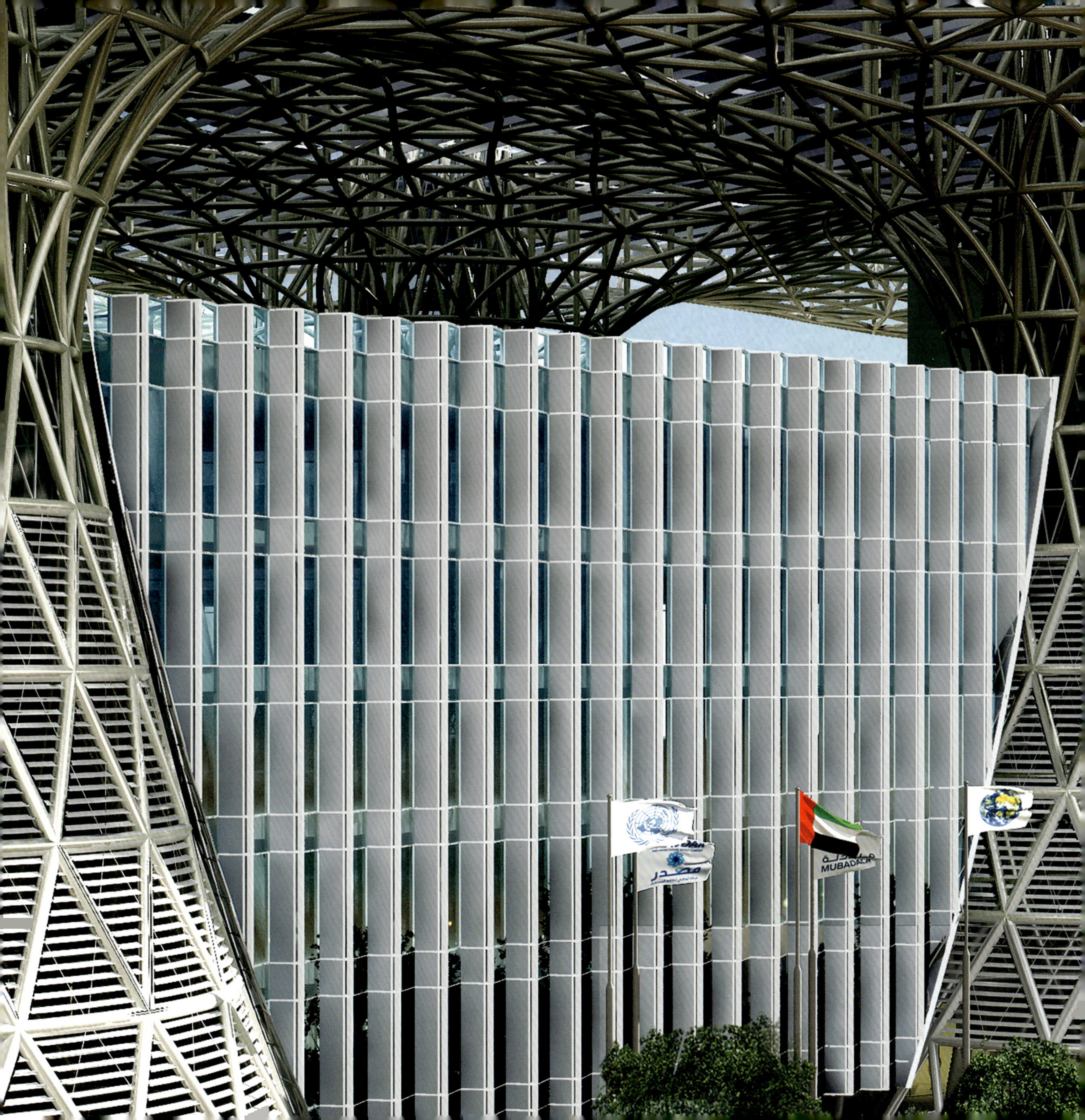
مصدر

Sawtooth Facade

One of the key distinguishing features of the building is the high-performance sawtooth facade that allows access to daylight and views, while mitigating glare and solar heat gain. The design of the wall orients the highest transparency vision glazing toward cardinal north or south, where daylight is at its highest angles and can best be redirected into the interiors.

The east- and west-facing non-vision glazing features a 16.44mm thick insulating unit. This facade results in more daylight, better views, a lower cooling load, and increased energy generation. The sawtooth facade is also more structurally sound and sustainable than alternatives, reducing the structural steel required for mullions.

To limit heat transfer, strict details were developed to decouple the outer surface from the interior spaces. The facade was designed to balance daylight, heat gain, power generation, and cross ventilation

SAWTOOTH FACADE RENDERING

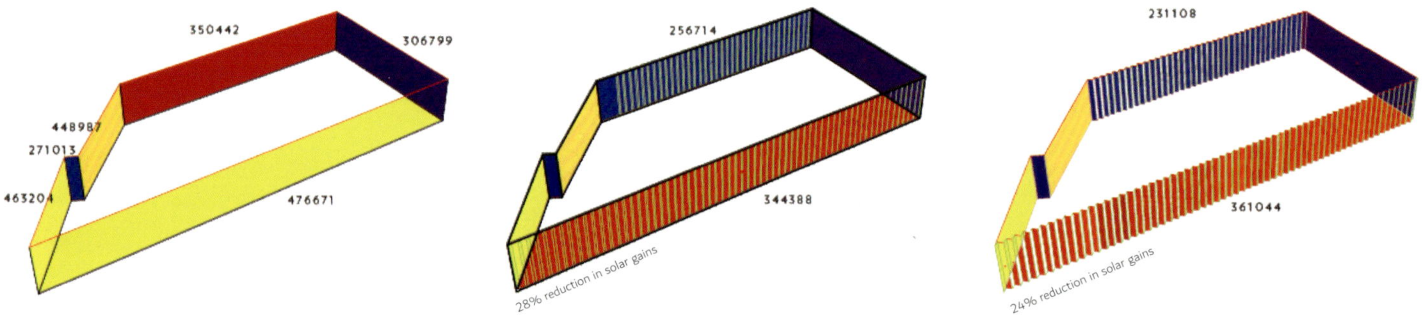

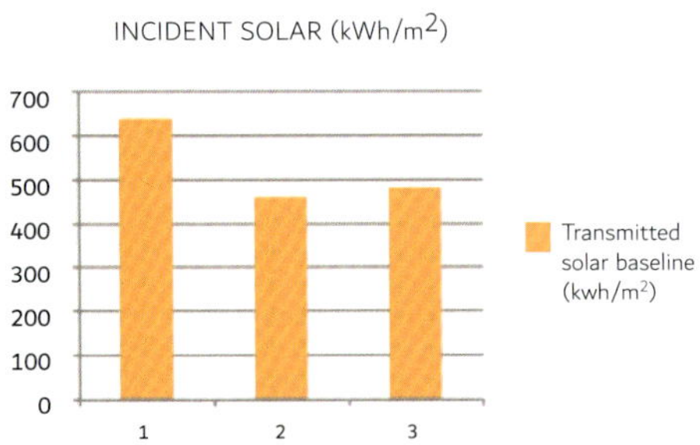

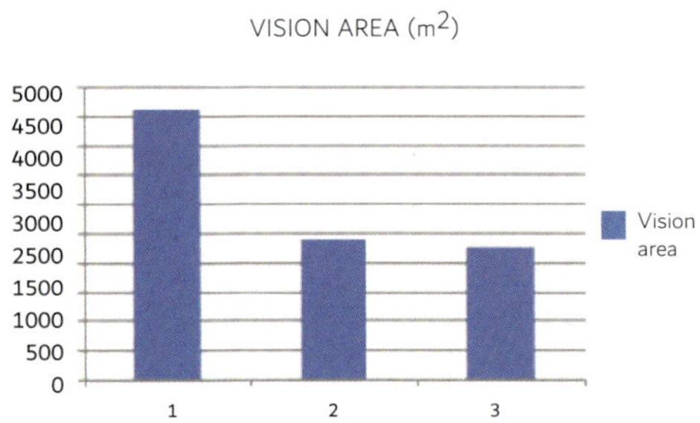

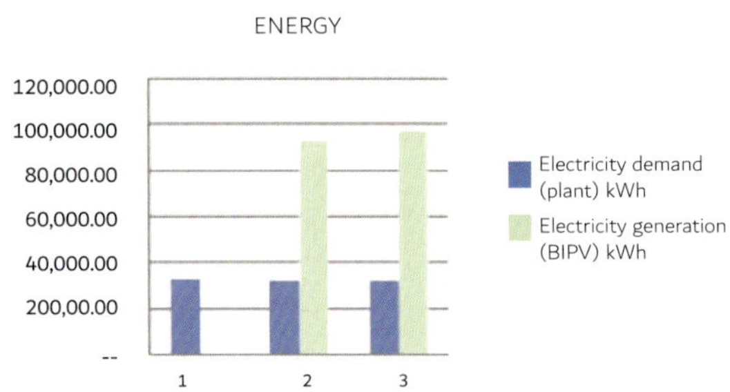

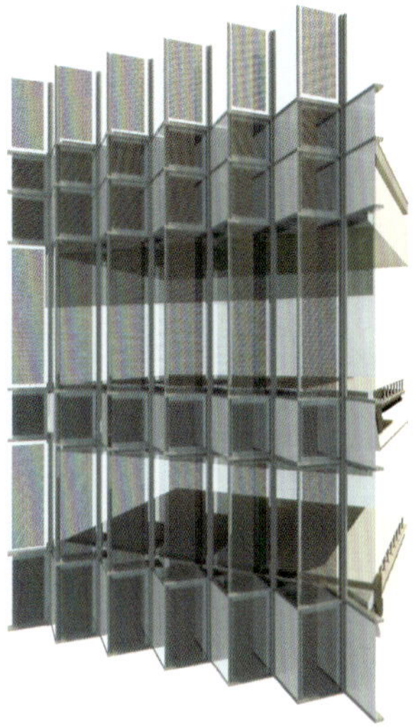

FACADE DETAIL

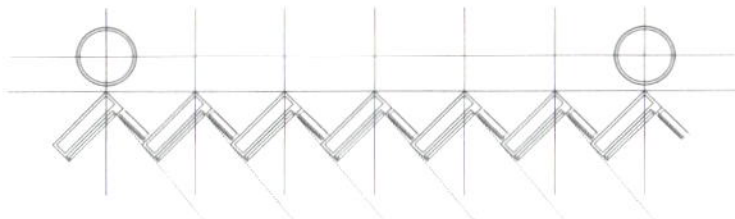

TYPICAL PLAN

FACADE MOCK UP

14 TRELLIS FACADE

Project: Al Wasl Plaza

Location: Dubai, United Arab Emirates

Climate Zone: BWH - Arid, Desert, Hot

Program: Mixed-Use

Status: Built

Client: Dubai Expo2020 LLC

Date: 2018-2021

Strategies: Solar Control, Daylight, Ventilated, Luminous, Modular

Al Wasl, which translates as "meeting place," is the centerpiece of Expo2020 Dubai, the international exposition that ran from October 2021-March2022 in Dubai, United Arab Emirates. The space was the central public amenity for the main expo events. Now in the post-expo, or Legacy, phase the space is being transformed into a spacious garden that hosts events of all scales; from small gatherings to large artistic happenings that are enhanced with state-of-the-art technology.

Visitor comfort is factored into the design of the plaza by using techniques to calibrate the temperature under the trellis with the outside temperature, ensuring a comfortable environment. The aim is to achieve a thermal comfort reduction of 4-8° Celsius cooler than exposed areas through a combination of strategies that include shading, micro-climate management, and thermal mass cooling. Light-colored materials were selected to ensure that solar radiation is reflected away from the plaza level. Additionally, the lightweight UV-resistant fabric canopy reduces solar heat gain by 50%.

Al Wasl Plaza is surrounded by five mixed-use office and hotel buildings, which also help increase the comfort levels of the space. Cool air from the buildings is recycled into the plaza, increasing air movement, and creating a cooler, less humid environment. Airflow is further encouraged through the porous canopy material, allowing warm air to rise and escape and cooler air to sweep through from below, accumulatively lowering the temperature. The trellis skin achieves the approximate daylight needed for the plants so that the tree cover grows to provide additional protection from the sun's rays, while evapotranspiration creates a localized cooling effect that pools at the pedestrian level. At the center of the space, reflecting ponds provides evaporative cooling.

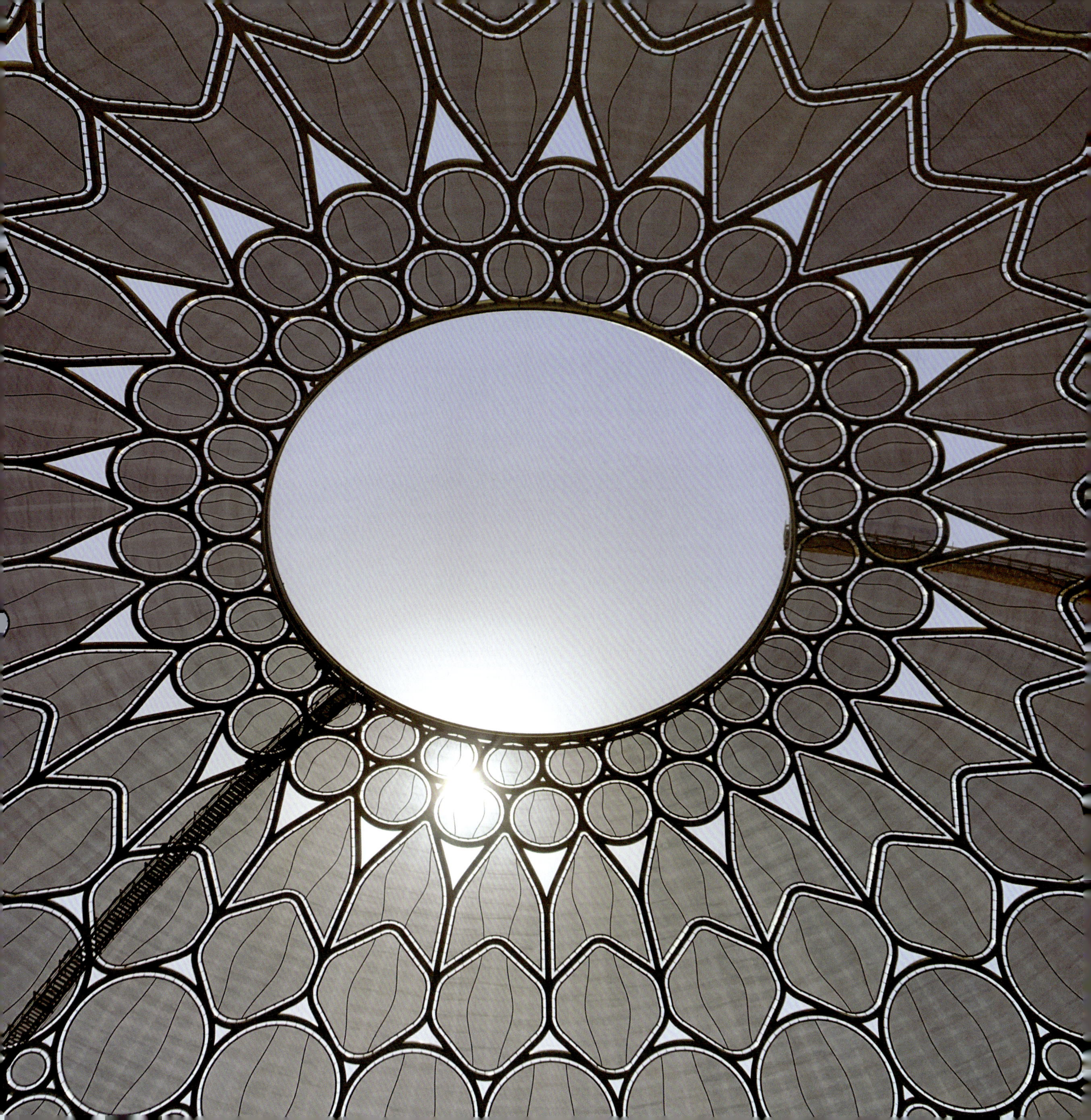

Trellis

The pattern of the 65-meter-high domed trellis, which covers the plaza, is inspired by the shape of the Expo2020 logo. The distinctive form is based on the translation of a 4000-year-old Bronze Age ring that was recently discovered in the United Arab Emirates. The dome is translucent and serves as an immersive 360° projection surface that will be visible to those inside and outside of the trellis.

Constructed of fabricated steel, the trellis has "petals" of PTFE fiberglass mesh that reduce the impact of the intense Dubai sun, while simultaneously allowing diffused light into the gardens below. The petals are embedded with dynamic, sparkling LEDs that can simulate starlight for evening shows.

The trellis has gaps between the structural frame and fabric that increases air flow and casts varying patterns of sunlight and shade on the garden floor. This combination of direct light, 50% light, 30% light, and full shade, with carefully placed water features, as well as the shade of the surrounding buildings, creates an environment that is active and is both physically and visually cooler than the adjacent exterior spaces.

At the top of the trellis is a 35-meter-wide oculus, which casts sunlight to the garden surface. Plant species were selected to correlate with the arcs of sunlight that the garden receives throughout the year. Palms span from east to west across the plaza, soaking in this "designed" arc of sunlight.

LEGACY PLAZA GARDEN RENDERING

AL WASL PLAZA ELEVATION

TRELLIS INTEGRATED PROJECTORS

TRELLIS PROJECTION

PROJECTION DIAGRAM

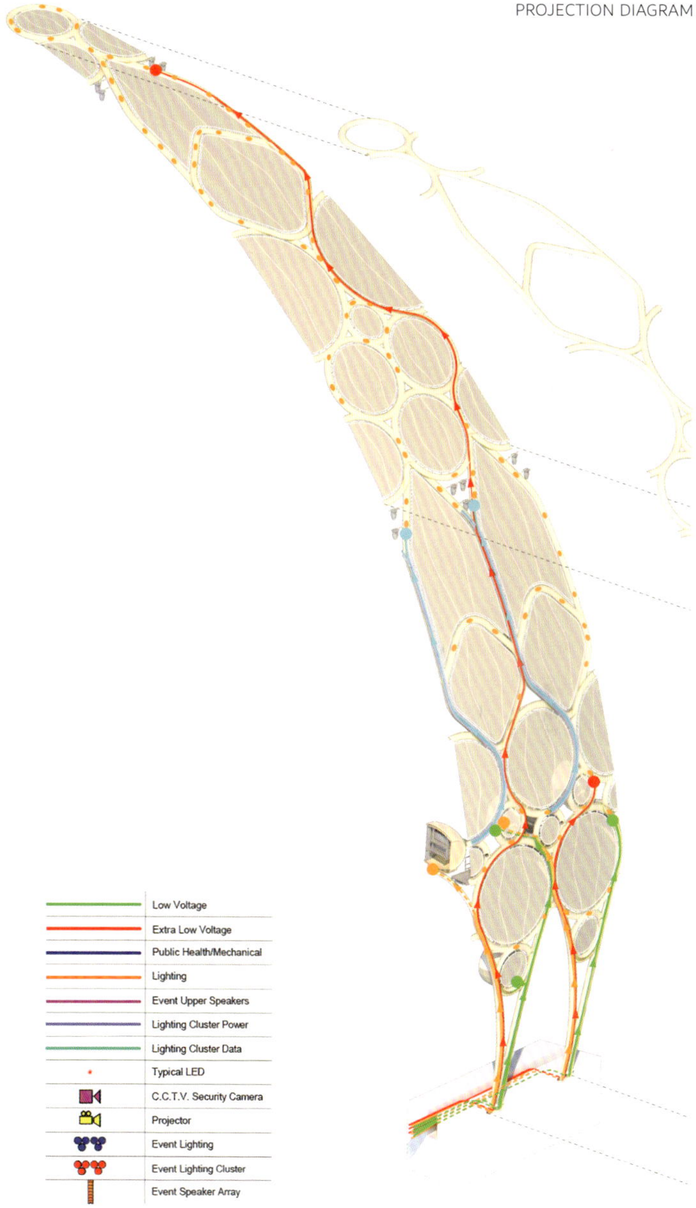

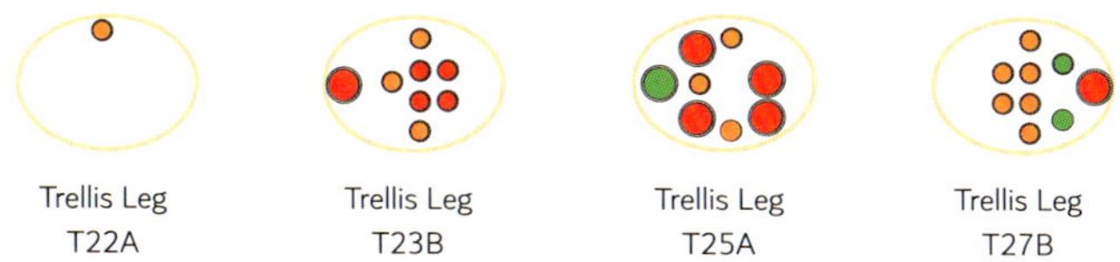

15 SCREEN FACADE

Project:	Uptown Tower
Location:	Dubai, United Arab Emirates
Climate Zone:	BWH - Arid, Desert, Hot
Program:	Mixed-Use
Status:	Construction
Client:	Dubai Multi Commodities Centre (DMCC)
Date:	2017-present
Strategies:	Solar Control, Daylight, Ventilated, Modular

Beauty, strength, value, and endurance are coveted attributes of all built endeavors. The Burj 2020 District is rooted in these principles. AS+GG's Uptown Tower, now under construction, is the first building in the Burj 2020 District, located in the Jumeirah Lake Towers Free Zone in Dubai. Alongside the Dubai Expo2020, the Burj2020 complex will serve as the southern gateway into the city and the Dubai Multi Commodities Centre Company (DMCC). The 190,000 sm 72-story mixed-use Uptown Tower includes office, residential, and hotel functions. The retail podium includes spaces for vehicle parking, MEP rooms, back of house spaces, a ballroom, and conference rooms, as well as separate entrances for the tower's functions.

Architecturally, AS+GG's design concept combines our deep understanding of the challenges associated with supertall towers and the environmental performance issues associated with Dubai's climactic conditions. We see these two issues as opportunities to develop a complex that has a unique architectural expression and is a physical symbol for Dubai in the 21st Century. The result is the next generation of mixed-use development: a self-sustaining, intelligent structure that combines optimal performance with aesthetic beauty. Uptown Tower advocates a progressive, environmental position that is intelligently planned and technologically advanced

The tower features a large garage structure. The parking garage's location, and visibility from the street and adjacent towers, required a design that was both attractive and modern, and aligned with the language of the Burj 2020 development. A unique, functional screen wall was design to protect the structure from excess sun, while allowing for natural ventilation and visual interest.

Screen Wall

The architectural expression of the screen wall for the vehicular helix is generated using the same architectural language of the main tower with triangular/diamond shaped panels. The screen is composed of independently hung aluminum panels that are stamped with an anodize aluminum coil and folded at the center to generate the desired diamond shape geometry.

The panels are folded back along the edges to create the stiffness necessary for them to hold their form. Using a butterfly fitting, each panel is hung from a stainless-steel structural cable. These cables are then tensioned to steel brackets, which are cantilever from the concrete structure of the helix ramp.

Panelization Program

One of the design objectives for the screen wall is to create the illusion of movement within the helix. For this purpose, the panels have been separated into nine groups that are folded in specific angles. They range from 5° for the group with the smallest opening to 85° for the largest opening group.

The panels are organized vertically along the surface of the helix. Those with the smallest openings are located closer to the edge of the wall; the widest groups are located along the center. Transitions from one group to the other are softened by using a gradient system and staggering the panels.

Because the panels are arranged in a circular formation, the light reflecting from each panel is different and changes as one moves around the site.

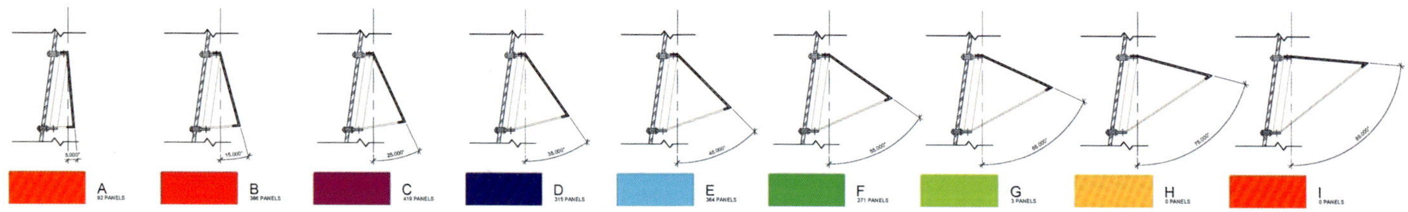

SYSTEM TYPE H.1 PANEL TYPES

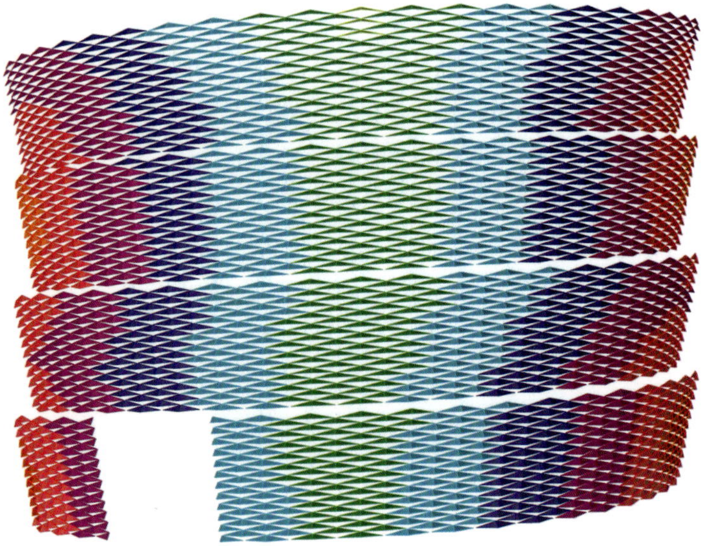

SYSTEM TYPE H.1 PANEL AXON

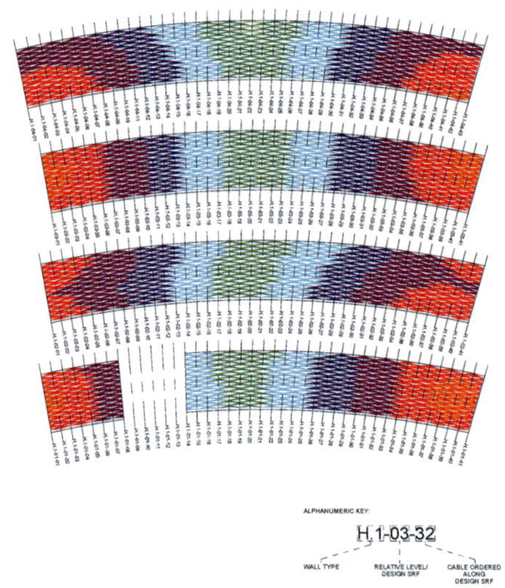

SYSTEM TYPE H.1 UNROLLED GEOMETRY

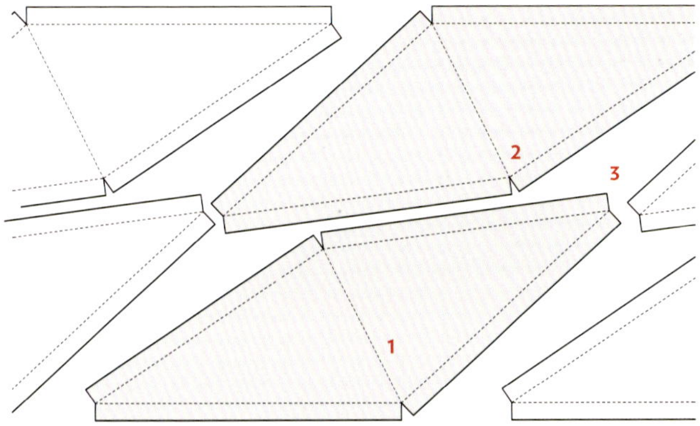

LAYOUT / PLAN

1. Anodized Aluminum Panel
2. Cut
3. Fold

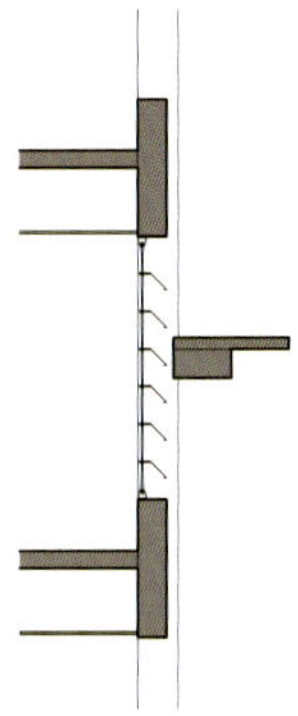

SYSTEM TYPE H.3 SECTION
(Typical)

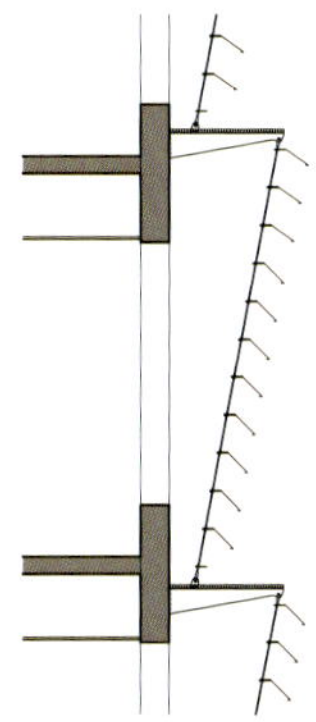

SYSTEM TYPE H.1 SECTION
(Typical)

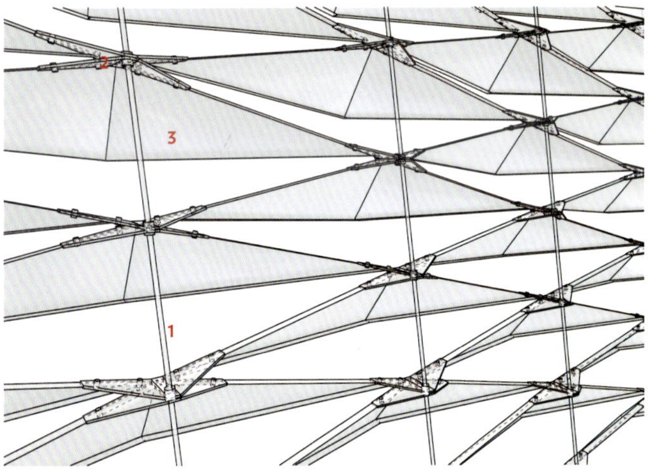

CONNECTION DETAIL AXON VIEW

1. Stainless Steel Cable
2. Stainless Steel Fittings
3. Anodized Aluminum Panel

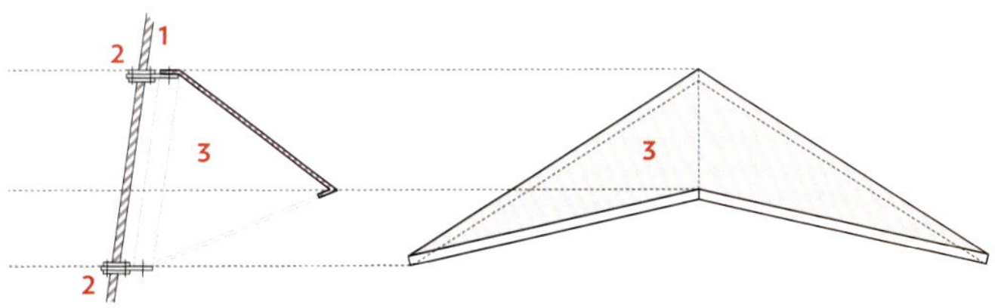

PANEL SECTION

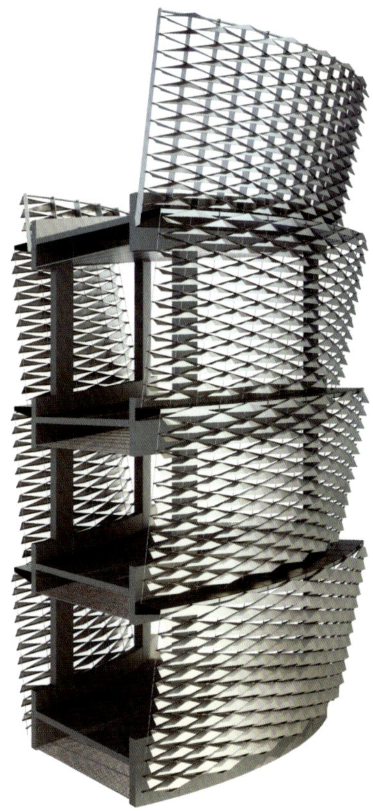

PANEL ELEVATION

16 THERMAL MASS FACADE

Project:	Kuwait University Master Plan
Location:	Shadadiyah, Kuwait
Climate Zone:	BWH - Arid, Desert, Hot
Program:	Education
Status:	Concept
Client:	Kuwait University
Date:	2009
Strategies:	Solar Control, Daylight, Solar Power, Thermal Mass, Ventilated

This dramatic competition entry for Kuwait University's central administrative facilities complex is a subdistrict of the main campus and includes an administration building, a conference center, a convocation hall, a cultural center, a library, a visitor center, and a grand mosque. The main buildings are collected under a central roof, forming a monolithic massing that creates shaded landscaped connections between the buildings.

The campus recalls traditional regional design in several contemporary ways. The duality of light and shade in the desert landscape is explored through a central design theme by creating courtyards and shaded spaces, both indoors and outdoors. Islamic-inspired geometric patterns are incorporated in courtyard trellises and building facades, resulting in interesting dappled light patterns and shadows.

The scheme's superior energy performance represents a modern vision of proven vernacular responses to the intense regional climate. Buildings and the lower public realm are self-shaded from intense high-angled sun through responsive angled facades. Orientation can reduce solar gains by over 20% when combined with an expansive roof system, which, by being permeable, controls daylight penetration and ventilation. To take further advantage of the climate, solar energy is harnessed through a 19,000 m^2 building integrated photovoltaic system that generates approximately 4,560 MWh of electricity.

Building Geometry

Several schemes were studied to understand the optimal exterior wall slope that can reduce the solar incidence of the building facades. By angling the walls downward, the self-shading effect significantly reduces the direct radiation on the surfaces, as well as creates shaded exterior spaces along the building entrances. The roof of the building is also sloped to maximize solar incidence on the photovoltaic panel arrays. The selected facade slope angle of 65° reduces radiation by a range of 30-45%, depending on the orientation. A combination of sloping planes and solid roof overhangs allow higher percentages of glass to be used on the exterior wall, without compromising the interior comfort.

SOLAR ANGLE ANALYSIS

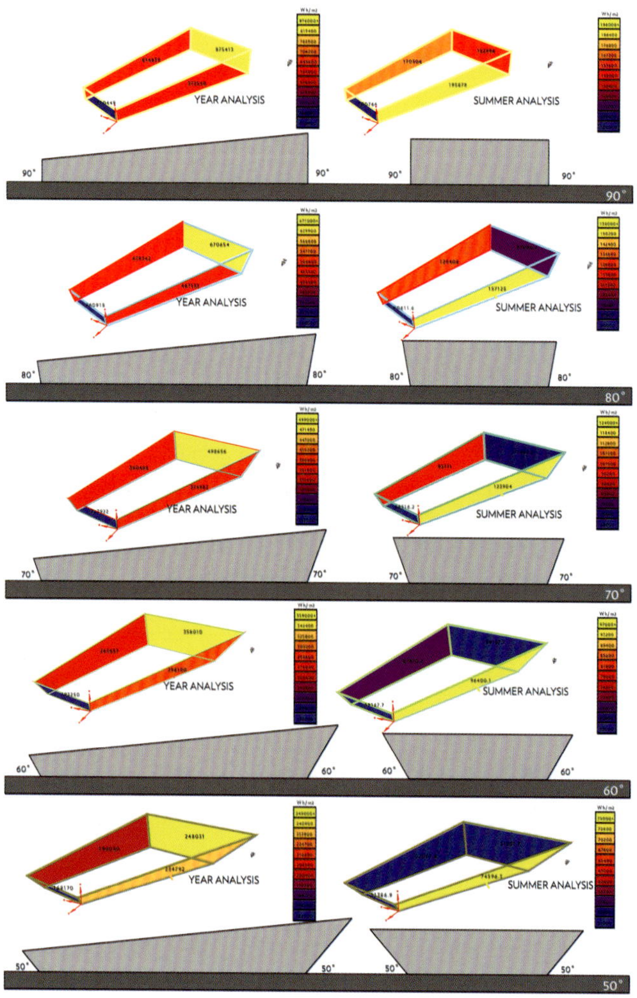

YEARLY TOTAL RADIATION (Wh)

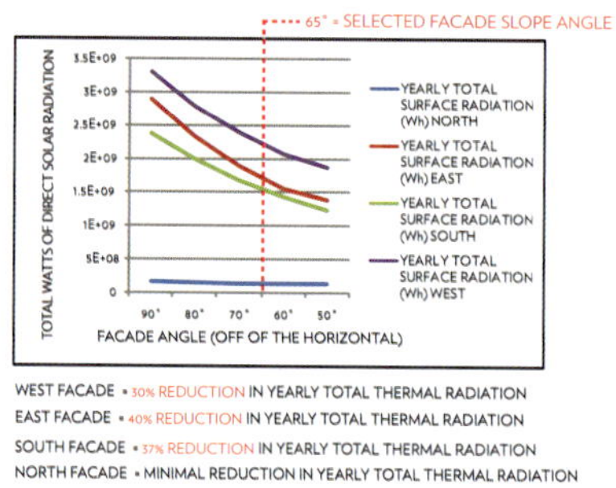

SUMMER TOTAL RADIATION (Wh)

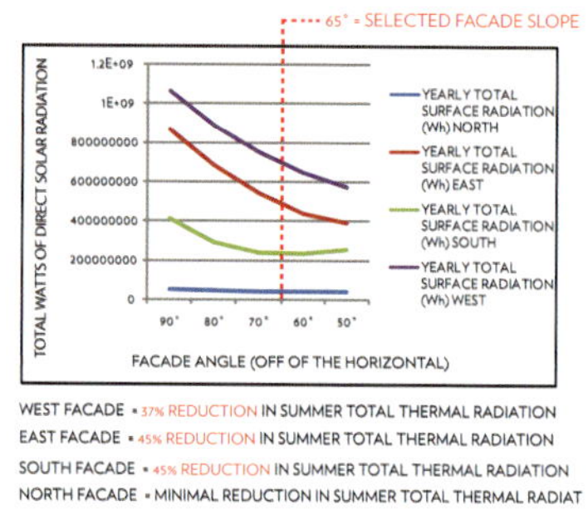

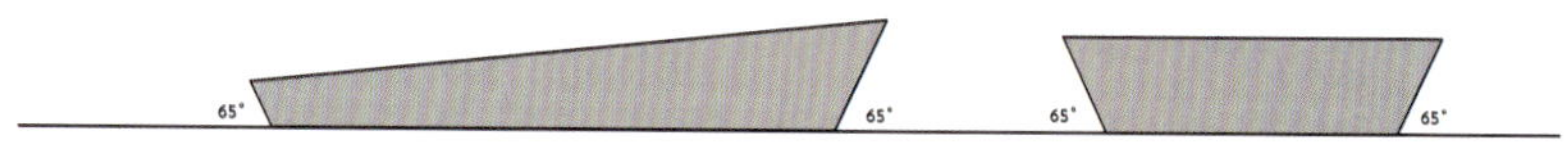

EAST WING CENTRAL ADMIN + CULTURAL CENTER

WEST WING CENTRAL LIBRARY + CONFERENCE CENTER

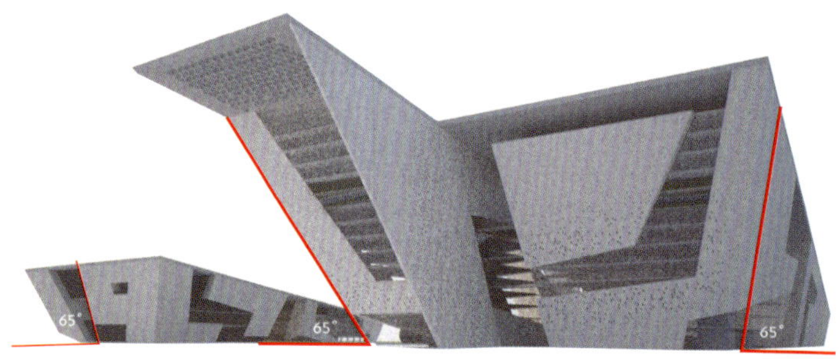

SOUTH FACADE ANGLE WEST FACADE ANGLE EAST FACADE ANGLE

Thermal Mass Wall

The buildings use inward-focused, regional planning and design principles that incorporate landscaped courtyards throughout the complex. Through shading and integral landscaping, temperatures are moderated during the day, keeping internal spaces cool. At night, when the cooler desert air settles into the courtyard, it is absorbed by the monolithic thermal mass walls. The following day, as temperatures rise, the cool air is released into the space, allowing a further reduction in temperature.

ANGULAR FACADES

COURTYARD / VENTILATION

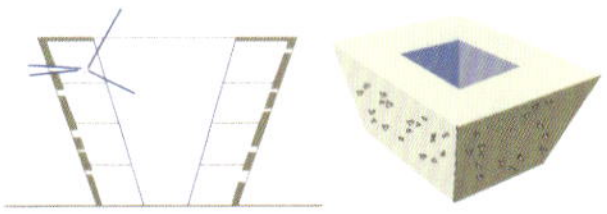

THERMAL MASS / VIEWS

EXPANSIVE ROOF / SHADING

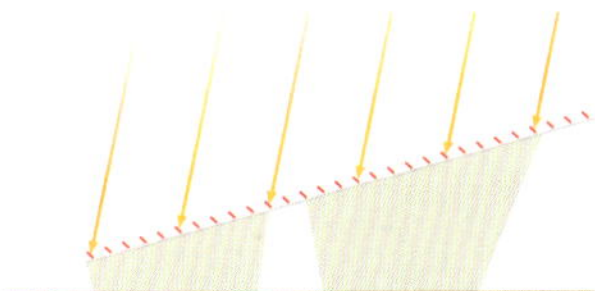

PHOTOVOLTAICS

GARDENS

EAST WING SECTION

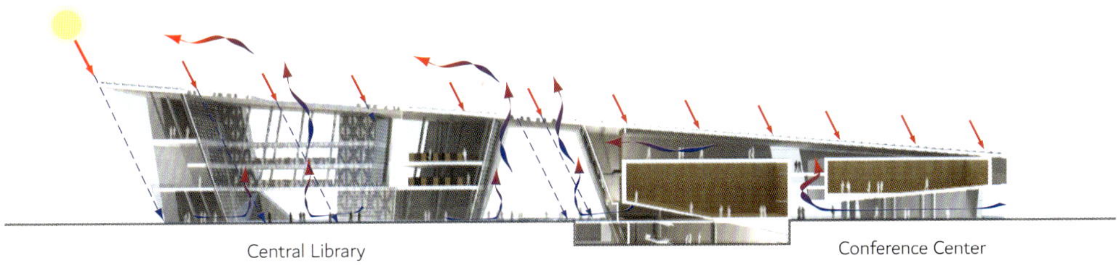

WEST WING SECTION

17 LOUVERED FACADE

Project: Gang Xia Tower

Location: Shenzhen, China

Climate Zone: CWA - Temperate, Dry Winter, Hot Summer

Program: Mixed-Use

Status: Built

Client: Shenzhen Centralcon Real Estate Co. Ltd.

Date: 2010-2016

Strategies: Solar Control, Daylight, Ventilated, Modular

Gang Xia Tower is the newest icon in Shenzhen's Futian Central District. As viewed from Jintian Road, the 199-meter, 38-story tower's softly curved corners make a powerful architectural statement that is at once dynamic, elegant, contemporary, and timeless.

The experience of the building is defined by its simplified floor plate, spacious 4.5-meter floor-to-floor heights, landscaped gardens, and floor-to-ceiling windows that provide vast westward views of the adjacent Civic Center Park, a focal point of the city's sparkling new business district.

At less than 2,000 m^2, the floor plate is compact and efficient, eliminating the need for fire zone separations and other features that would have increased costs. The design rigidly adheres to the constraints of optimized lease spans, high-quality elevator service, overall energy efficiency, and highly durable materials.

Sunshade Design

The tower's design expresses a deep understanding of local environmental conditions through the refinement of passive technologies. The primary design challenge was to maximize views of the park, which require an overall north-south orientation for the tower, while mitigating harsh solar heat gains and uncomfortable glares that are common in Shenzhen's sub-tropical climate.

To meet this challenge, a unique aluminum stainless steel-and-glass envelope was developed, which features a unified grid system of 1.5m unitized curtain wall panels, each module with recessed high-performance operable windows and horizontal sunshades. The modular fenestration system, with four smaller-proportioned windows stacked vertically on each floor, allows for significantly shallower sunshades. An energy study on the integration of shading louvers estimated a 7-8% decrease in cooling loads each year. The results equate to a "free" year of energy costs every 13 years.

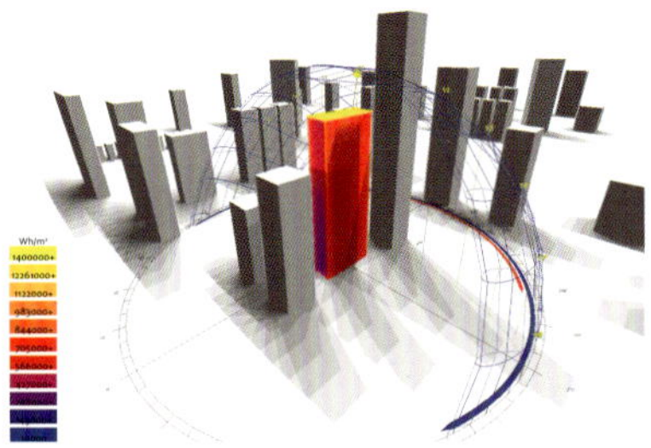

SOLAR RADIATION

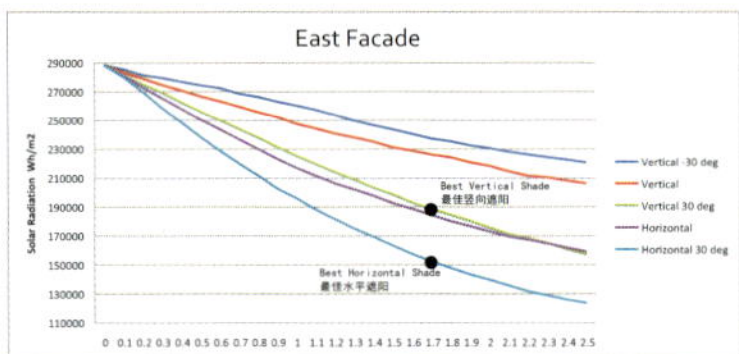

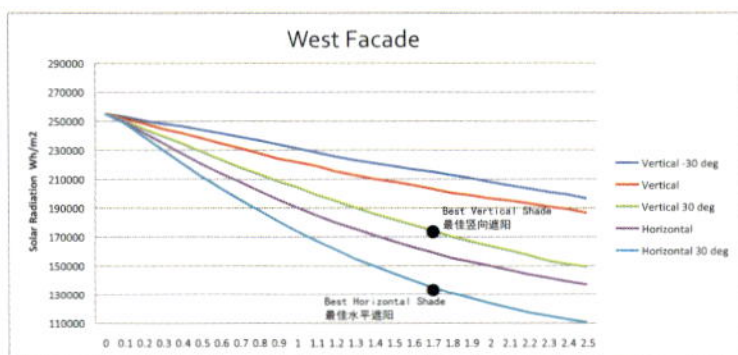

SOLAR GAIN ON FACADE VS. LOUVER LENGTH
(3m spacing)

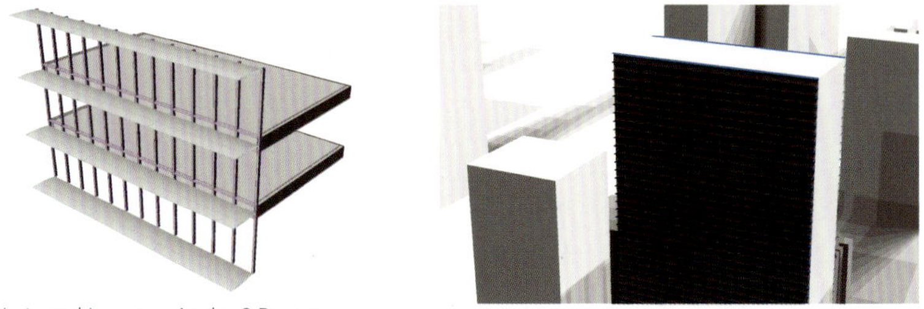

Horizontal Louvers - Angle : 0 Degrees

Horizontal Louvers - Angle : 30 Degrees Down

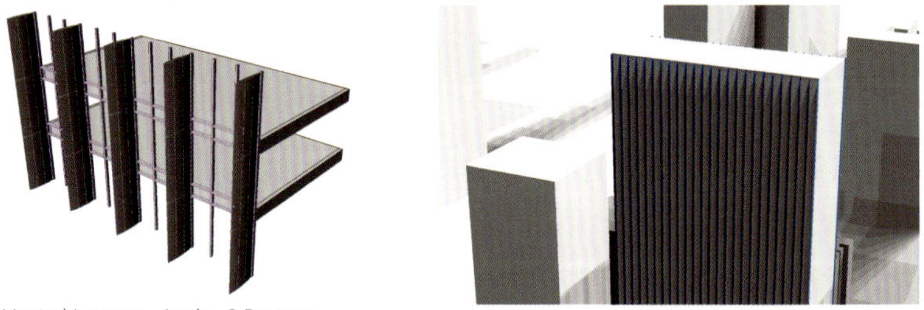

Vertical Louvers - Angle : 0 Degrees

Vertical Louvers - Angle : 30 Degrees North

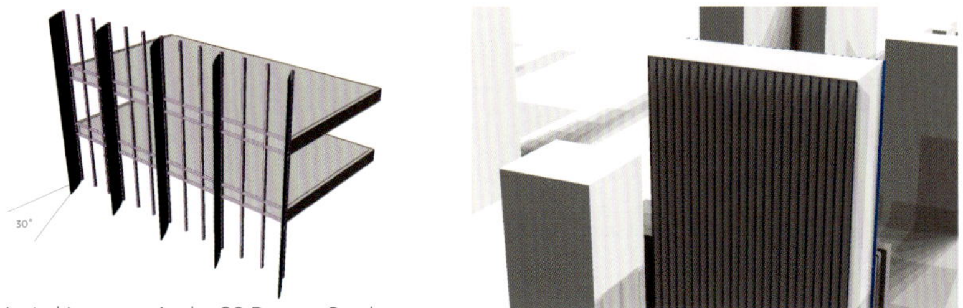

Vertical Louvers - Angle : 30 Degrees South

LOUVER STUDIES

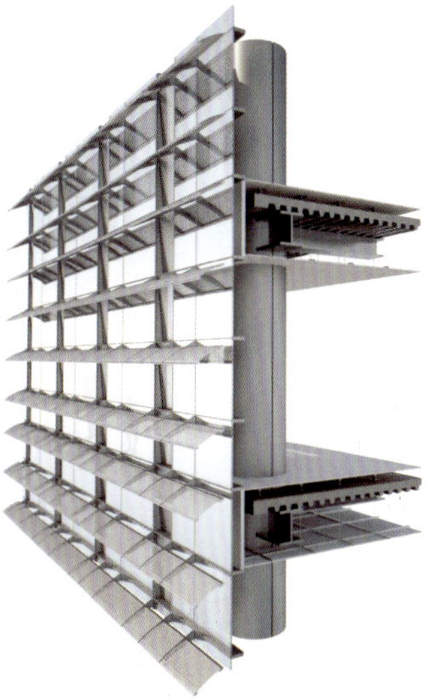

FACADE DETAIL

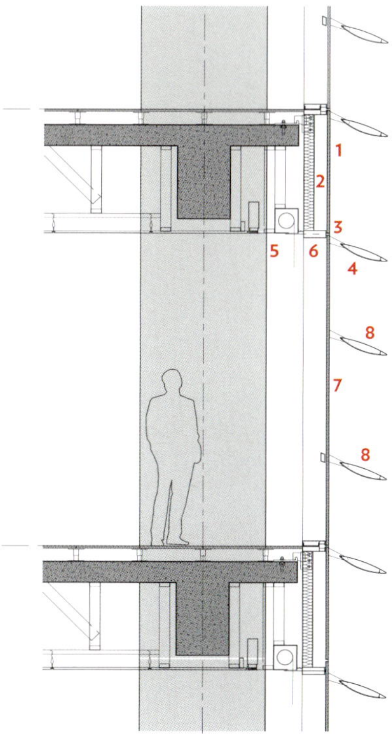

SECTION

1. Spandrel Glass
2. Insulated Metal Panel
3. Metal Bracket
4. Perforated Metal Sunshade
5. Window Shade
6. Metal Mullion
7. Vision Glass
8. Removable Sunshade

18 FIN FACADE

Project:	Central Park Tower
Location:	New York, United States
Climate Zone:	CFA - Temperate, Without Dry Season, Hot Summer
Program:	Mixed-Use
Status:	Built
Client:	Extell Development Company
Date:	2015-2021
Strategies:	Daylight, Ventilated, Modular

A beacon of glass and steel rising from the famed Billionaire's Row in New York City, Central Park Tower is one of the most prestigious addresses in the world. The tower is now certified by the CTBUH as the world's tallest residential tower. The building, which features prominent views of Central Park, is over 1500 feet tall with 179 residences, many of which are full-floor units.

The building's form responds to the conditions and opportunities presented by the site's context and the project's functional program. At the base of the tower, the form is respectful to both the human scale and the scale of the adjacent structures, and features of a 300,000 sf, seven-story Nordstrom department store and mechanical floors. The podium is framed by a steel blade wall articulation on the east and west sides that extends upward through the tower.

Grand living and entertaining spaces are strategically positioned in the corners of the residences to maximize multiple panoramas and citywide views. Structural elements are discreetly located between the residential units, resulting in floor-to-ceiling windows, unencumbered views, and gracious layouts. Residential units and their related views become grander at higher, more prominent locations. As the tower emerges, set back from the base, a landscaped outdoor amenity space is exposed. Some individual units also have private outdoor balconies.

Super-Mullion System

The tower shaft incorporates a vertical expression with flat, high-performance insulated glazing on a five-foot module. The glazing is articulated by contoured super-mullions that are used to catch the sun's light at varying angles and distribute the mullion's structural integrity to both sides of the glass. The super-mullions also provide exterior space for the facade access equipment. Integrated operable glazing panels are stacked vertically on the facade for a clean secondary vertical expression.

At the mechanical floors, rhythmic angled vents act as required ventilation without subtracting from the vertical expression. Adjacent to the central vertical shaft, two volumes rise, distinguishing themselves from the main tower as a horizontal expression. Each floor module is distinguishable by a 3D frame, which at the spandrel and edges, sets back by 5.5 inches to provide depth and separation from the high-performance insulated glazing plane. The two volumes rise to different elevations, allowing for a play in the composition.

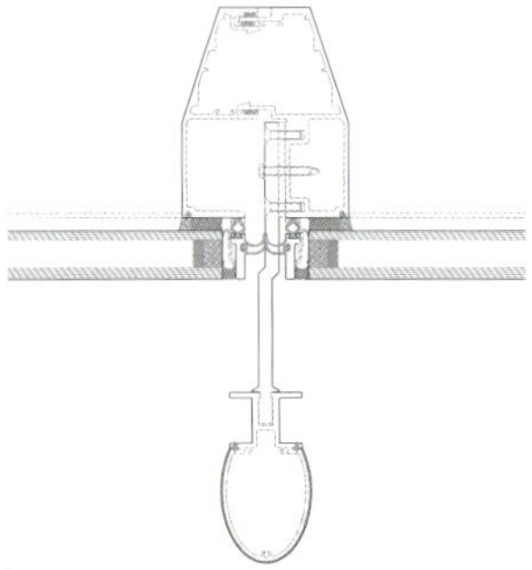

OPTION 1 - ELLIPSE WITH GAP

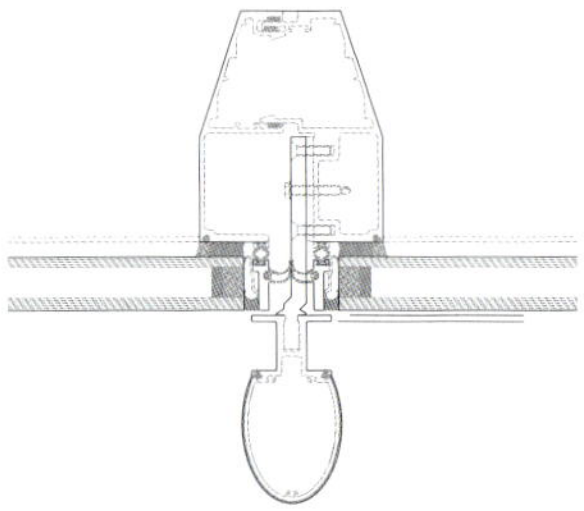

OPTION 2 - ELLIPSE WITHOUT GAP

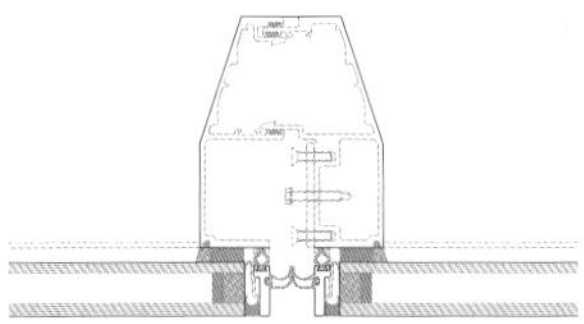

OPTION 3 - BUTT GLAZING

SUPER-MULLION OPTIONS STUDY

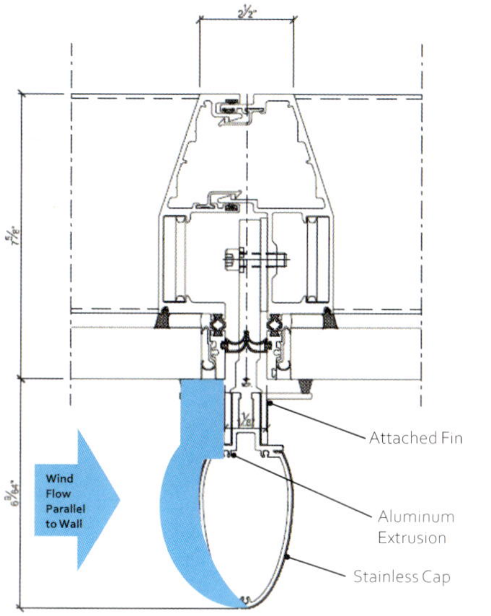

1

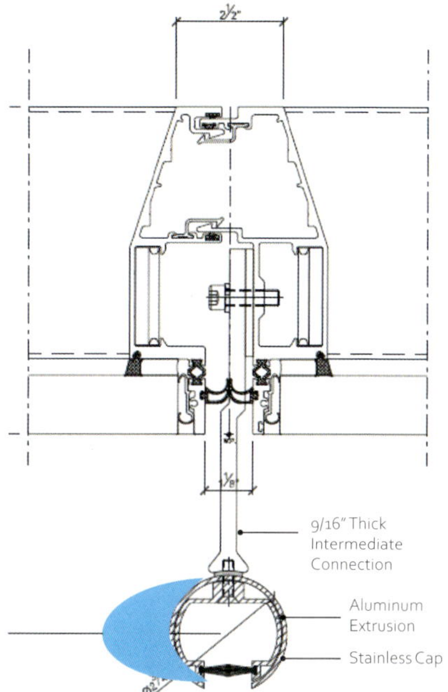

2

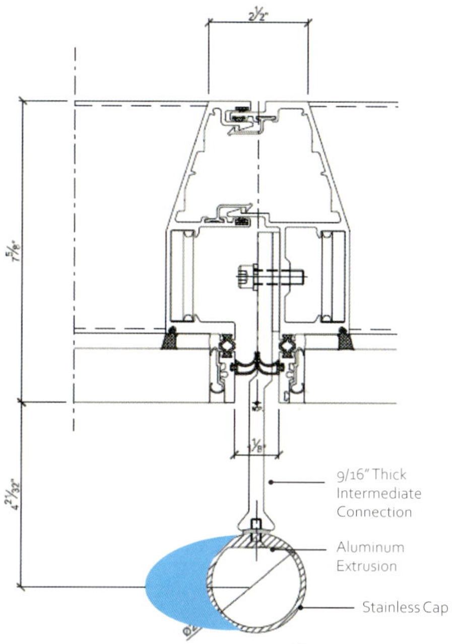

3

INITIAL PROPOSED DESIGN - ELLIPSE WITHOUT GAP
(Not Recommended)

FINAL DESIGN - ROTATED OVAL WITH GAP
(Recommended)

1. Wet snow accumulation on windward side of protruding mullion
2. Fin with gap geometry as track: anticipated reduced wet snow accumulation on windward site of protruding mullion
3. Fin with gap geometry as internalized track: anticipated reduced wet snow accumulation on windward site of protruding mullion

Snow + Ice Studies

Snow and ice studies were performed to determine the best design for the super-mullions. Specialty consulting engineering firm RWDI was engaged by the client to simulate the effect of the elements on the mullion geometry. The conditions of the site were tested using a physical mock-up of a portion of the facade. The results informed the design of the mullions, confirming that providing a gap between the facade and the mullions reduces ice formation. Additionally, it prompted changing the geometry from the original elongated oval to the completed built design, which is better able to shed ice and snow.

19 FACET FACADE

Project:	Chengdu Greenland Tower
Location:	Chengdu, China
Climate Zone:	CWA - Temperate, Dry Winter, Hot Summer
Program:	Mixed-Use
Status:	Construction
Client:	Greenland Group
Date:	2011- present
Strategies:	Solar Control, Daylight, Ventilated, Luminous, Modular

Located in the center of Chengdu's growing Dongcun district, Chengdu Greenland Tower is inspired by the unique ice mountain topography of the region. The tower translates the mountain ridges that reflect the light from the sky and the valleys that reflect light from the earth as a supertall light sculpture, creating a connection between earth and sky. The 468-meter-tall tower was designed to be the region's tallest building and the fourth tallest in China.

The tower is an environment-friendly and sustainable new city icon, designed for the specific local climate conditions. The facade has careful integration of the ventilation system behind the metal rods to allow air movement for typical tenant space and air exchange for building mechanical systems. The high-performance facade shines with a layer of elegant metallic glow from the carefully detailed exterior stainless steel rods that self-animate with the changes of weather, the surrounding buildings, and when viewing from different angles. At night, the tower comes alive with unique lighting animations from a specially integrated channel lighting system.

The architecture and structure are one, as the design fully considers the structural requirements of a supertall building in a high seismic zone, using a geometrical plan, a tapered form, and a high-performance bracing system to ensure the structure's stability and efficiency. The tower's form has superior aerodynamic performance from the tapered and faceted cylinder geometry that efficiently disrupts the wind and prevents large vortices from shedding in a coherent pattern, thereby reducing high inertial wind loads.

Tower Geometry

When designing a structure at this height, a variety of practical issues need to be considered and adopted into the architectural form. One key element is how the tower's structure responds to wind loading. The tower's form is essentially a tapered, faceted cylinder. This shape confuses the wind, preventing large vortices from shedding in a coherent pattern. These well-correlated vortices can produce a high-dynamic response, which results in high-inertial wind loads and elevated motions, both perceivable by occupants. Compared to a more traditionally shaped box or rectangular building, Chengdu Greenland Tower has superior aerodynamic performance because it disrupts the wind more efficiently over the tower's height.

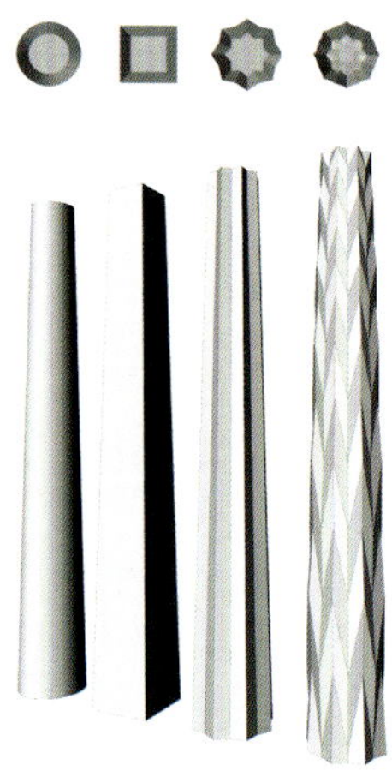

TOWER GEOMETRY
SAME VOLUME

The faceted geometry also minimizes the vertical surface area of the exterior wall, with a well-balanced annual solar heat gain that optimizes the daylight quality to the interior space. Tilting up and down with a gradual changing scale facing toward the sky, the building facets disperse the direct glare in the sunny days, and diffuse ambient light on cloudy days.

The sculpted form creates a unique reflective effect that gives the tower its overall design character. However, the technical issues of resolving such a complicated shape in the curtain wall posed challenges. One challenge was at the point in which the tips of the geometry intersect. To solve this, the design includes a stainless-steel clad channel reveal that serves two distinct purposes.

The first, is to facilitate the installation of the glass joints where several panels come together. These reveals allow detailing that ensures proper protection against water infiltration and excessive movement in the facade panels. The second, is to provide a location where festive lighting can be installed and remain out from view from the inside of the tower.

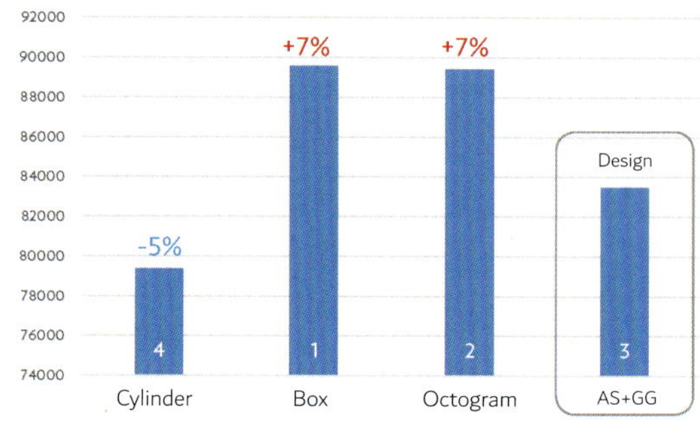

FACADE AREA

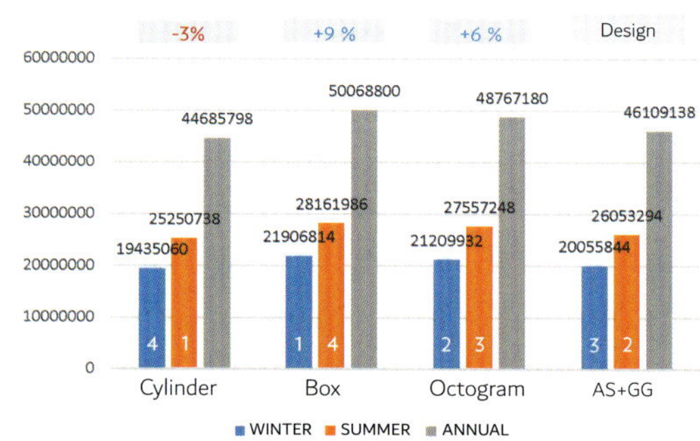

TOTAL SOLAR RADIATION (KhW)

Exterior Wall

The exterior wall was designed to be highly efficient in both cost and energy performance. Panel sizes and types were studied to optimize minimal variations for a more efficient construction. The wall's defining features are exterior round stainless steel pipes, designed to capture the sunlight as it hits the tower. Various configurations were studied before deciding on the final design.

EXTERIOR WALL DIAGRAM

1. Integrated Lighting Channel
2. Polished Stainless Steel Rod
3. Integrated Ventilated Mullion
4. Insulated Shadow Box Assembly
5. Insulated Vision Glass

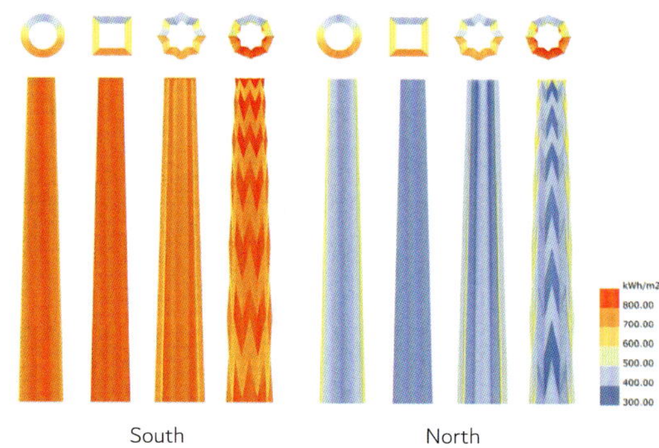

FACADE ANNUAL SOLAR RADIATION

Structural Integration

Chengdu Greenland Tower has a unique shape likened to the configuration of a pyramid distributed along the building's height and is symmetrical in the center. Each floor plan is slightly different and can be separated into three groups: octagon, 16-side polygon, and 32-side polygon. The 16-side polygon is the basic form, while the octagon and 32-side polygon are mutated versions that fit inside the original. To integrate to the architectural profile, one composite column is placed at each corner of the 16-side polygons.

Each composite column, which contribute to the tower's overall lateral stiffness when the columns connect to the core, slopes at 5 degrees from the vertical line. Following an alternate pattern, the composite columns slope toward and away from the core, creating the unique building profile.

The main tower includes a gravity system and a lateral system. Some of the structural members belong only to the gravity system or the lateral system, but it is also common that some—like the core wall—are key components of both the gravity system and lateral system. From a structure point of view, any tall building is a cantilever element.

Under lateral loads (wind and seismic loads), the overturning moment on the tower increases proportionally to the square of the building's height, while the tower deflection increases proportionally to the building height by the fourth power. Lateral system elements include the core wall, composite columns, outrigger trusses, and the exterior diagonal bracing.

The core dimension for the plan is approximately 28m x 28m from the base to Level 54. From Level 54 to Level 65, the flange wall slopes inward, and the core dimension reduces gradually. At Level 65 and above, the core dimension for the plan is 24m x 24m. The thickness of the flange wall at the bottom is 1m, reducing to 0.4m at the top. The web wall thickness is 0.8m at the bottom and reducing to 0.4m at the top.

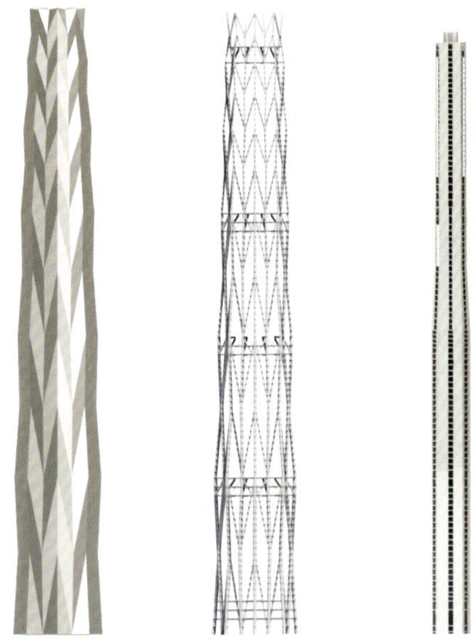

FACADE STRUCTURE CORE

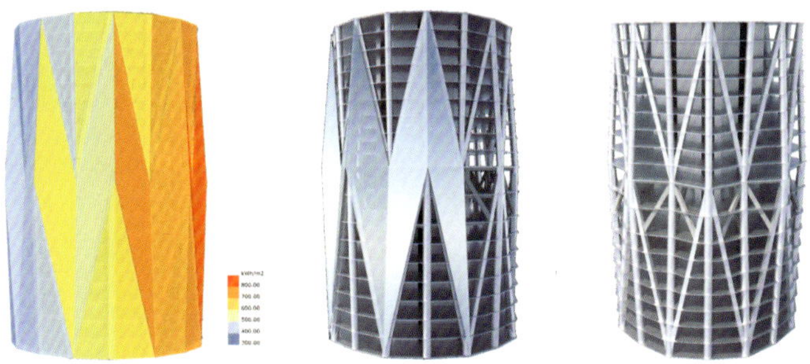

SOLAR HEAT GAIN FACADE STRUCTURE

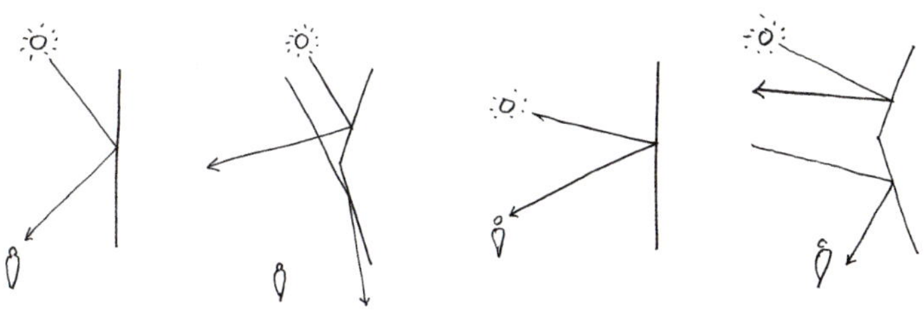

STRAIGHT: HIGH ANGLE SUN FACET: HIGH ANGLE SUN STRAIGHT: LOW ANGLE SUN FACET: LOW ANGLE SUN

CONSTRUCTION 2019

20 ACTUATED FACADE

Project:	Shenzhen Bayview Tower
Location:	Shenzhen, China
Climate Zone:	CWA - Temperate, Dry Winter, Hot Summer
Program:	Mixed-Use
Status:	Concept
Client:	China Merchants Shekou Industrial Zone Holdings Co.
Date:	2019
Strategies:	Solar Control, Daylight, Solar Power, Wind Power, Intelligent, Luminous, Modula

Shenzhen Bayview Tower sets a new standard for high-performance, environmentally responsive architecture. The building's shape and exterior expression are designed to protect from, and take advantage of, the local environmental conditions. The building responds to the natural forces of the site with the goal of achieving a delicate balance with nature.

The silhouette of the building draws inspiration from the undulating natural forms of the surrounding Nanshan Mountains and the Shenzhen Bay. Both the mountains and the water are important symbols and physical characteristics of the Shenzhen landscape. By borrowing inspiration from these natural forms, the building creates a direct relationship to its context. From across the bay, the tower appears as a new peak between the water and the mountains. At night, the tower is a beacon of light that anchors the entrance to the bay.

The form of the tower was designed for efficiency, not solely measured in its floor plate, but also in its structure and environmental system performance. By combining efficiency and comfort with an aerodynamic form suitable for a supertall tower, the building is more cost effective, user friendly, and easier to maintain than standard buildings of this size. In supertall towers, the forces and acceleration experienced by the structure are heavily influenced by the form of the building. Therefore, it is critical that the form of the building be developed with aerodynamics (wind engineering) in mind.

The form of Shenzhen Bayview Tower was developed and optimized with the goal of creating a highly efficient building, both functionally and structurally. By reducing the wind force on the building, the form minimizes the amount of structural material—and the associated embodied carbon—that is needed for construction.

High Performance Exterior Wall

A preliminary massing analysis of the site indicated that reducing the mass at the top of the building by stepping back the form is more effective at mitigating the wind loads than tapering the building. To further reduce wind forces, wind slots are incorporated into the massing of the building. These wind force reductions minimize the amount of structural material, and the associated embodied carbon, which is needed for construction. The combination of these optimizations gives the building its distinct and iconic form.

Another major component to the design of the building's facade is the retractable awnings that shade the building from direct sunlight and generate electricity from their BIPV. These high-performance awnings are automatically deployed by sensors throughout the building as the sun moves across the sky. They are connected to the building's management system and fold into each bay when they are no longer needed or during extreme weather. The design draws inspiration from traditional awnings that have adorned buildings in sub-tropical and tropical regions for generations.

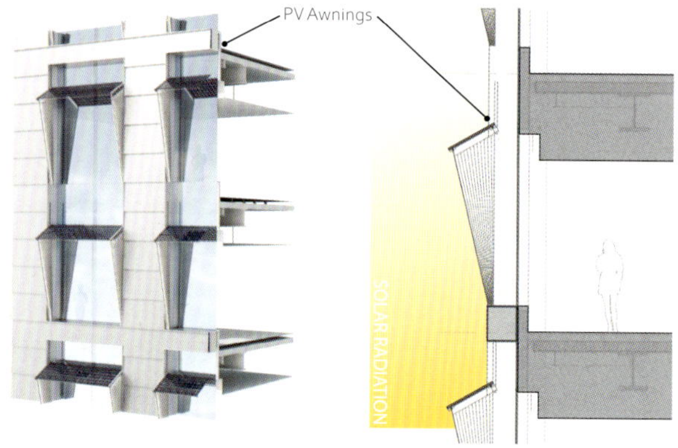

SOLAR REDUCTION

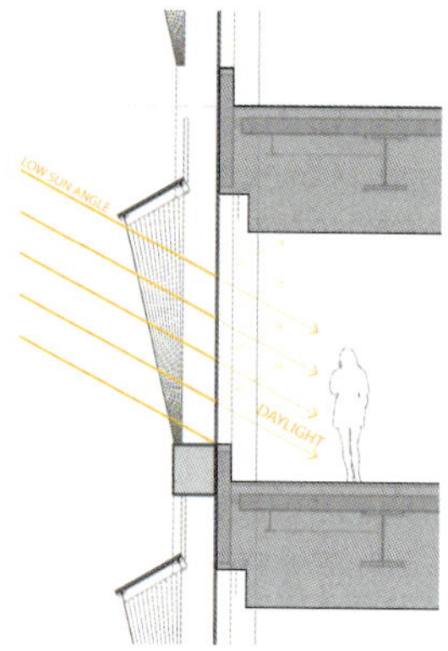

GLARE MITIGATION + DAYLIGHT

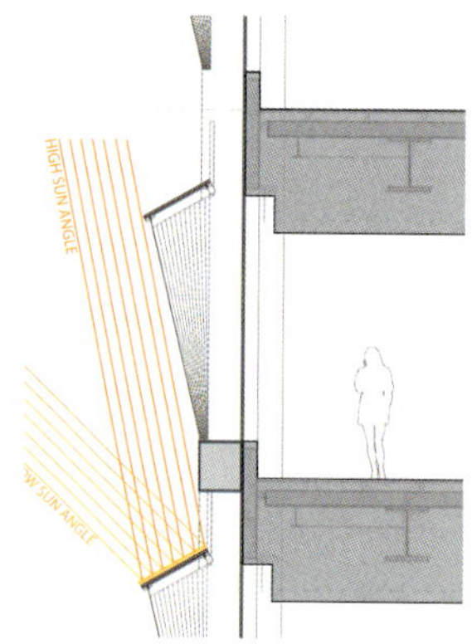

PV POWER GENERATION

PARAMETRIC BAY VIEW STUDY

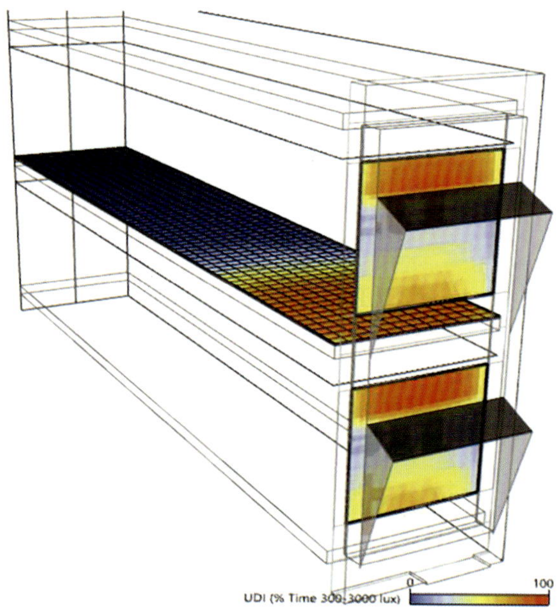

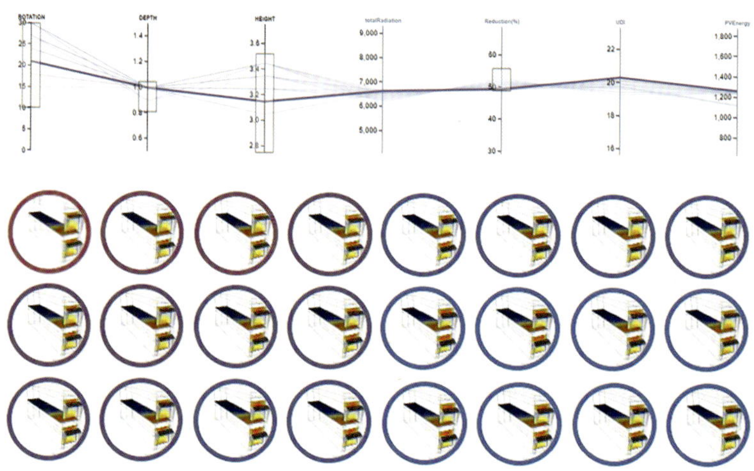

AWNING COMPARISON STUDY

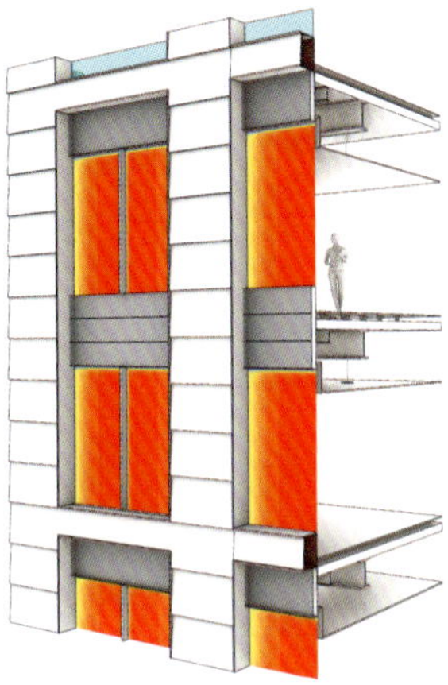

WITHOUT AWNINGS

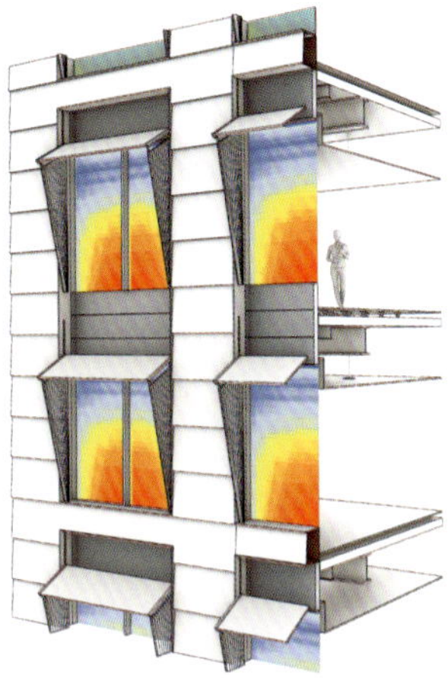

WITH AWNINGS
43% Overall Solar Radiation Reduction

Heat Gain Reduction + Power Generation

In addition to providing solar protection to the building, the BIPV on the exterior awnings generate renewable solar energy. The PV array at the top of the observatory is optimally oriented to maximize renewable solar energy generation throughout the year. The total renewable energy produced from PV is estimated to be 3.8% of the total building's annual energy consumption.

The building also incorporates 16 wind turbines located on the AOR floors at points where wind vortices are maximum. Wind velocity was studied for each of the AOR floors using CFD Analysis. The small notches allow the installation of two 1.7m vertical axis wind turbines and the larger notches allow for a single 6m turbine. The vertical axis turbines are a proven technology that can handle wind of variable direction and velocity. The total renewable energy produced from wind is estimated to be 1.8% of the total building's annual energy consumption.

EXTERIOR WALL RENDERING

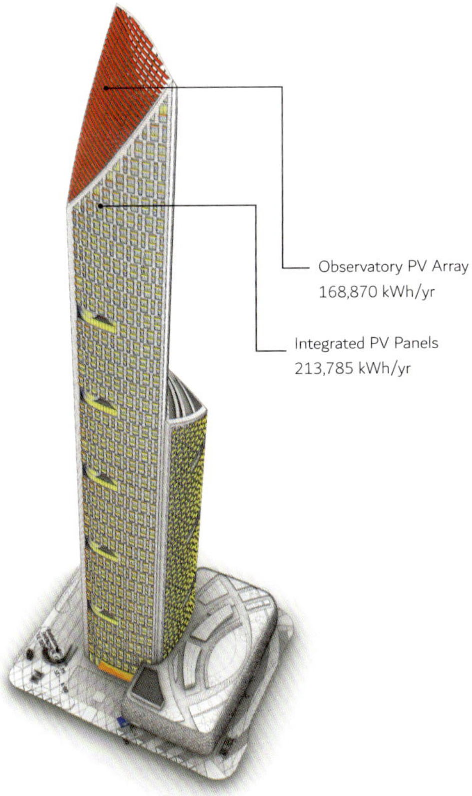

21 UNDULATING FIN FACADE

Project:	Runmao Tower
Location:	Nanjing, China
Climate Zone:	CFA - Temperate, Without Dry Season, Hot Summer
Program:	Mixed-Use
Status:	Design
Client:	China Jinmao Holdings Group Ltd.
Date:	2017-present
Strategies:	Solar Control, Daylight, Luminous, Modular

Runmao Tower, officially named South HeXi Yuzui Financial Tower, will be the center of a world-class, waterfront business district in Nanjing. The work-live community will be a new global destination and vibrant center for culture, nature, entertainment, and technology.

The development intends to raise property values with networks to access the riverfront, public transit, and many new cultural, natural, and technological opportunities. The district encourages increased interaction, inviting the user to experience the district either as a work-live environment or as a visitor to one of the many public parks and art centers.

At the heart of the CBD, the architectural design of the new supertall tower was inspired by the Yangtze River. The river reflects light, throwing out textures and dimensions, much like the tower's exterior, which is shaped to mitigate wind vortices, optimize views, and enhance both the structure and the program. Its mixed-use office program also features a unique observatory amenity with a stunning viewing platform.

Building Performance

The tower is designed and positioned to take advantage of the wind, sun, and rain that is specific to the site. The LEED-Gold design incorporates multiple green spaces that enhance the tower and the surrounding development, allowing users to experience the tactile sensations of the landscaping elements. It has been shown in human-comfort studies that access to green spaces promotes a sense of well-being among tenants, while simultaneously improving air quality and the local micro-climate.

The building reaches its LEED targets through a variety of strategies including a high-performance, Low-E insulated curtain-wall system with uniquely designed fins that are integrated into the building's geometry. Their positioning on the east and west facing facades efficiently reduces solar heat gain, providing effective protection to the indoor environment, while controlling glare and maintaining access to daylighting.

Visually, the exterior wall adds a rich layer of undulating texture that enhances the tower's spatial qualities and experience from the exterior and the interior. Stainless steel was chosen as the material used to ensure long-term durability.

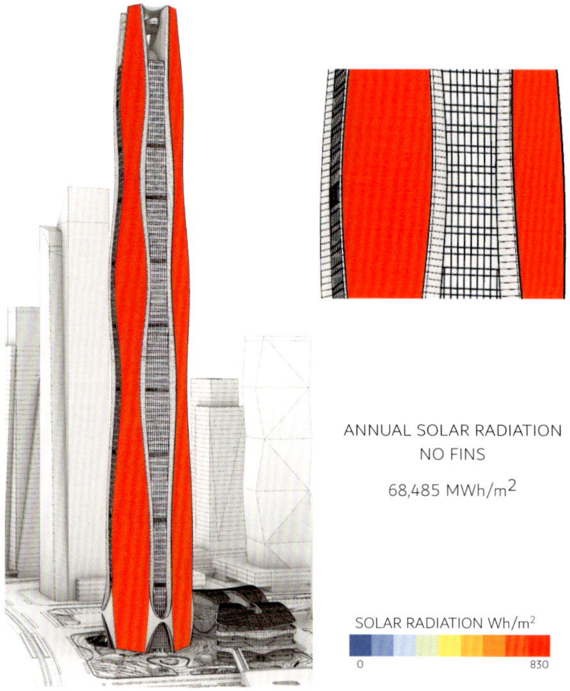

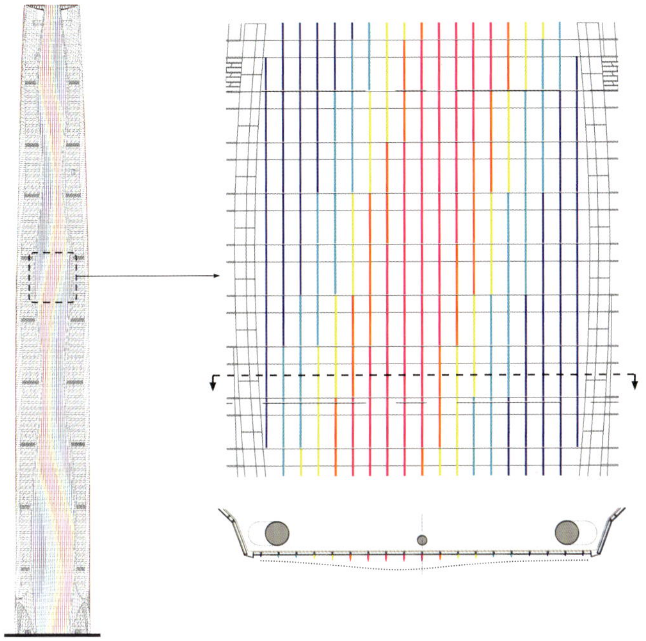

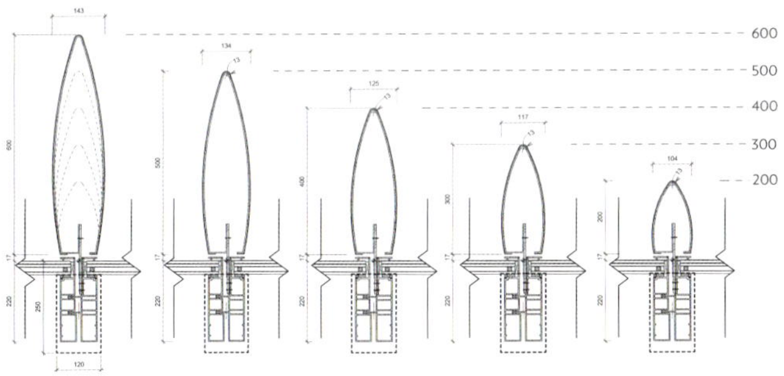

CURVED FIN WITH FIVE STEPS

Fin Design

The fin design was studied through numerous iterations of computer modeling and physical mock-ups. A gently curved, petal-like shape was selected to achieve the best balance of visibility, constructability, performance, and cost. The fins are rationalized in five different modules to create an undulating effect. Functionally, the bowed fins increase the structural integrity of the tower, create visual interest, and optimize the reflectivity of both direct sun and diffused light. The fins that are perpendicular to the facade have interior spaces with optimized exterior views. As the sun moves around the building, the intricate paneling of the facade subtly animates from bright to dark, creating a visually stunning experience for users of the district.

22 GLASS FIN FACADE

Project: Ahlamana

Location: Riyadh, Saudi Arabia

Climate Zone: BWH - Arid, Desert, Hot

Program: Mixed-Use

Status: Construction

Client: Saudi Binladin Group

Date: 2009-present

Strategies: Solar Control, Daylight, Thermal Mass

Ahlamana serves as a gateway into the overall KAFD development, marking one of its entrances. Connected by a series of elevated pedways, it is intricately linked to the surrounding parcels. Programmatically, the building contains retail, residential, and office spaces. Ahlamana—the Arabic word for "our dream" is a reference to an Arabic concept that informed the design—consists of a 78-meter-tall office tower and a 105-meter-tall residential tower, with the towers connected by two retail podium structures. The building's podium also features KAFD's only outdoor restaurant.

Although one of the design goals was to attract retail shoppers from neighboring parcels, the function is separated from the residential and office programs. This is accomplished by elevating the residential program above the retail, separating potential shoppers from residents living in the development, thereby increasing the residents' privacy. The further separation of some residences also enhances circulation flows for all users. The office component is semi-isolated from the retail and completely disconnected from the residential component.

Ahlamana's chief sustainability strategy is its deployment of a louvered travertine screen wall that protects the office tower's western facade from the harshest solar radiation. The residential tower also presents a mostly solid stone wall toward the west, minimizing solar heat gain and reducing energy consumption for air-conditioning. The buildings' other facades consist of high-performance vision glass, which alternates in a subtle pattern using slightly opaque fritted glass panels that allow for views of KAFD toward the north and south, while effectively reducing solar heat gain.

Exterior Wall

The skin treatment was designed through computer modeling that focuses on protection from the harsh sun and heat common in Riyadh. The design solution, to use building integrated shading controls, allows for natural daylighting within the spaces. Daylighting can also be controlled by maintaining 9m lease spans and moving typically artificially lit features, such as stair towers and corridors, to the perimeter of the building, allowing light to penetrate.

The use of thick stone walls keeps the building cool and shades the windows from direct sunlight. Strategically placing the protective stone walls toward the western setting sun and the daytime southern sun also helps reduce cooling costs. Glass curtain walls are used on the north side of the building, allowing cooler northern light to penetrate the spaces, increasing energy efficiency.

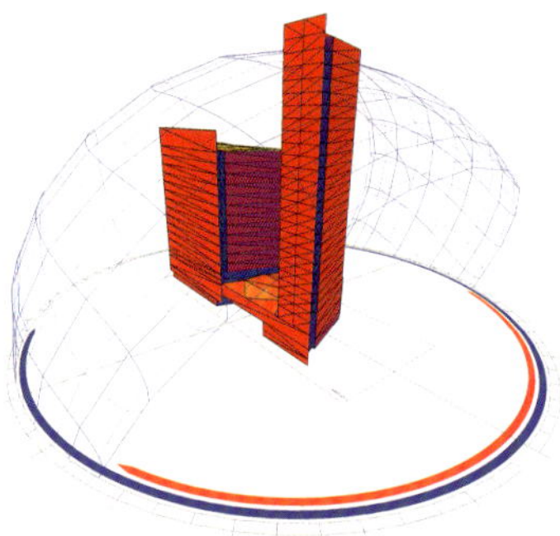

SOLAR ANALYSIS SOUTHWEST

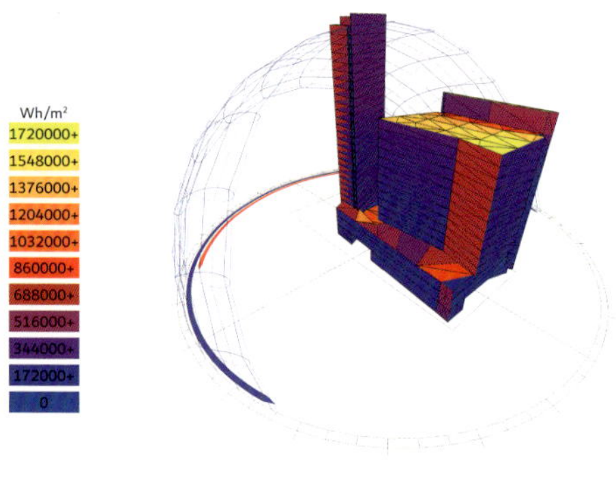

SOLAR ANALYSIS NORTHEAST

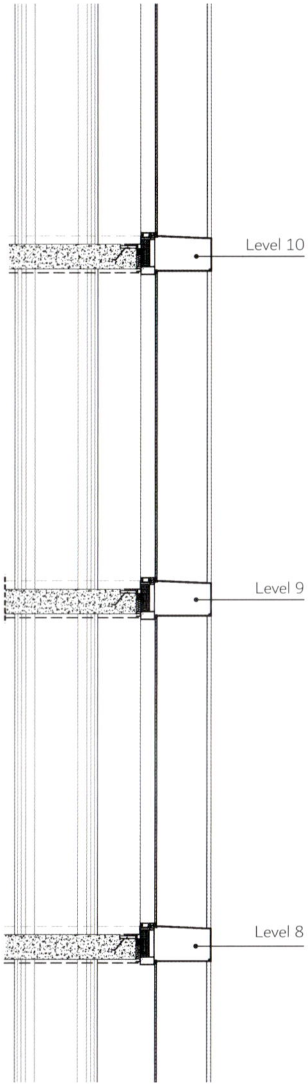

PARTIAL WALL SECTION

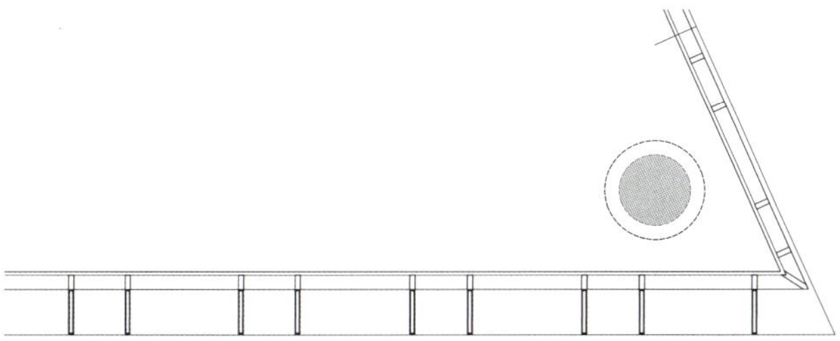

PARTIAL PLAN

CONSTRUCTION 2018 (ABOVER + BELOW)

23 TRANSFORMATIVE FACADE

Project:	KLIFD Iconic Tower
Location:	Kuala Lumpur, Malaysia
Climate Zone:	AF - Warm, Sunny, Abundant Rainfall
Program:	Mixed-Use
Status:	Concept
Client:	1 Malaysia Development Berhad
Date:	2010
Strategies:	Solar Control, Daylight, Solar Power, Intelligent, Luminous, Modular

KLIFD Iconic Tower was designed as an endearing symbol for Kuala Lumpur. The tower's design is formed by the physical and environmental opportunities present on the site. The tower is mixed-use with office floors and features a five-star boutique hotel on its upper floors.

The building is oriented toward the east and west to minimize the impact of strong lower sun radiation. Its envelope is a dynamic folded form that serves dual purposes: the downward slope of the glass minimizes solar heat gain and glare while permitting daylight; the upper fold faces upward toward the sky to absorb of solar energy. The tower's skin reduces heat gain by controlling daylighting while capturing solar energy. The triangulated modulation on the west facade is a response to increase interior views and protect the outdoor spaces with a rich combination of large communal terraces and smaller private balconies.

The site's landscaping responds to the park at the west side of the tower, flowing through and up the tower from the lobby level to the Sky Club at the tower's apex. The tower's refined top is another gesture toward the park and features a louvered PV system that is oriented for maximum solar energy harvesting.

Solar Radiation

A unitized self-shading design on the north and south facades responds to the environmental site conditions. The vision glass slopes inward at an angle of 15 degrees. This angle was selected for its high solar performance, while not requiring an expensive specialist glazing protection treatment. BIPV form the spandrel panels and are angled optimally at 30 degrees on the north and 40 degrees on the south.

As the facade curves toward the east, the slope of the vision glass transitions from 15 degrees to 30 degrees to increase the solar exposure on the surface. Concurrently, the slope of the PV becomes shallower, although the power generation potential remains largely the same due to the increased surface area.

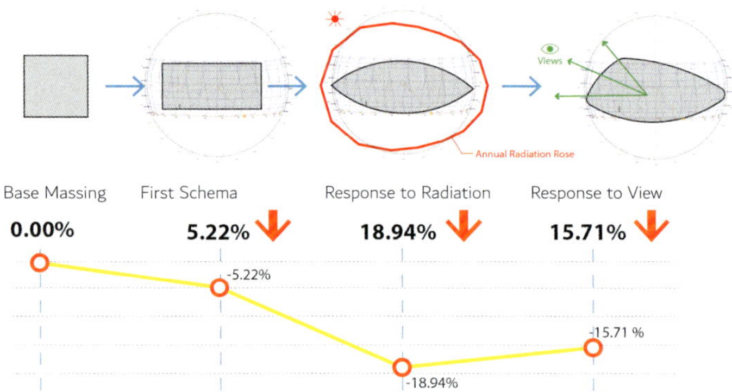

SOLAR RADIATION PLAN DIAGRAM

The west facade serves multiple purposes by allowing the best views across the park and acting as the primary means of minimizing solar heat gain. The walls on this elevation are designed in three different ways: one portion is recessed and protected by a retractable exterior wall shading system; the second, outermost portion of the wall, folds with inward sloping vision glass and outward sloping PVs; and the third is oriented almost directly north and downward. View oriented balconies offer outdoor spaces with magnificent views to the Kuala Lumpur skyline to all floors.

The roof of the tower is designed as a multi-functional envelope that provides shelter from the sun and rain, generates electricity, and creates a naturally ventilated semi-conditioned space. Operated by the BMS, louvers made from an integrated semi-transparent photovoltaic film provide shade and rain protection when in the closed position. Rather than forming a shingled roof, the louvers are married with clear glass vertical glazing, which allows indirect natural lighting into the space, creating a bright well-lit environment that also reduces heat gain and glare.

NORTH AND SOUTH FACADE

EAST FACADE

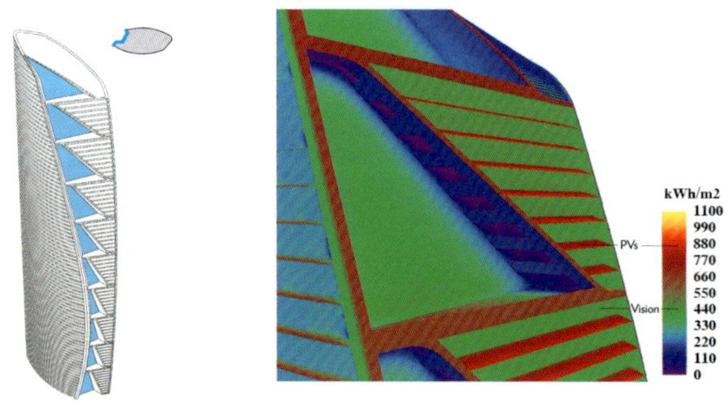

WEST FACADE

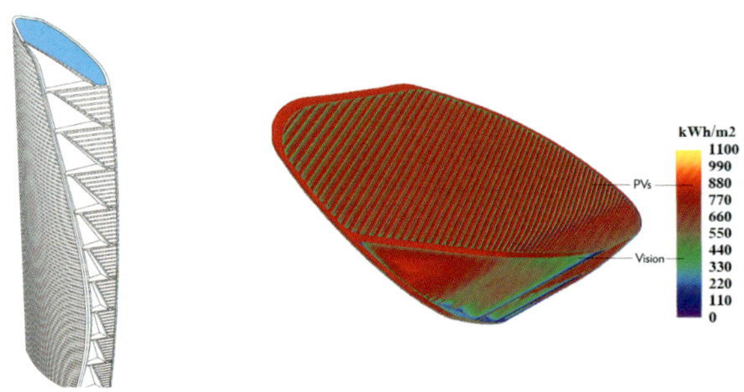

ROOF

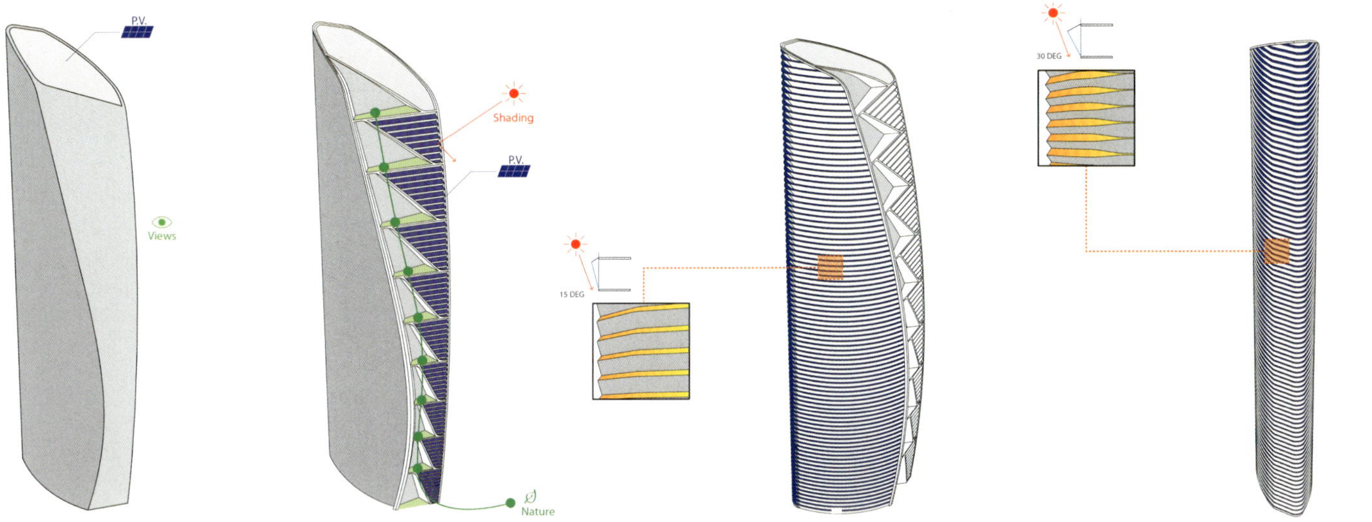

BASE

WEST FACADE TREATMENT
+137% PV Energy Production
-13% Envelope Cooling Load

NORTH AND SOUTH FACADE TREATMENT
+940% PV Energy Production
-52% Envelope Cooling Load

EAST FACADE TREATMENT
+1169% PV Energy Production
-50% Envelope Cooling Load

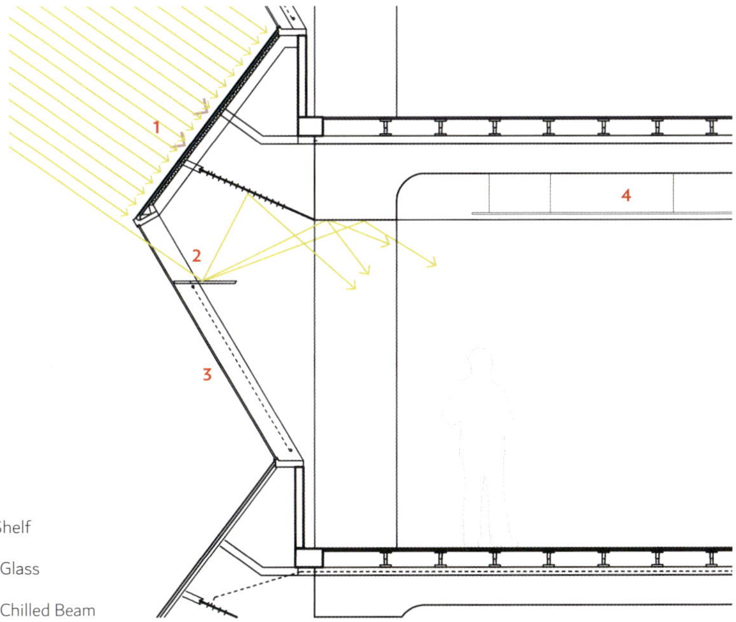

SECTION

1. PV
2. Light Shelf
3. Vision Glass
4. Active Chilled Beam

24 SOLAR SHIELD FACADE

Project:	Jeddah Tower
Location:	Jeddah, Saudi Arabia
Climate Zone:	BWH - Arid, Desert, Hot
Program:	Mixed-Use
Status:	Construction
Client:	Jeddah Economic Company
Date:	2010-present
Strategies:	Solar Control, Daylighting, Solar Power

At over 1,000 meters (3,280 feet) and with a total construction area of 530,000 square meters (5.7 million square feet), Jeddah Tower—formerly known as Kingdom Tower—will be the centerpiece and first construction phase of the $20 billion Kingdom City development in Jeddah, Saudi Arabia, near the Red Sea. Expected to cost $1.2 billion to construct, Jeddah Tower is a mixed-use building that features a luxury hotel, office floors, serviced apartments, luxury condominiums, and the world's highest observatory.

Jeddah Tower's ground-level entrances are covered with extensive canopies that give the tower massing a strong base and improve directed solar protection. The canopies receive a high concentration of solar energy because of the tower's convex surface geometry so sun studies and heat gain analysis were conducted to determine their optimal shape. Further refinement of the canopy design led to a PV cladding component to harvest solar energy.

Concentrated Solar Radiation

Glass buildings, depending on the specification of the glazing system and the amount of insulated spandrel panels, reflect significant amounts of incident solar radiation and if positioned wrong are a nuisance to adjacent buildings and public areas. While this is a common phenomenon, convex curved geometries present unique challenges because they can focus reflections onto concentrated locations at varying times of the year. This effect is especially pronounced if the curved facade has a generally south facing orientation when located in the northern hemisphere.

Jeddah Tower is fully glazed with three straight wings that are connected by circular segments to create a plan that has convex curves on three sides. One of the convex surfaces is oriented in a precisely southerly direction. Therefore, the final building is oriented so that the convex segments face north-northwest, north-northeast, and south.

Realizing that the geometry would likely lead to the concentration of solar energy, a series of investigations were undertaken. First was to confirm and study the opportunities of the building geometry of the site's specific location and orientation. Second was to determine the area of solar convergence, the climactic conditions, when solar convergence would occur, and for what length of time.

These investigations suggested the greatest impact is on the south canopy at the base of the tower. The information gained helped to design the final detailing of the lower canopies to protect the temperature sensitive roofing materials, gaskets, and sealants, and to access other potential uses for this heat gain including solar hot water and solar photovoltaic electricity generation.

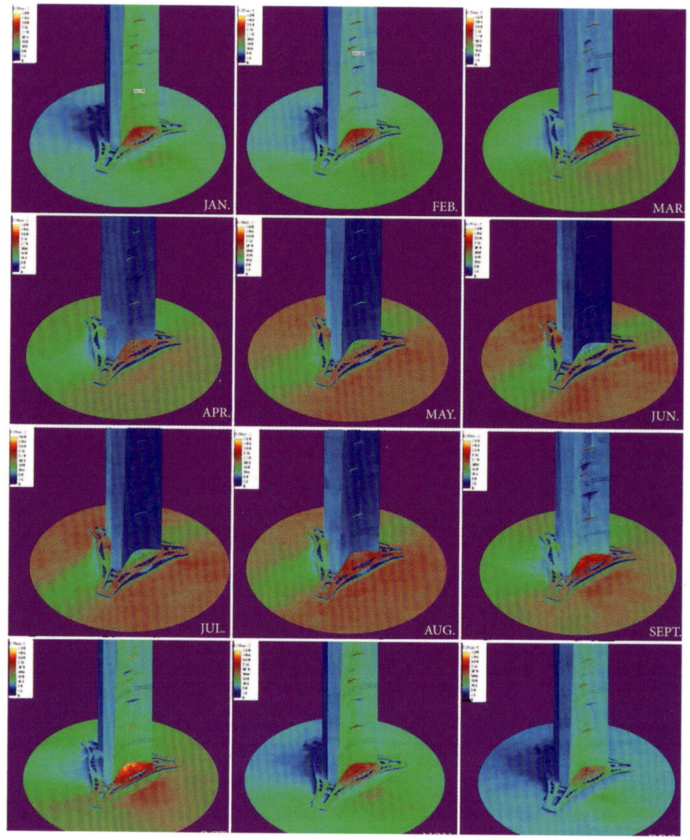

SOLAR RADIATION ANALYSIS

SOLAR PV CANOPY RENDERING

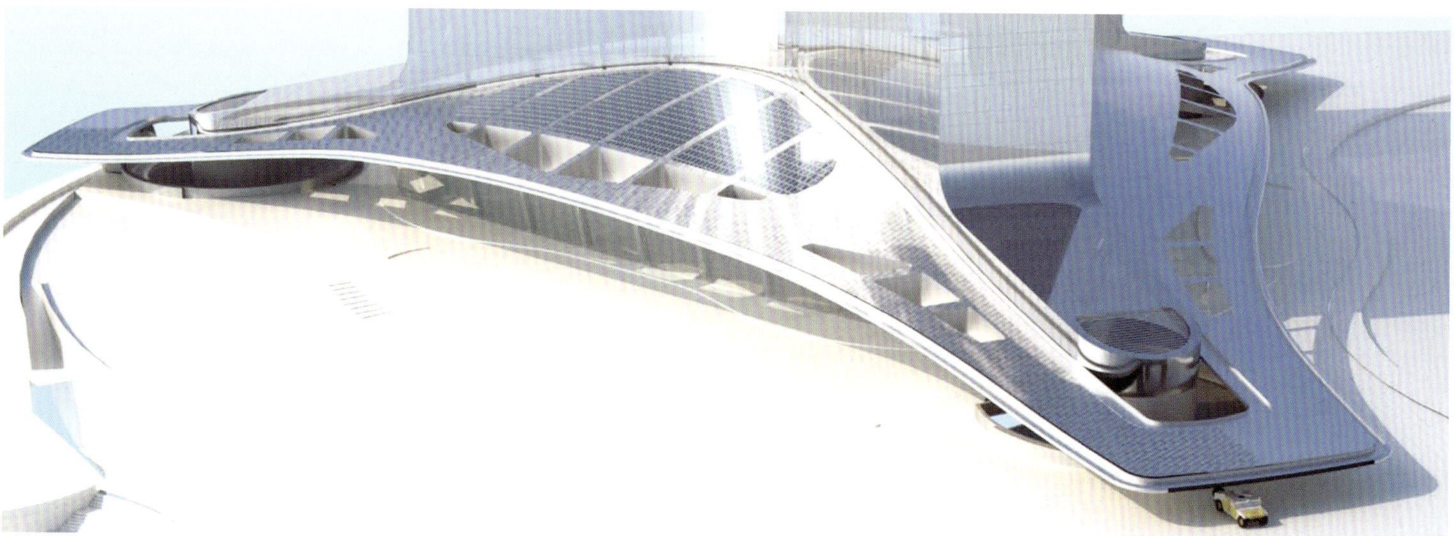

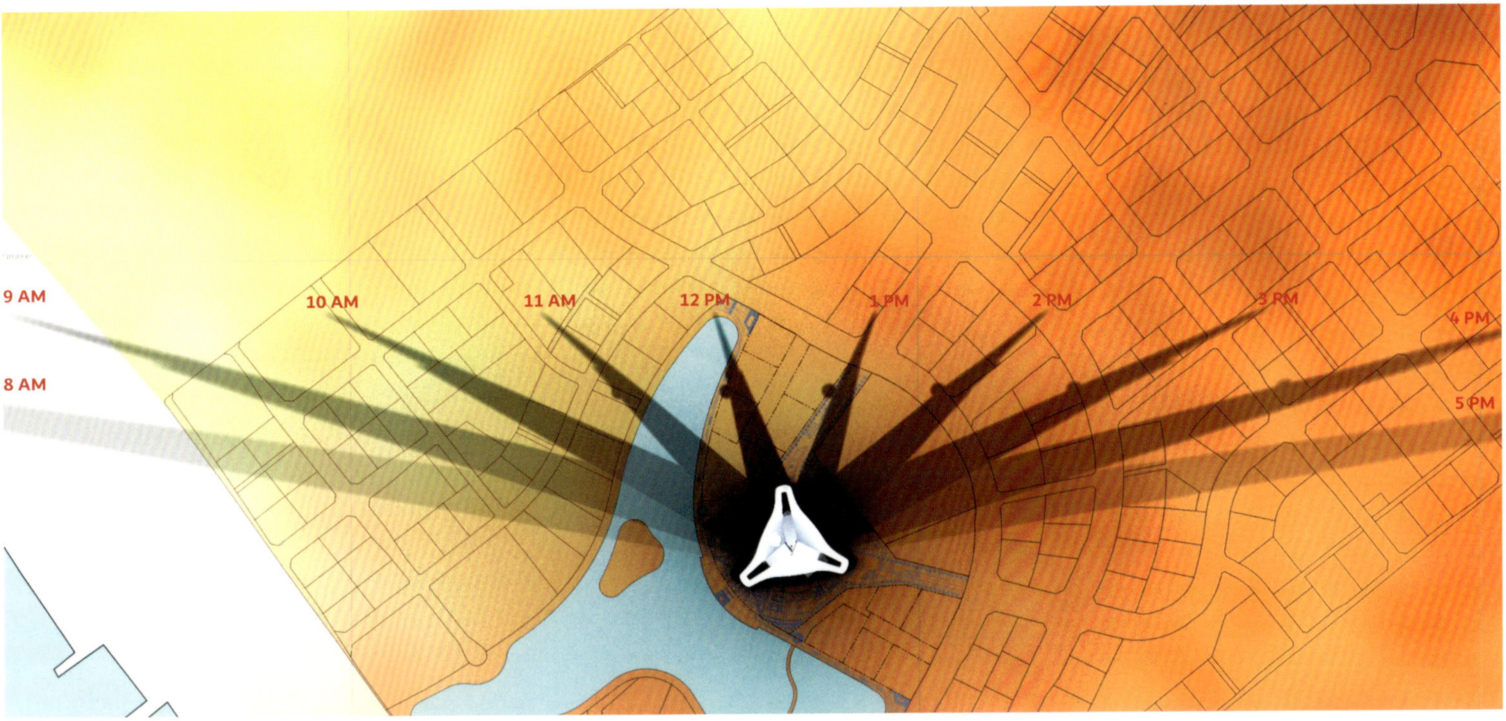

MARCH 21 / SEPTEMBER 21

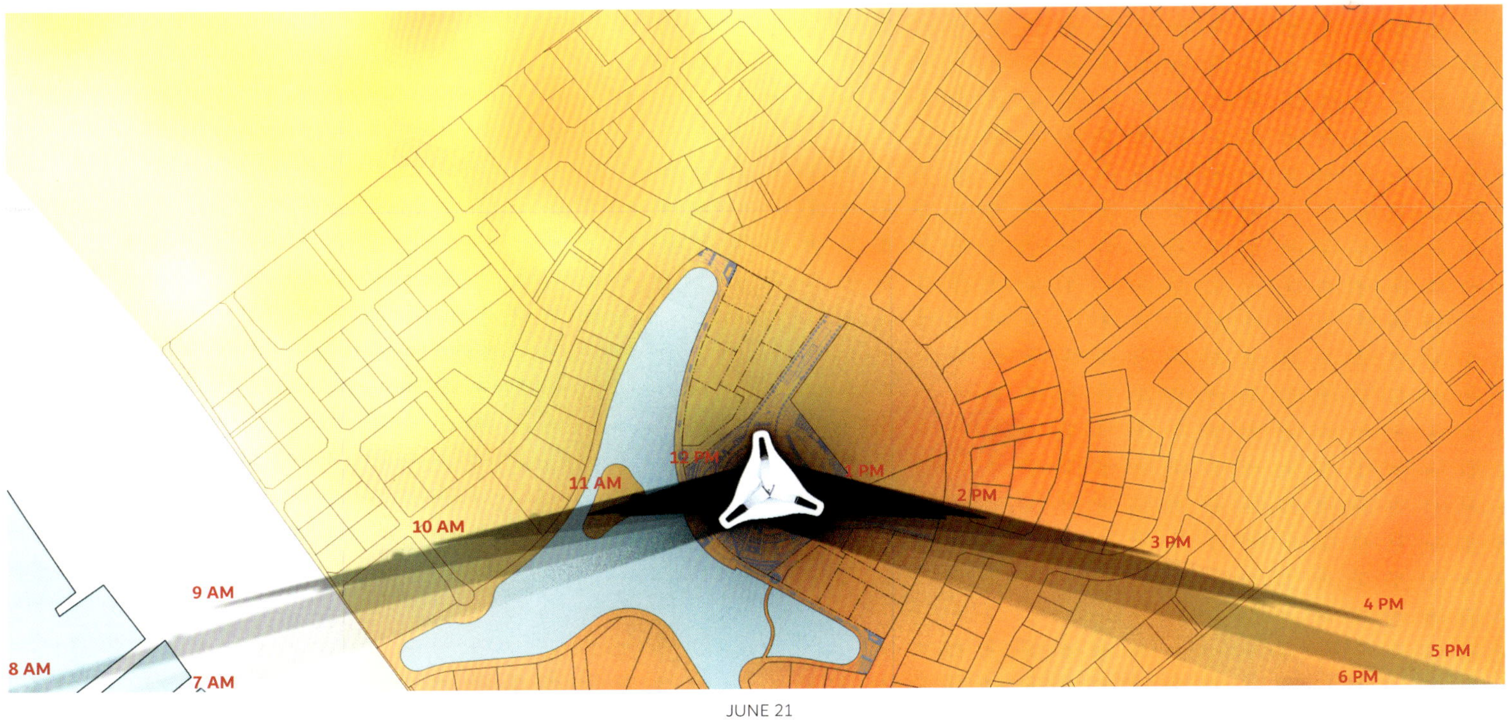

JUNE 21

Power Generation

Using real world weather data to accurately predict cumulative solar exposure on the canopies, a bi-directional scattering function (BDSF) of the building's facade system was created using radiance software to quantify the solar load on the canopies for a year and each individual month.

Solar and thermal loads were quantified, along with an estimate of the thermal energy production potential of solar hot water and power generation of solar photovoltaic systems. This process greatly informed the final design detailing of the canopy.

The studies show that November 15th produces the maximum temperature on the south canopy and May 28th produces the highest temperatures on the northwest and northeast canopies. The simulations show that the south canopy reaches the highest temperature of 134°C with the northwest and northeast canopies at 132°C and 117°C, respectively. Based on the simulated results for surface temperatures of 135° C or greater, and a better than average yield for various solar energy strategies, the result is recognized as both a potential problem and a potential opportunity.

PV manufacturers have documented that excessive heat can reduce the efficiency of solar panels. It is currently unknown if developing solar technologies will better handle increased heat loads. Based on the results of the study a payback analysis indicated that—even with 15-20% efficiency losses—the panels have a payback of 8-20 years.

Assuming more resilient products will become available in the coming years, the design seeks to understand how we can replace the system in the future.

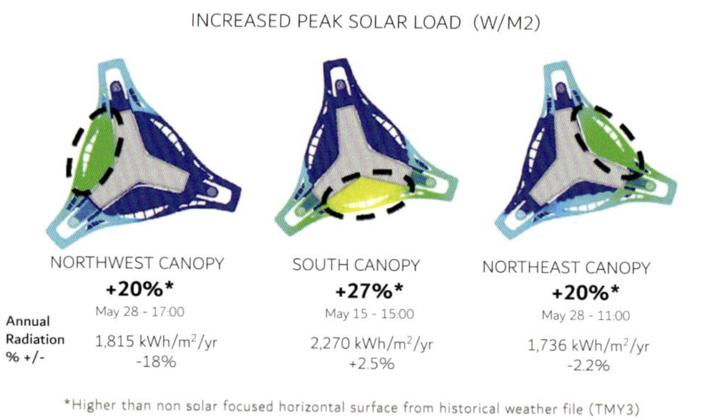

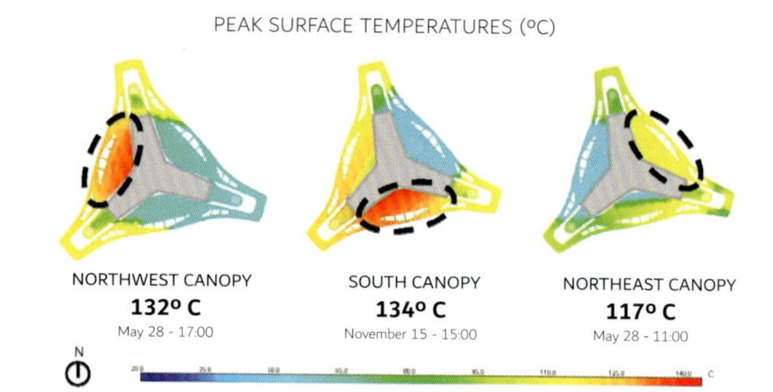

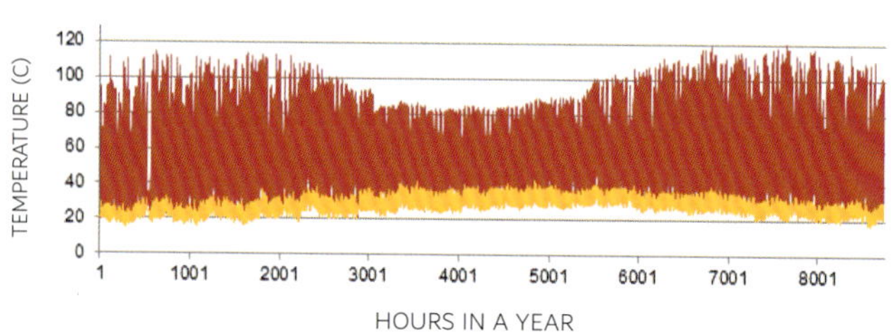

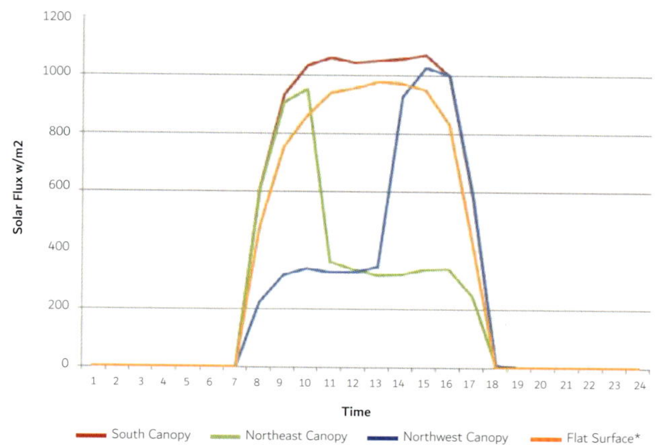

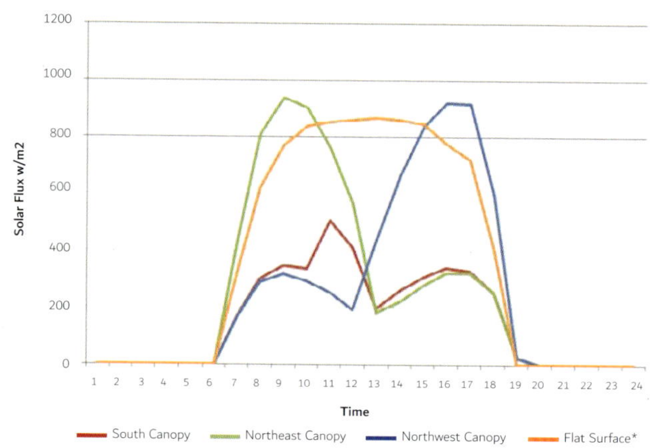

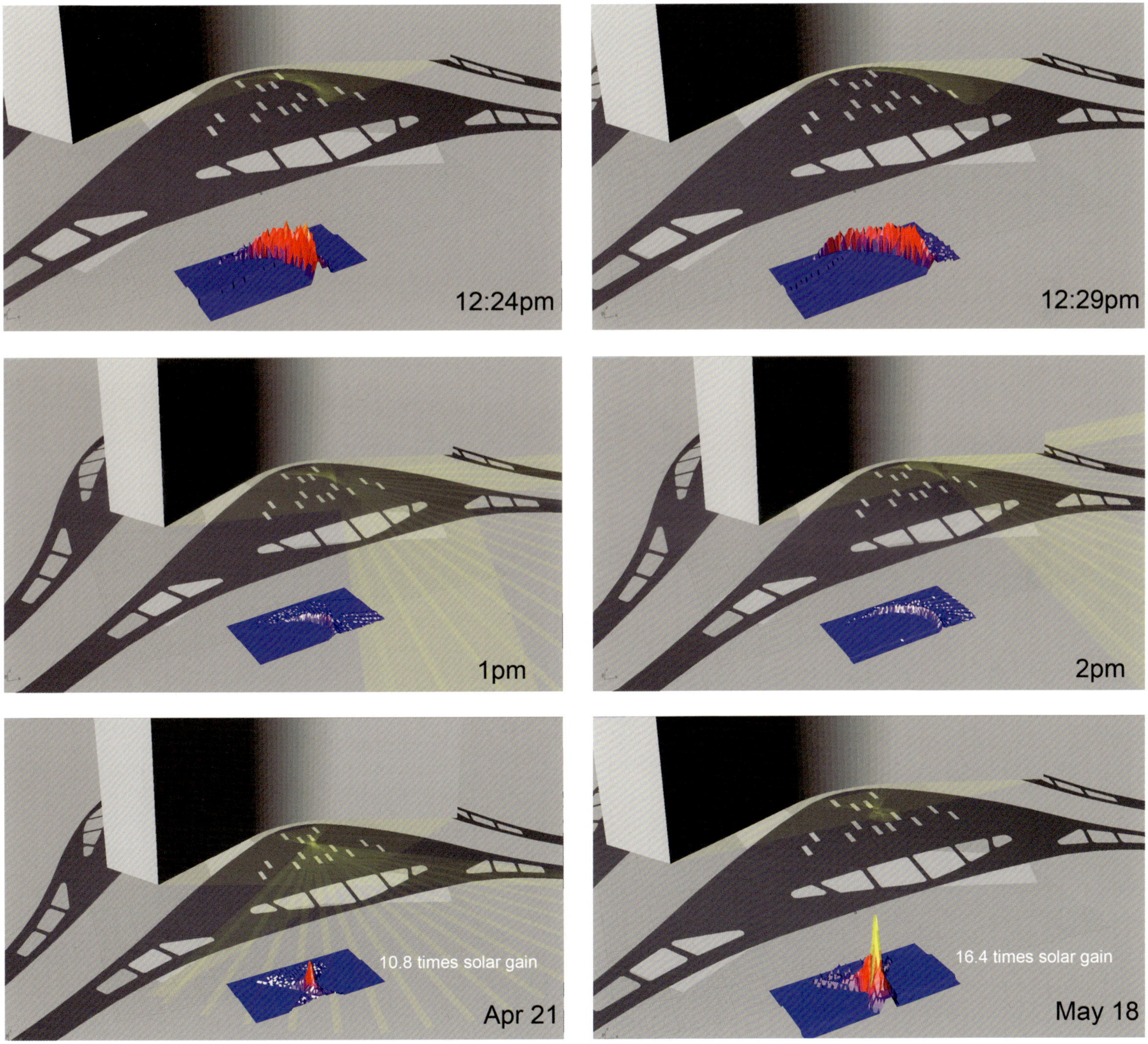

SOLAR RADIATION + SOLAR CONCENTRATION

25 BIOPHILIC FACADE

Project:	Biophilic Tower
Location:	Suzhou, China
Climate Zone:	CFA - Temperate, Without Dry Season, Hot Summer
Program:	Mixed-Use
Status:	Concept
Client:	Zhongnan Group
Date:	2012
Strategies:	Solar Control, Daylight, Ventilated

The Biophilic Tower represents a new paradigm for skyscrapers: a self-sustaining, intelligent building that combines optimal performance with aesthetic beauty, and focuses on a human being's innate attraction to nature.

The mixed-use complex features a 700.8-meter tower and retail and conference center podium with a total above-ground area of approximately 431,000 m^2. The tower contains approximately 369,000m^2 total gross floor area with 189,200 m2 of office space on levels 4-62; 74,325 m^2 of apartment space on levels 65-91; 46,500 m^2 of hotel spaces on levels 94-112; and 8,450 m^2 of club/observation programs on levels 115-118. The observation program occupies the highest levels of the building with the main observation floor at elevation +556.8m with an interior atrium to +700m.

One of the tower's main features is a continuous vertical garden environment that wraps around the building from grade to the pinnacle. Each of the 119 floors has access to this lush atrium space, giving occupants a direct multi-sensory connection to nature.

The tower design uses fractal patterns—designs that appear the same from near as far—that can positively affect human neural activity, increase work productivity, and physical and mental health. The design uses a common fractal pattern, the Voronoi diagram, to add another layer to the natural environment that is created within the tower.

Design Concept

The Biophilic Tower's has three key design concepts in mind:

- Nature in the space: integrating water elements, courtyard gardens, and views of nature from inside.
- Nature of the space: adapting to human psychological and physiological responses to different spatial configurations to improve concentration and productivity.
- Natural analogues: using materials and patterns that evoke nature, including building elements that mimic shells and leaves, furniture with organic rather than geometric shapes, and visible wood grain.

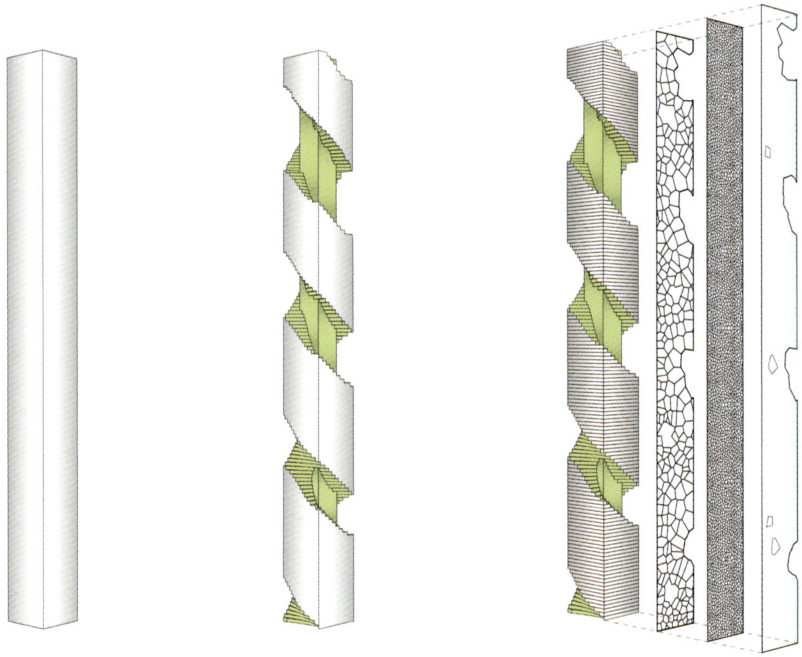

1
Begin with an elegant, simple shape.

2
Apply layers of screens at various scales at various scales to create a rich and culturally connected facade.

3
Use natural elements such as gardens and water features to carve an interior atrium throughout the height of the tower.

BIOPHILIC TOWER CONTEXT RENDERING

Biophilic Wall

In nature, a spiral is often a structural or organizational tool. The tower's design uses a spiral to organize the continuous garden space that wraps up and around the tower. As the space spirals, the occupant has views of the atrium rotating both toward and away from them. This technique creates a visual connection that links each space to another along the height of the tower. The tower also creates a connection to the traditional wood window screens throughout the facade design. These screens, and the tower's curtain wall, are designed to encourage shade and are decorated with natural patters that are visually comforting and culturally relevant to Suzhou.

SKY LOUNGE WITH EXTERIOR DETAIL RENDERING

INTERIOR + EXTERIOR ATRIUM VIEW RENDERING (RIGHT)

Tower Massing

The tower is shaped to take full advantage of the natural light available on the site. By carving the atrium space deep into the massing of the building, natural light is allowed to enter the building beyond the perimeter envelope and penetrate deep into the floor plates. At the same time, the tower offers stunning views east to Jinji Lake and west to the Old City.

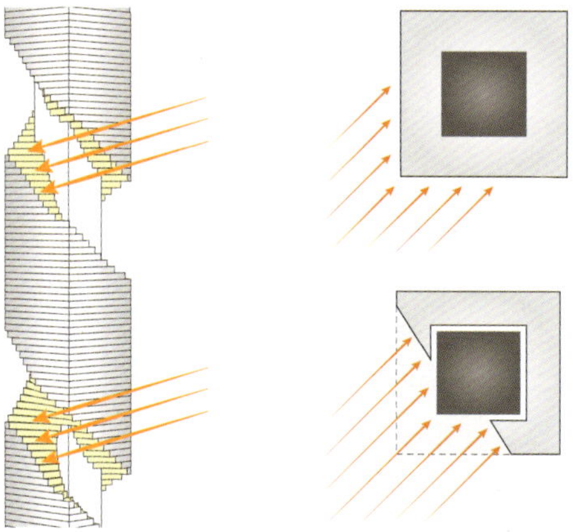

DAYLIGHT ACCESS

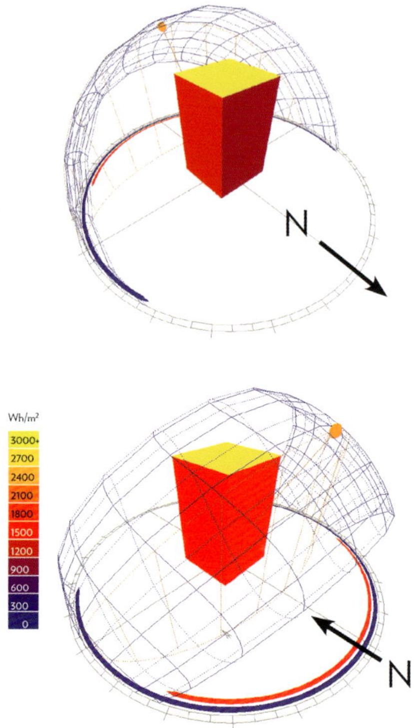

ANNUAL SOLAR DIRECTION

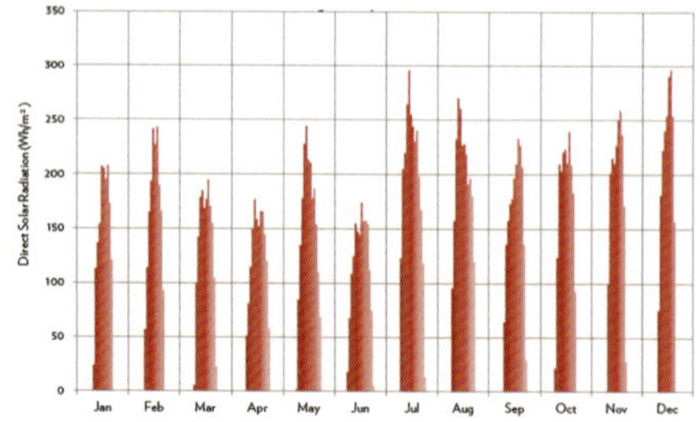

AVERAGE HOURLY DIURNAL SOLAR RADIATION

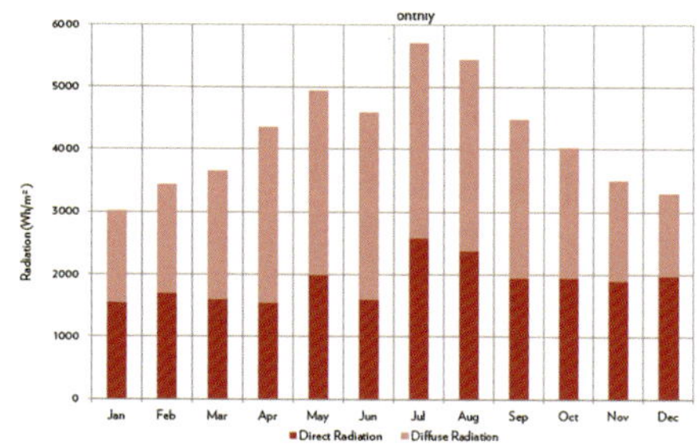

AVERAGE MONTHLY SOLAR RADIATION

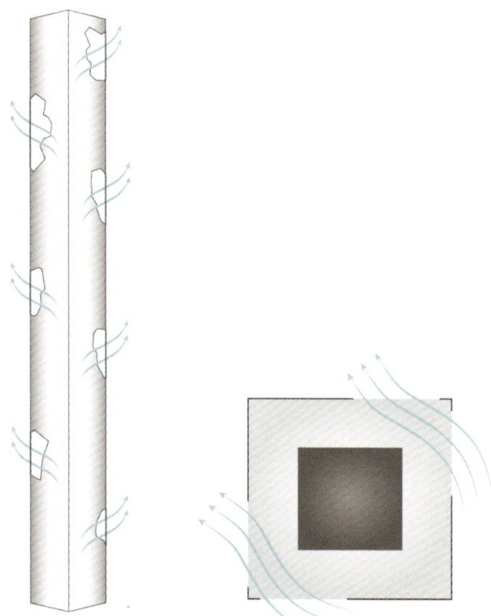

WIND EXPOSURE

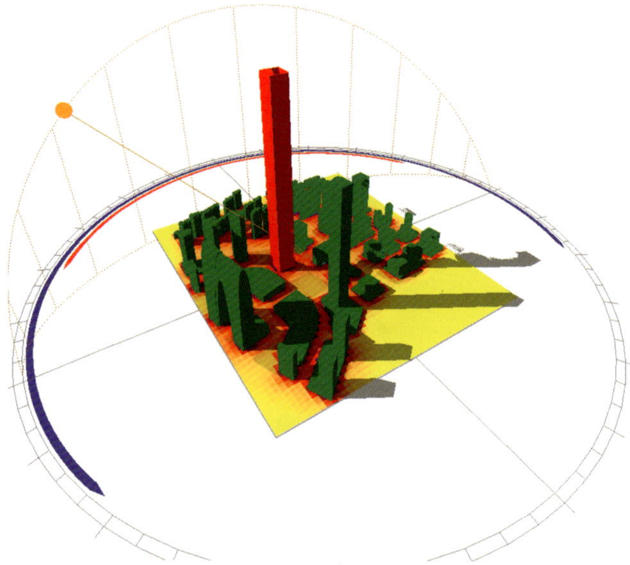

DISTRICT SOLAR INSULATION AVAILABILITY

detail studies

26 MULTIFACETED FACADE

Project:	FKI Tower
Location:	Seoul, The Republic of Korea
Climate Zone:	DWA - Continental, Dry Winter, Hot Summer
Program:	Office
Status:	Built
Client:	Federation of Korean Industries
Date:	2009-2014
Strategies:	Solar Control, Daylight, Solar Power, Ventilated, Modular

First occupied in January 2014, the new head office building for the Federation of Korean Industries (FKI) is a major new addition to the skyline of Seoul, Korea. FKI represents major Korean companies such as Samsung, LG, and Hyundai Motors. The 50-story, 240-meter tower features an innovative exterior wall, designed specifically for the project. The building's unique skin helps reduce internal heating / cooling loads and glare, while collecting energy through BIPV, which are integrated into the spandrel panel areas of the southwest and northwest facades.

FKI Tower's multifaceted BIPV exterior wall system combines maximum access to views, energy efficiency strategies, and energy generation technologies. The optimization of the panels was a driving factor in the architectural expression and is an architecturally appealing way to meet the district's zoning requirements of an orthogonally contextual building.

Further incentive to the design was given because the local electric utility company (KEPCO) provides a favorable 5-to-1 buyback rate for onsite green-energy generation. The payback for the BIPV panels, which would have typically been 30-35 years, was reduced to seven years due to these incentives.

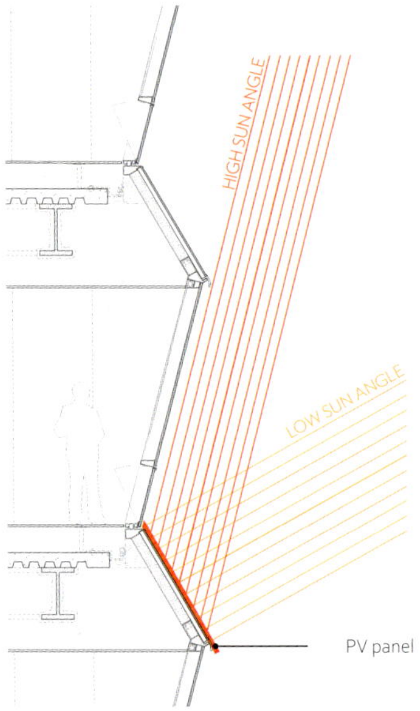

PV POWER GENERATION

The specific angle of the PV panel maximizes the power output potential of the tower.

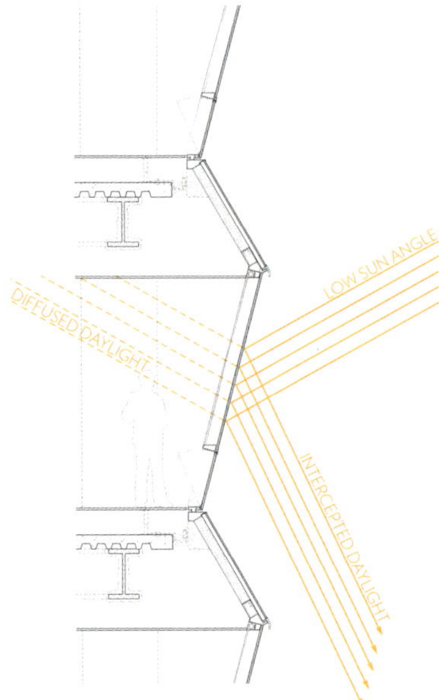

GLARE MITIGATION

The positive tilt of the vision glass panel allows for the deflection of low sun angle glare.

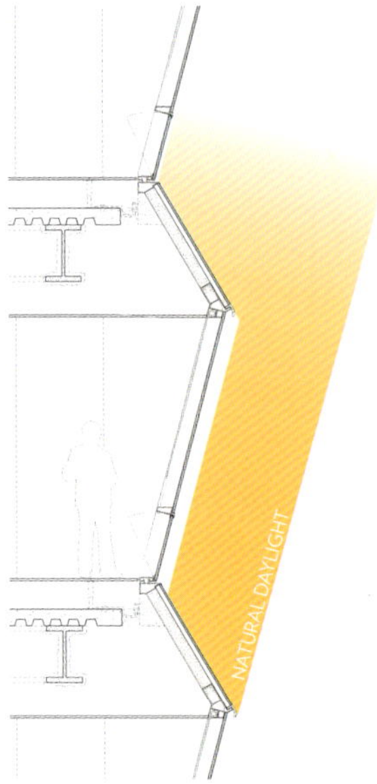

SOLAR REDUCTION

The specific angle of the PV panel maximizes the power output potential of the tower.

Comfort + Glare Reduction

One of the benefits of turning the spandrel panel toward the sky and the vision panel toward the ground is the reduction of glare and heat from direct sunlight. Even in the early morning and late afternoon periods, the building uses the geometry of the exterior wall to partially self-shade the perimeter spaces, which would normally be inundated with direct sunlight.

The configuration gives building occupants the flexibility to open the shades and allow indirect natural light to illuminate the interior spaces. With a maximum lease span of 12m, the majority of building occupants benefit from natural light. It also reduces the building's dependency on artificial light, thus reducing the overall energy consumption of the tower.

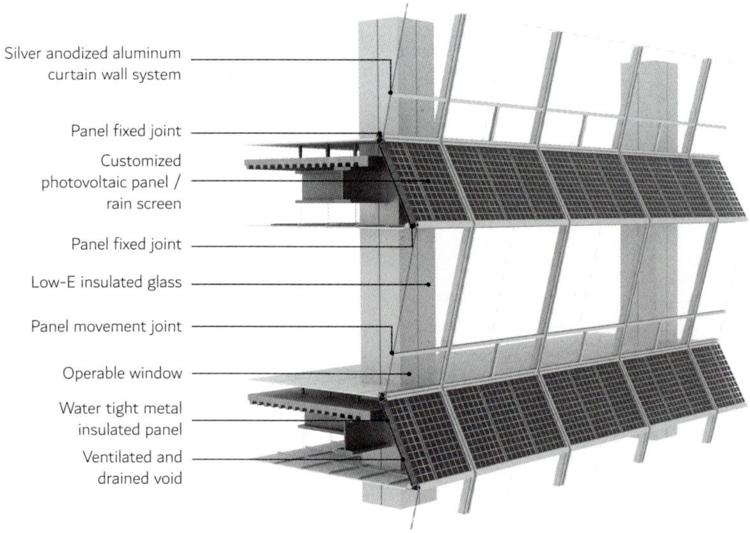

PHOTOVOLTAIC SYSTEM AREAS

Spandrel Area: 16,377 m^2

Number of cells: 240,156 5"x5" Monocrystalline silicon

Exterior Panel Design

Because not all of the faces of the building are currently suitable for BIPV, it was important to propose a design where BIPV panels are interchangeable with insulated spandrel panels for maximum flexibility in the use of BIPV without a significant change in the symmetry of building expression. The design also allows the BIPV to be replaced with similar appearing spandrel panels, or in the areas where the sky gardens occur, the spandrel panels are clear glass that allows for increased natural daylight.

During design phase, the weight of large tilted glass panels became a challenge. Due to the weight of the glass, the deflection of the tilted floor-to-ceiling glass exceeded allowable guidelines, necessitating a reduction in the glass size area. This was accomplished by adding operable panels at the base. Therefore, the panel size was designed at 1500mm x 2400mm to reduce deflection and allow the use of a standard glass thickness.

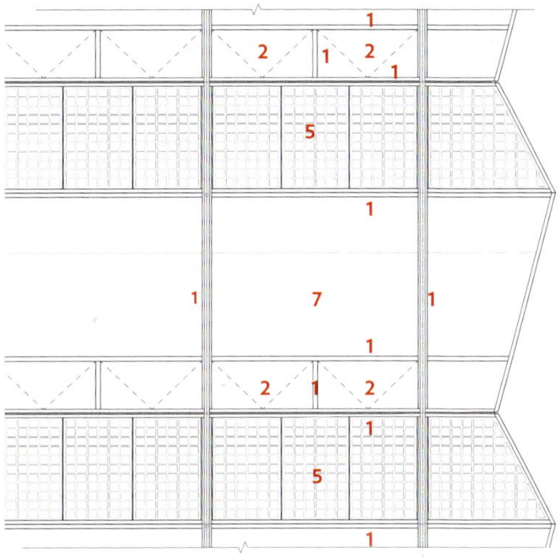

TYPICAL WALL SECTION DETAIL

1. Silver Anodized Aluminum Curtain Wall System
2. Automatic Project-in Operable Window
3. Load Bearing Connection with 2HR Fire Safing Insulation
4. Metal Insulated Panel
5. Photovoltaic Panel
6. Shading Control System
7. Low-E Insulated Glass
8. Lateral Connection with Vertical Control
9. 2HR Fireproofing (TYP)

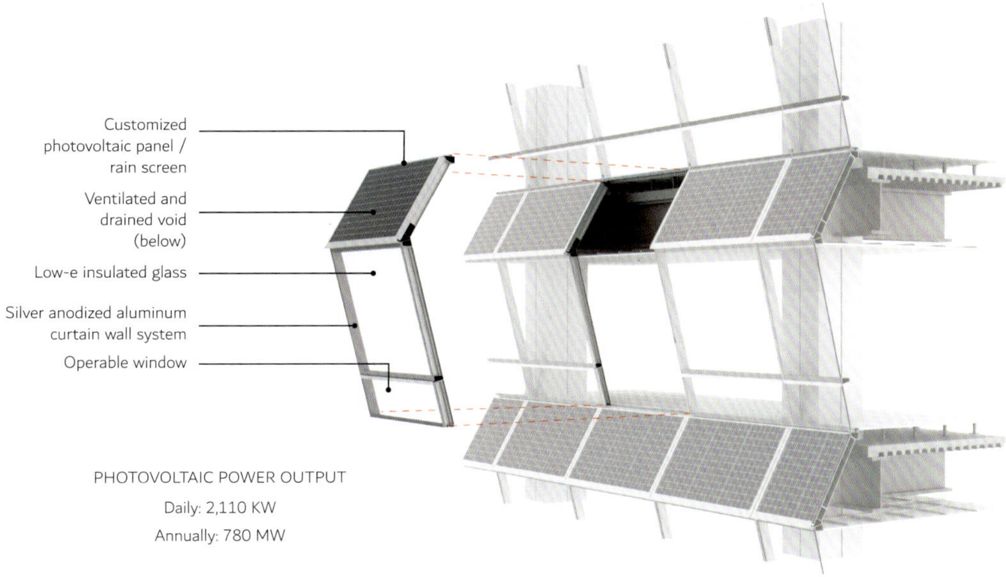

PHOTOVOLTAIC POWER OUTPUT

Daily: 2,110 KW

Annually: 780 MW

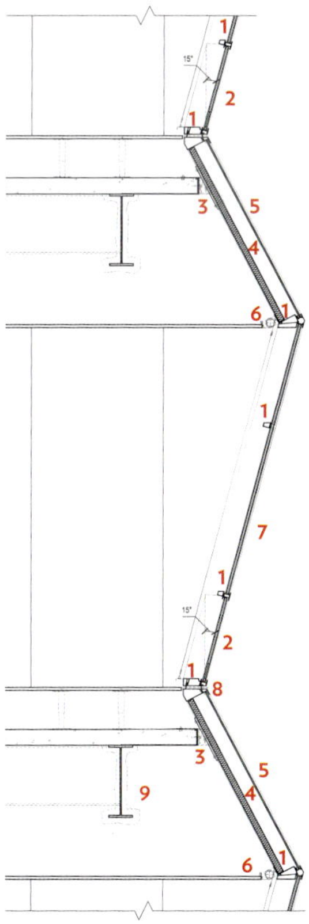

Energy Studies

The search for balance between the performance of the BIPV and human comfort became a function of the relationship between the angle of the vision glass and the spandrel panel. Research determined that the system would function best with an angle between 10-15 degrees. The highest performance was at the 15-degree slope. It saves nearly 4% of cooling load and over 20% of surface solar radiation. As expected, the performance of the PV panels continues to improve as the angle of the spandrel panel increases.

In large office buildings, even in temperate climates, summer cooling loads are greater than winter heating loads, so design for shading is critical. Tilting the facade beyond 15 degrees causes the heating loads to increase at an accelerated rate, due to the increased surface area. Therefore, the 15-degree slope, where the heating penalty and cooling gain are approximately even, was determined to be the optimal solution.

An economic advantage in maintaining the glass slope to 15 degrees or less from vertical is defined as "vertical glass," as per the International Building Code (IBC) as opposed to "sloped glass," which imposes more stringent design criteria. The other factor is the physical comfort of the inhabitants standing against a glass wall that is tilting outward.

A study was done to determine the psychological impact of outward sloping glass at the exterior wall on the building occupants. A full-scale mock-up was built and tested. The study determined that the angle of 15% was not a problem to the occupants' comfort or safety.

BIPV Area at Tower Elevation

- Area per module is 1.56 m² (0.95m x 1.648m)
- Total BIPV area at elevations is **4,476 m²** (1.56 m² x 2,859)

BIPV Area at Tower Sky Light

- Area per module is 1.59 m² (0.878m x 1.821m)
- Total BIPV area at sky light is **991 m²** (1.59 m² x 620)

BIPV Power Generation

- Average Solar Exposed Hours per day on site is 3.5 hours
- Total energy generation per day is **2,552 KWH / day**
- Expected Overall Energy Consumption of tower is **35,500 KWH / day**
- BIPV generates **4-7%** energy of tower on site

WALL TILT COMPARISON ANALYSIS

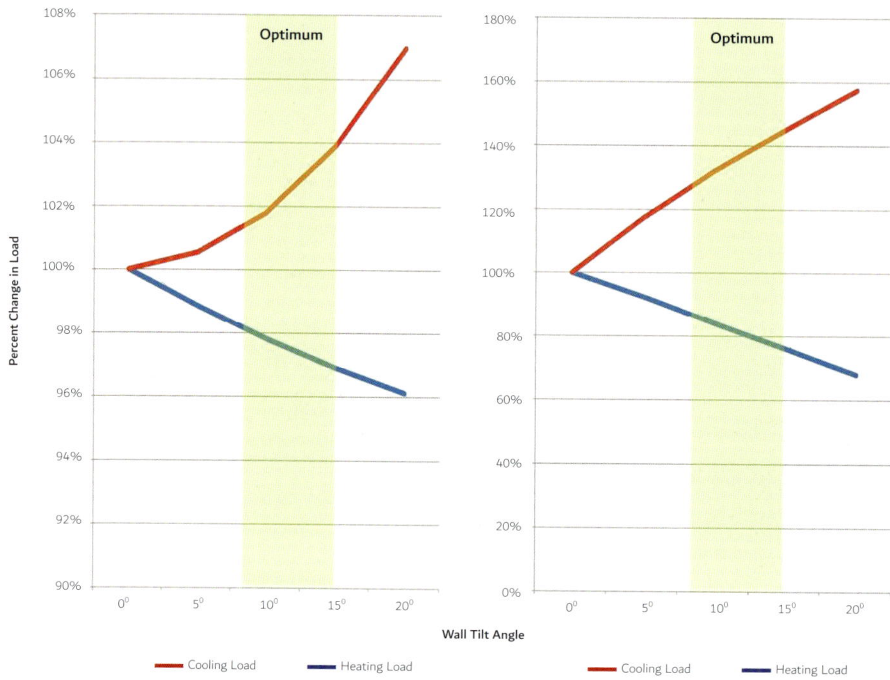

Effect of wall tilt on heating and cooling loads

Effect of wall tilt on surface solar radiation

WALL TILT STUDIES

The best performance was at the 15° slope, saving nearly 4% of cooling load and over 20% of surface solar radiation.

5% TILT   10% TILT   15% TILT

Surrounding Buildings Shading Analysis

As part of the initial design process, an Ecotech® model was used to determine the optimal areas for BIPV on the proposed building, given the surrounding buildings which partially shade the site. It was determined that BIPV is best used on the southeast and southwest faces above Level 14, all south facing surfaces, and covering the rooftop of the tower.

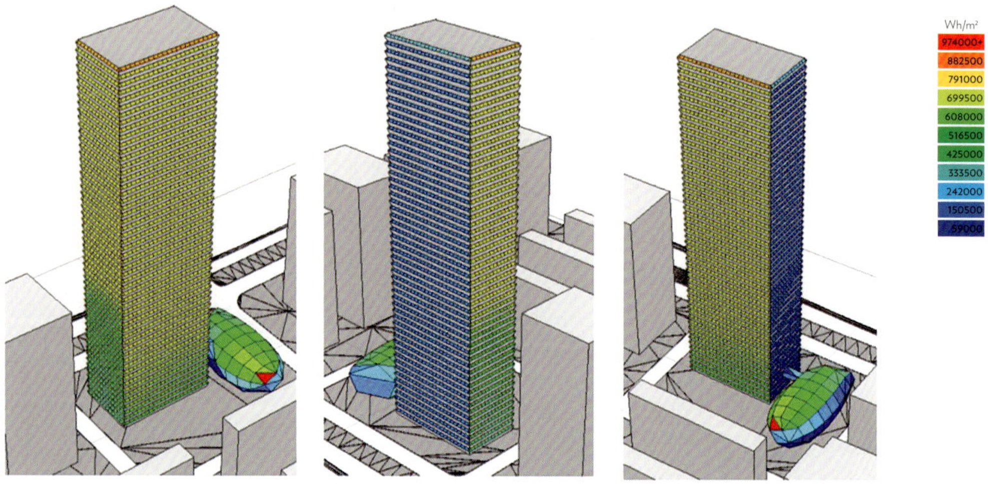

South West East

DIRECT RADIATION ANALYSIS

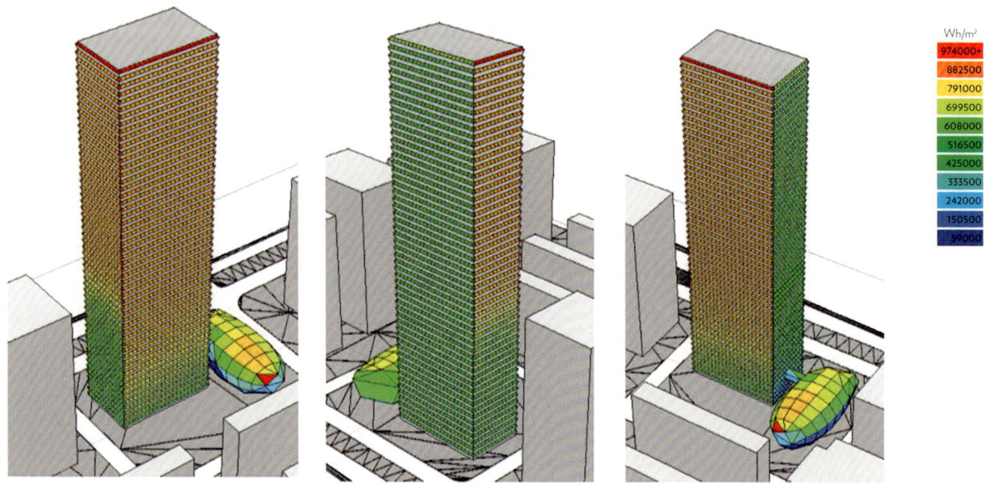

South West East

TOTAL RADIATION ANALYSIS

Sky Gardens

In addition to the BIPV energy wall, the building features an array of interior multi-story sky gardens for the use of tenants occupying these floors. The atrium spaces enhance the workplace environment with natural elements of wood, bamboo, and other native plants. Floor-to-ceiling windows offer an abundance of natural light that spills from the atrium spaces into the interior offices and corridors, as well as providing extensive views of neighboring Yeoido Park, the Han River, and the surrounding city.

TYPICAL SKY GARDEN

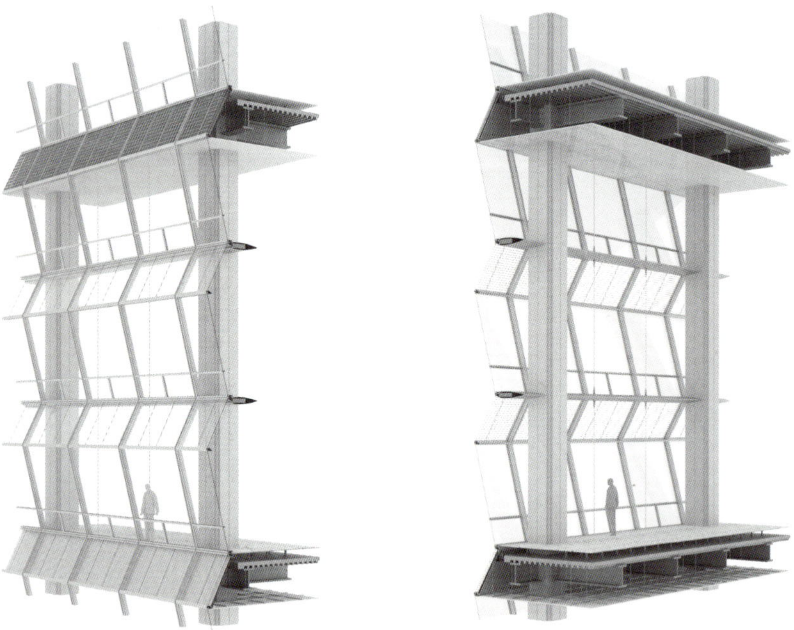

LIGHTSHELF DETAIL

SKY GARDEN EXTERIOR RENDERING

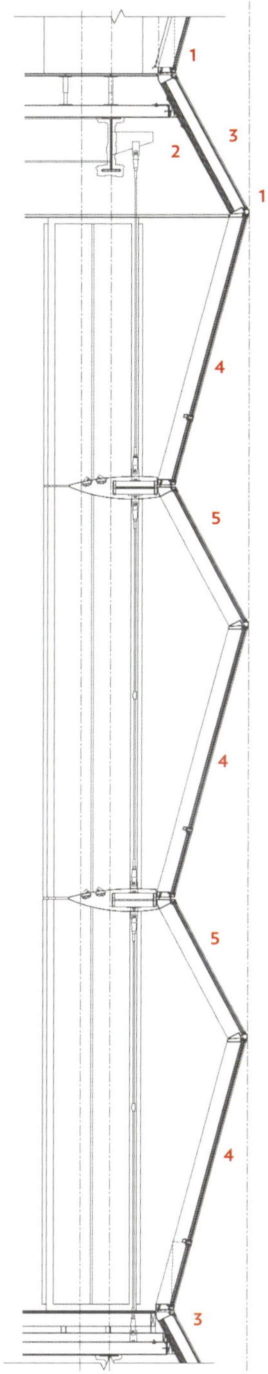

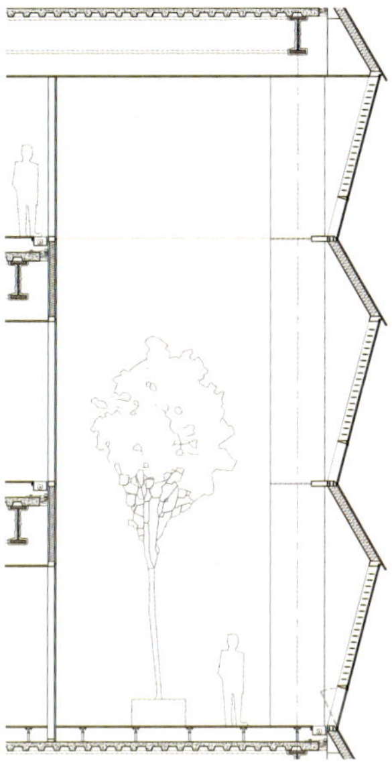

ATRIUM SECTION

TYPICAL SKY GARDEN

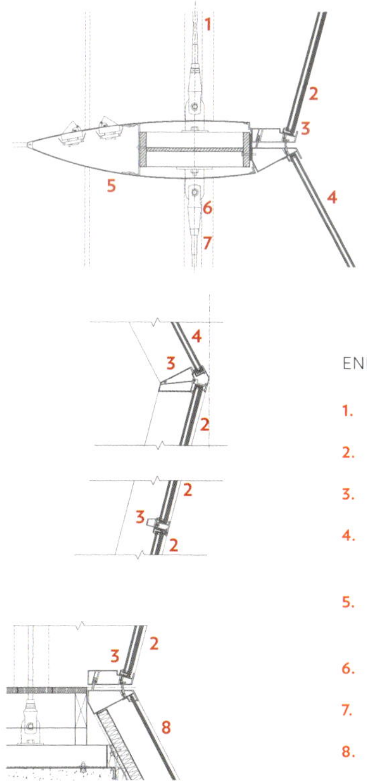

ATRIUM WALL SECTION DETAIL

1. Silver Anodized Aluminum
2. Shadow Box with Insulated Sheet Metal Panel
3. Tower Spandrel Glass - Laminated glass with ceramic frit to match appearance of PV Cells
4. Low-E Insulated Glass
5. Low-E Insulated Glass w/Dot Pattern Silkscreen

ENLARGED DETAILS

1. Stainless Steel Rod
2. Low-E Insulated Glass
3. Silver Anodized Aluminum
4. Low-E Insulated Glass with Dot Pattern Silkscreen
5. Extruded Aluminum Sheet Cladding with Silver Anodized Finish
6. Stainless Steel Structural Tie Rod System
7. Stainless Steel Treaded Rod
8. Tower Spandrel Glass - Laminated glass with ceramic frit to match appearance of PV Cells

Roof BIPV

When analyzing the roof skylight PV, it was important to account for self-shading of the PV panels and to allow enough open area of glass for natural light for the sky garden below. Three configurations were studied. While power output per square meter of PV was similar, it was found that a 10 degree tilt allows more PV panels in a smaller area, thereby creating a larger overall output.

EXTERIOR AND ROOF PV

SKY GARDEN WITH ROOF PV

ROOF PV EXTERIOR

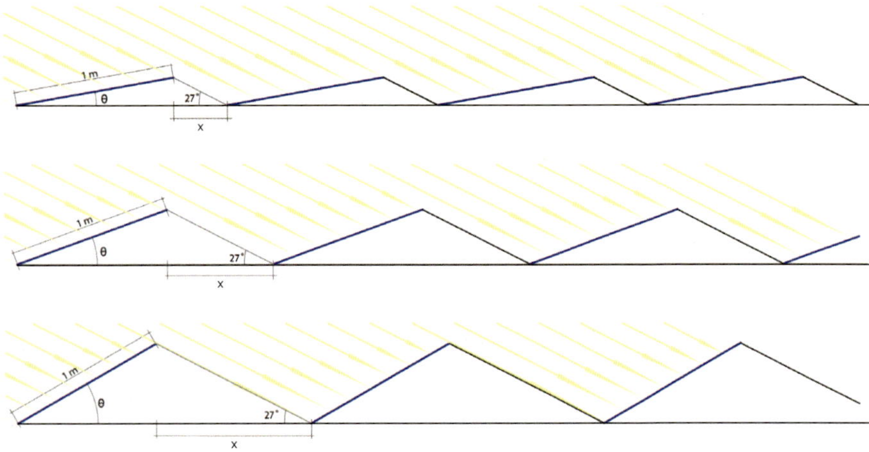

θ = Tilt (degrees)	x = Spacing (m)	Energy (kWh/m²)
10 deg	0.34	192
20 deg	0.67	195
30 deg	0.98	194

ROOF PHOTOVOLTAIC ANGLE STUDIES

ROOF PV INTERIOR

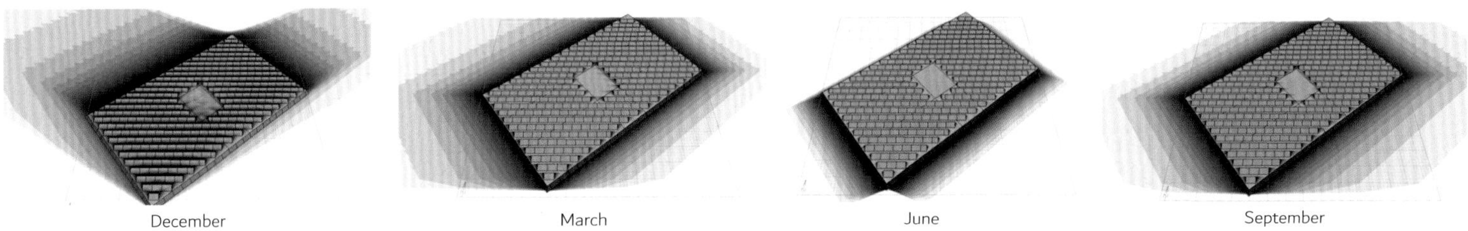

ROOF SYSTEM DESIGN: SHADOW STUDIES

27 VISTA FACADE

Project:	Burj Vista
Location:	Dubai, United Arab Emirates
Climate Zone:	BWH - Arid, Desert, Hot
Program:	Residential
Status:	Built
Client:	Emaar Properties PJSC
Date:	2007-2019
Strategies:	Solar Control, Daylighting, Thermal Mass, Ventilated

Burj Vista is a residential development designed as a sophisticated anchor presence on Dubai's Boulevard, providing residents with unobstructed, front-row views of Burj Khalifa, the world's tallest building. The complex consists of two towers, at 22 and 69 stories, with the first two levels featuring high-end retail. As part of an urban plaza that includes public sculptures, an amphitheater frames views of the Burj Khalifa between the two towers at the amenities level to emphasize the concept of a "theatrical" experience for residents.

The need to maximize views of the Burj Khaifa in each unit, minimize overall energy consumption, and maximize the comfort of residents were key design challenges. The solution was to think about the volume, rather than the area, of the units. A collection of duplex units on the upper floors of the taller tower features a series of double-height observation rooms that work in tandem with outdoor terraces. The result is the configuration of an exterior wall that provides each unit with a rich combination of "observation" rooms and terraces that are aligned along facade that faces The Boulevard in a staggered configuration, maximizing views while keeping obstructions to a minimum.

In addition to the enhanced view configuration, the exterior wall responds to orientation with specific features that reduce heat gain in Dubai's warm climate, including insets for terraces and sloped glass exterior walls that maximize shading, reduce heat gain, and reduce collection of wind-born sand; high-performance coatings on exterior glass; utilizing a significant amount of GFRC cladding systems to minimize the amount of glass; orienting the towers to minimize solar exposure; and connecting landscaped event areas with shaded paths. These architectural decisions make Burj Vista's design specific to its program, location, and massing configuration, giving it a distinctive identity with high-performance characteristics.

Facade Strategies

The main drivers of the form, and the detail generation, are the protection from solar exposure and the maximization of views of the Burj Khalifa. There are four main facades surfaces, each exposed to varying levels of high solar radiation and having varying views.

Views toward the Burj Khalifa are the prime objective for marketability. In generating the plan's geometry, the building that faces the Burj is maximized in length and the resulting surface area. As noted in the corresponding diagrams, this section of the facade needs to be protected from the sun, yet open enough to provide views of the Burj.

The west facade has long-distances views toward the gulf and needs to resolve, and control, high west solar exposure. The northwest facade seeks to protect from low and intense solar radiation, particularly during the summer month. The facade facing north has a significantly reduced solar radiation and can be more exposed for increased views.

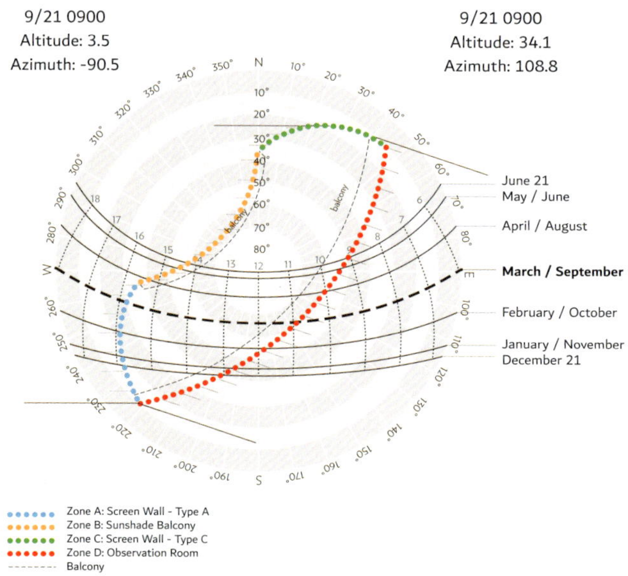

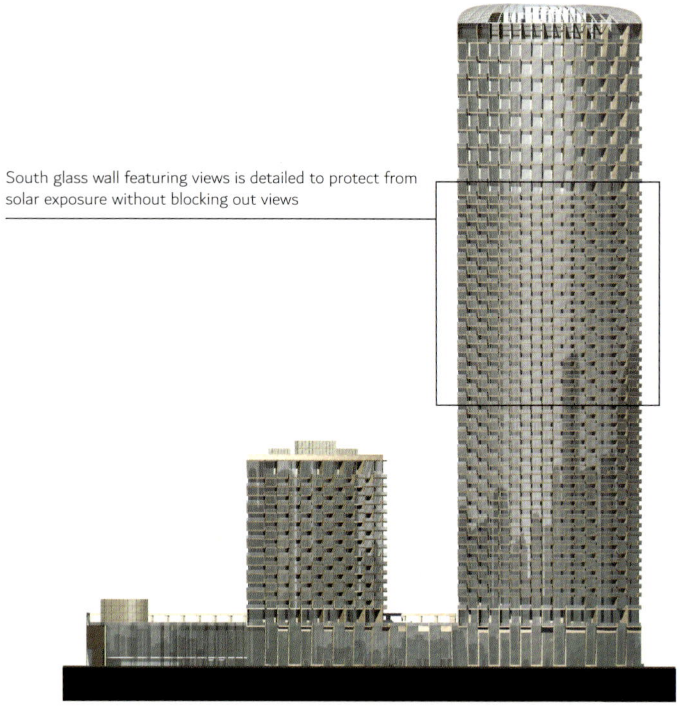

SOUTH-EAST ELEVATION

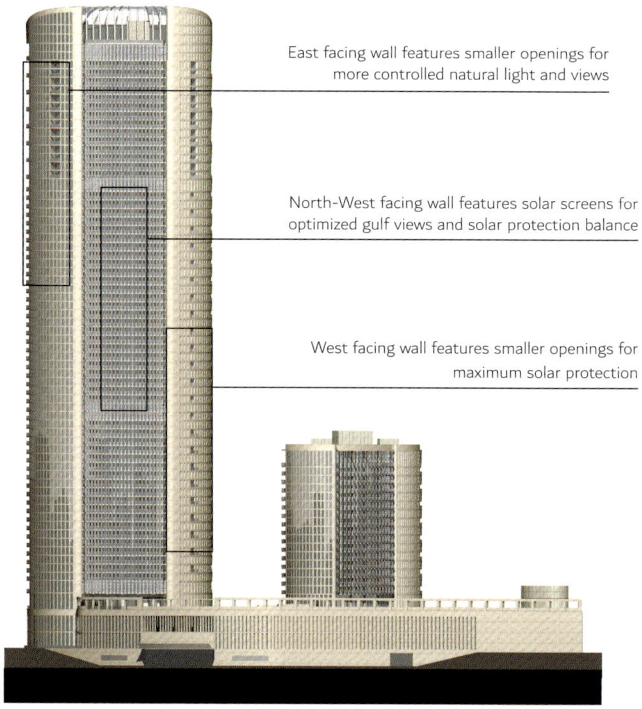

NORTH-WEST ELEVATION

Theatrical Experience

Burj Vista is set at an auspicious location, adjacent to the tallest building in the world, the Burj Khalifa, and its lushly landscaped park. A key design concept was how to maximize these focused, unobstructed views of the Dubai icon.

Another important consideration was how to provide this experience to every unit owner, regardless of unit size, and how the goal would affect the exterior facade.

The solution was to configure residential units facing the Burj Khalifa with at least one "viewing room" and one balcony carved out of the space. Each outdoor terrace has framed views of the tower, which also act as a protected shaded environment for the unit below.

BALCONY CONCEPT

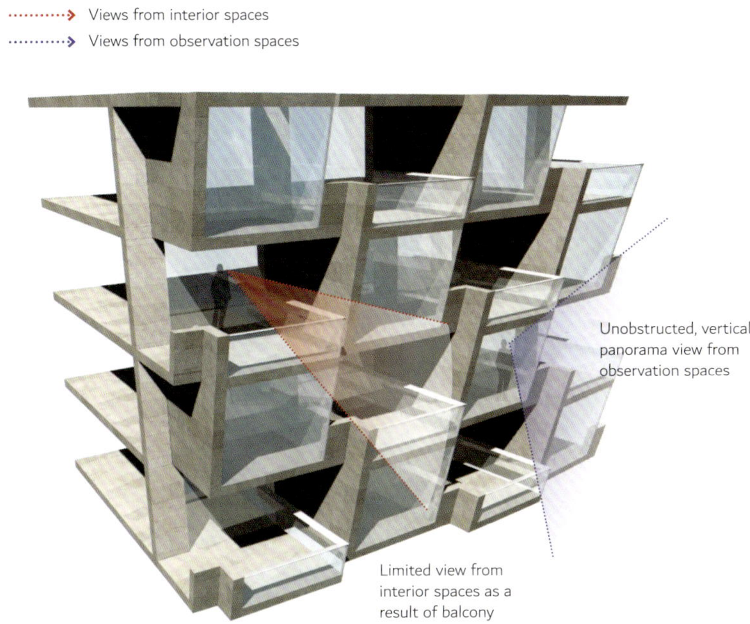

VIEW ANALYSIS

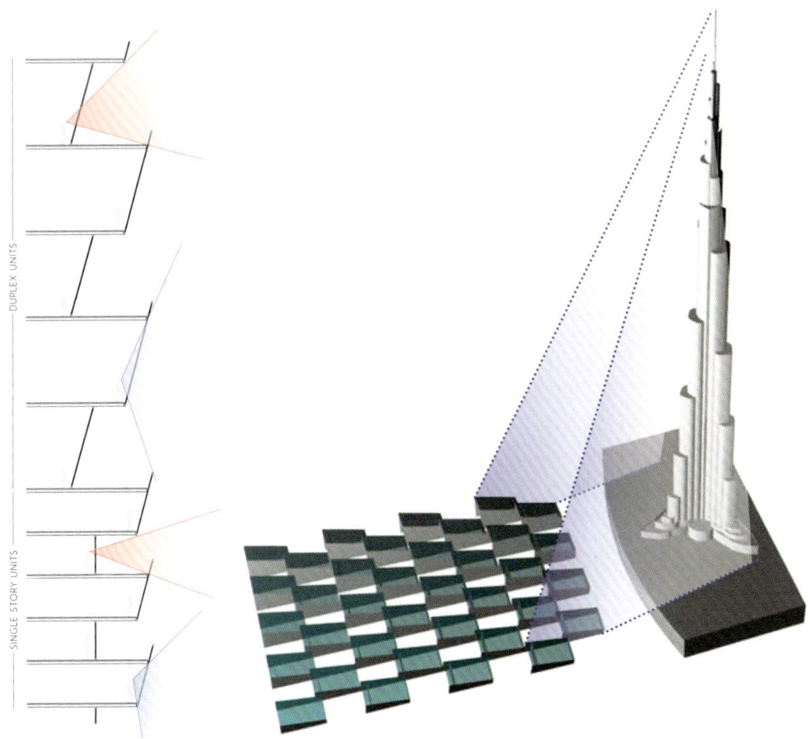

GFRC Cladding

Viewing rooms are clad with prefabricated, modular, locally produced Glass Fiber Reinforced Concrete (GFRC) on the south most facing surfaces. The localized use of this solid material enhances the performance of the exterior wall system in a variety of ways. It reduces the amount of solar radiation impacting the interior residential spaces, improving comfort levels and reducing energy use. Glare that is produced from the intensity of direct solar radiation is also significantly reduced.

Additionally, thermal conductivity of the wall system is reduced when compared to a vision glass system, given that insulation levels are enhanced within the thickness of the wall without impacting views. GFRC walls also provide privacy between units and rooms within the units. In the high solar intensity environment of Dubai, shade provided by GFRC and reduction of reflected solar radiation are highly beneficial to the performance of the building.

GFRC is also used to clad much the of the west oriented facade, where the low altitude of the sun is more difficult to control. In this section, narrow vertical glass openings placed deep into the GFRC passively reduce direct solar radiation. Furthermore, GFRC frames the windows on the facade, and on the articulated retail and amenity podium. Use of vision glass was limited to areas with significant view opportunities and to bring filtered daylight into interior spaces where needed.

GRFC SECTION + WEST ORIENTED FACADE (RIGHT)

South + Southeast Wall Design

The design intent for the south, southeast, and southwest walls was to utilize mostly solid walls, with a glass ratio that optimizes natural light and views, while controlling solar access into the units. The surfaces with direct views to the Burj Khalifa are clad in glass and sloped toward the ground to reduce the angle of incidence and solar radiation, as well as the cooling load on the building.

The south wall features significantly smaller, sloped windows, compared to the north wall, because of its increased exposure to sun and heat. Window opening detailing is responsive to the orientation, further enhancing solar protection. The glass wall that provides access to the terraces is fully shaded by the "observation room" above it. The contrast between the protruding "viewing rooms" and the shaded terraces generates a rich exterior expression.

SOUTHEAST WALL SECTION

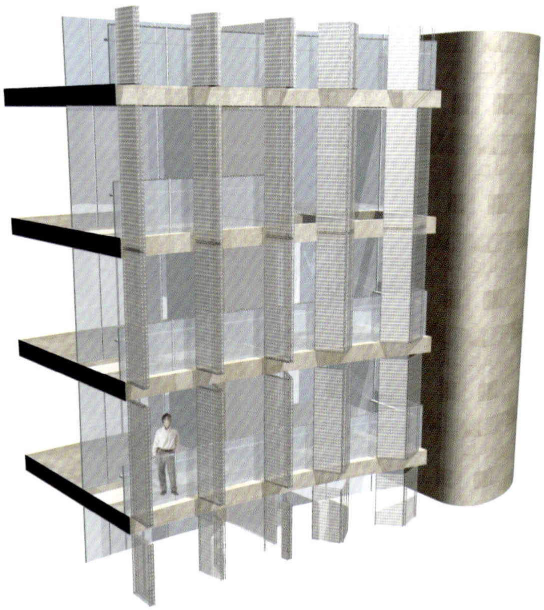

NORTHWEST WALL SECTION

North + Northwest Wall Design

The design of the north facade has reduced levels of solar radiation. Therefore, the facade can be less protected, allowing for more natural light and reducing the need for artificial light. The proportion of solid to glass walls is increased compared to the southwest elevation where the solid surface is increased.

The design intent for the northwest wall is to provide balcony areas that are shielded from the afternoon sun by using recessed glazing. This facade receives strong levels of solar radiation that are more difficult to control because of the low angle of incidence. A system of operable screens was conceived, which enables sweeping views during most of the day, while still protecting the interior spaces from strong solar radiation toward the end of the day.

SELF-SHADING BALCONIES

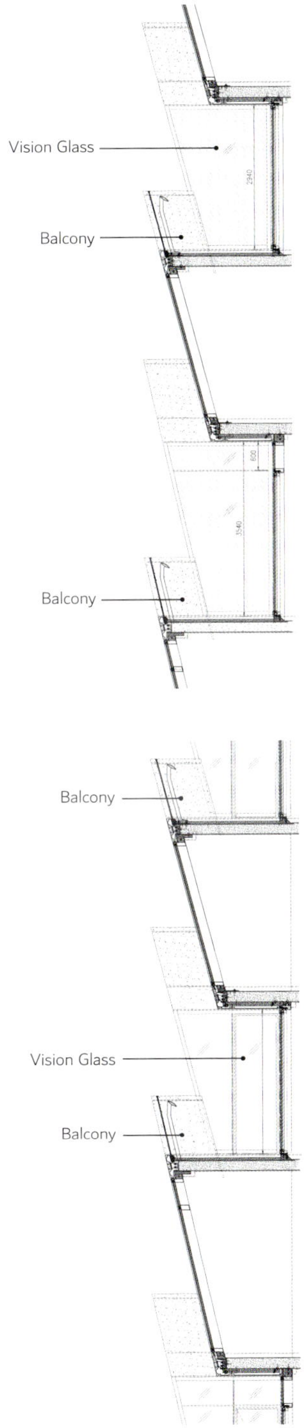

28 COMPOUND CURVE FACADE

Project: Kazakhstan Sphere

Location: Nur-Sultan, Kazakhstan

Climate Zone: DFB - Continental, Without Dry Season, Warm Summer

Program: Cultural

Status: Built

Client: Expo2017

Date: 2013-2017

Strategies: Solar Power, Wind Power, Luminous, Modular

The theme for the 2017 Expo, "Future Energy," was aimed at finding new ways to achieve qualitative changes in the energy sector, primarily for the development of alternative sources of energy and modes of transportation. Finding sustainable energy sources is a critical and growing global concern. A solution may spur economic growth and improve social standards, while reducing the burden on the environment. AS+GG's design for EXPO-2017 embraces the Future Energy concept by becoming the first post Industrial Revolution city, where energy consumed by the exposition community is provided by renewable sources.

The Kazakhstan Pavilion or "Sphere" is located at the center of the 25-hectare circular site. The pavilion symbolizes science as the foundation of Kazakhstan's future energy goals and aspirations. When the expo opened in 2017 the Kazakhstan Pavilion was the main destination and focal point on the overall development and of the Expo itself. In its present legacy mode, the building is a popular cultural destination known as Nur Alem: Museum of Future Energy.

The Sphere is approximately 87m tall with a spherical diameter of 80m with an exterior consisting of approximately 2,900 double curved panels. The sphere is panelized into 31 unique modules that repeat in a spiral pattern. It was important that the glass worked seamlessly with the geometry of the structural system, which is a curved grid wrapped around the sphere. The glass panel sizes were determined according to the main structural grid, with mullions anchored directly to the steel, so both pieces were designed together.

There are also 315 double curved panels that make up the side walls of the wind turbine inlet and 388 flat panels with integrated photovoltaics that make up the saddle surface of the scoop.

Design Process + Energy Modeling

Early in the design process, Building Information Modeling (BIM) was used to explore multiple iterations of the form in a virtual space. Each version was analyzed for design expression, energy impact, and structural integrity. The sphere's complex design required close collaboration with the structural consultant, ensuring that all opportunities for energy generation were investigated. Several were incorporated into the building's design.

After the initial form was chosen, more detailed analysis was conducted using Rhino/Grasshopper to further refine the form and to maximize sun exposure for the solar panels. Many investigations were completed and tested to integrate the BIPV panels, while balancing the requirements of other critical building components such as MEP surface area requirements, collision with other architectural elements, maximizing wind swept area for the turbines, and the rationalization the double-curved minimal surface geometry. Ultimately, BIPVs were installed at the top of the sphere to generate renewable energy for the building. During the testing phase, the energy model predicted 81,056 kWh/yr of electricity or 2.21% of total energy demand.

To further improve energy generation, an inlet was carved out of the building's top for integrated wind turbines. Several designs were modeled and tested to find the most appropriate form that responded to the programmatic requirements but also optimized the amount of energy generation, focusing on the wind energy that could be harvested from the surface of the sphere.

The design team worked closely with wind engineers to design and test multiple overall building forms and eventually the various shape of the wind inlet. Predominant southwest winds activate the turbines, which were also designed specifically for the harsh winter conditions in Nur Sultan. The turbines are predicted to produce a total of 52,700 kWh/yr of electricity or the equivalent of 1.6% of the building's total electricity demand or 0.9% of total energy demand.

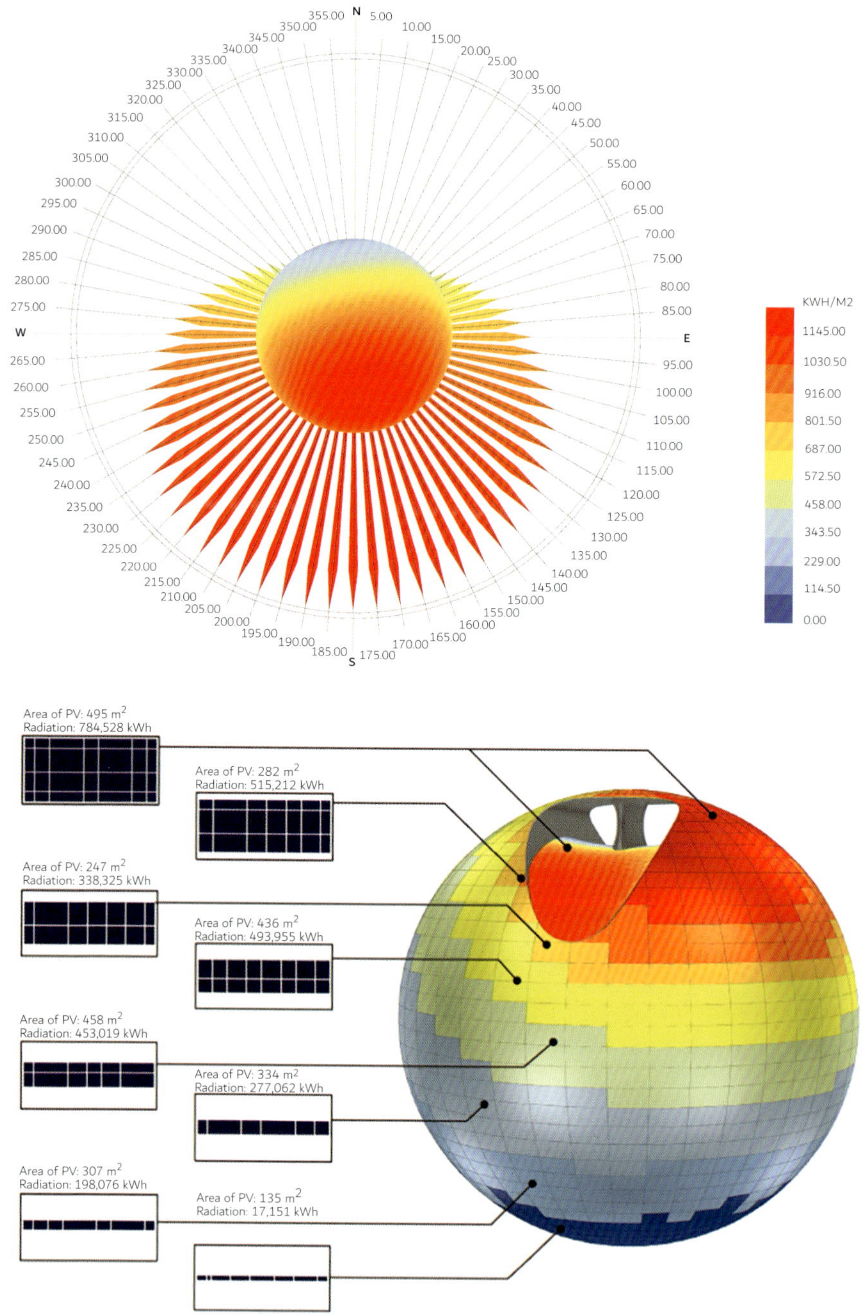

SOLAR RADIATION ANALYSIS

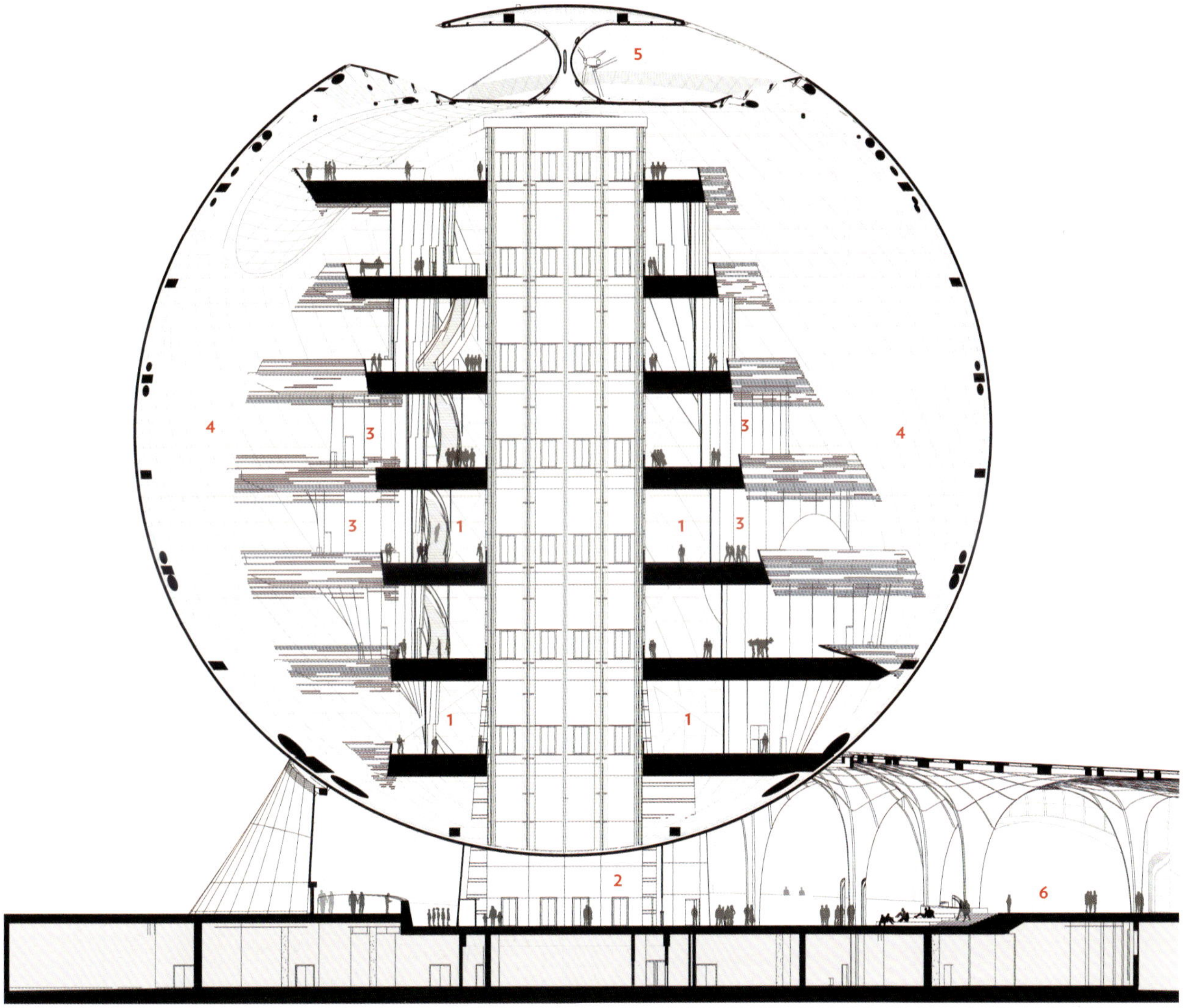

SECTION

1. Exhibit Space
2. Special Exhibit
3. Balcony
4. Atrium
5. Wind Scoop Turbine
6. Covered Street

Panelization Strategy

During the process of determining the overall geometry, and the additional geometric articulation of the sphere, the exterior wall, or cladding, for the extensive surface area was also being developed. With the goal of maintaining a smooth and refined spherical surface, the glass trapezoidal modules are detailed to be curved in two directions.

Double curved glass is created in a variety of ways, including using annealed glass or tempered glass. The design team researched and toured specialized glass facilities in Europe to find the ideal material for the facade.

The technology, while complicated, was readily available and achievable within the limited design schedule. It was critically important that the design and installation of the curved glass was done properly to achieve the design vision of a smooth sphere.

CONSTRUCTION 2015 (ABOVE AND RIGHT)

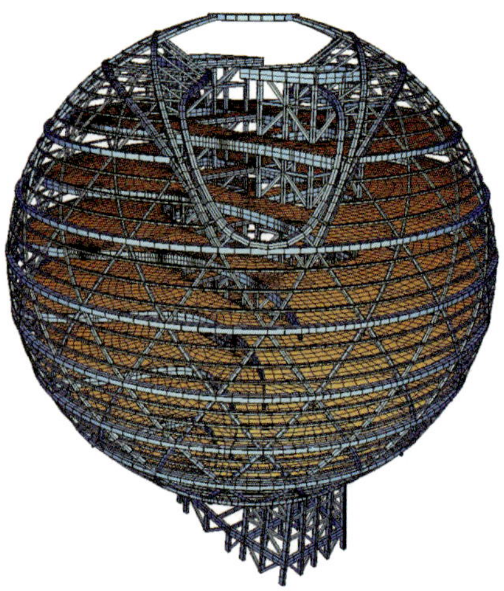

STRUCTURAL BIM MODEL

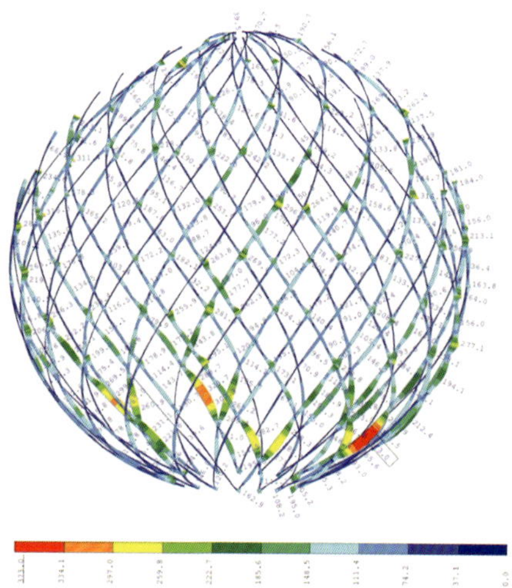

STRUCTURAL LOADS MODEL

STRUCTURAL PHYSICAL MODEL

Curtain Wall Design

The glazed unitized curtain wall consists of thermally broken double-curved insulated glass units, (IGU) with aluminum mullions supported by the building's primary structural tube system and secondary members.

The horizontal mullions support a perforated enclosure with a radiant heating tube system. The steel tube structural system is thermally isolated from the unitized glass wall. The inboard and outboard lite of the double glazed insulated glass unit are laminated glass units. The outboard laminated lite includes a pattern of ceramic frit.

The glass is an ultra clear low-iron glass with Low-E coating and ceramic frit in a varied pattern. An LED illumination/graphic system is integrated into the exterior curtain wall's mullion system. A BMS controlled shading system is integrated also into the exterior wall's mullion system.

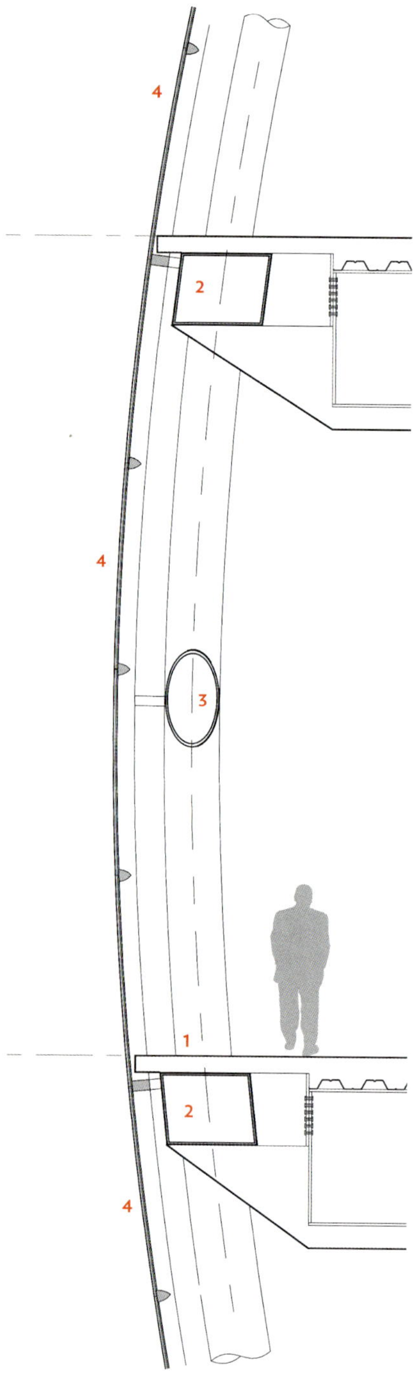

DETAIL SECTION DRAWING

1. Stainless Steel Grating
2. Primary Structural Ring Beam
3. Primary Diagonal Structural Member
4. Double Curved IGU With Laminated Low-Iron Glass

EXTERIOR WALL DETAILS

EXTERIOR WALL ATTACHMENT DETAIL

HORIZONTAL MULLION DETAIL

ATTACHMENT DETAIL DRAWING

1. Double Vision Glazing
2. Structurally Sealed Joint with Stainless Steel Toggle Glazing Clips
3. Led Strip For Light And Video
4. Aluminum Framing
5. Snap-In Cover
6. Steel Reinforcement
7. Adjustable Stainless Steel Anchor
8. Composite Stainless Steel Cladding
9. Fireproofing
10. Diagonal Steel Beam

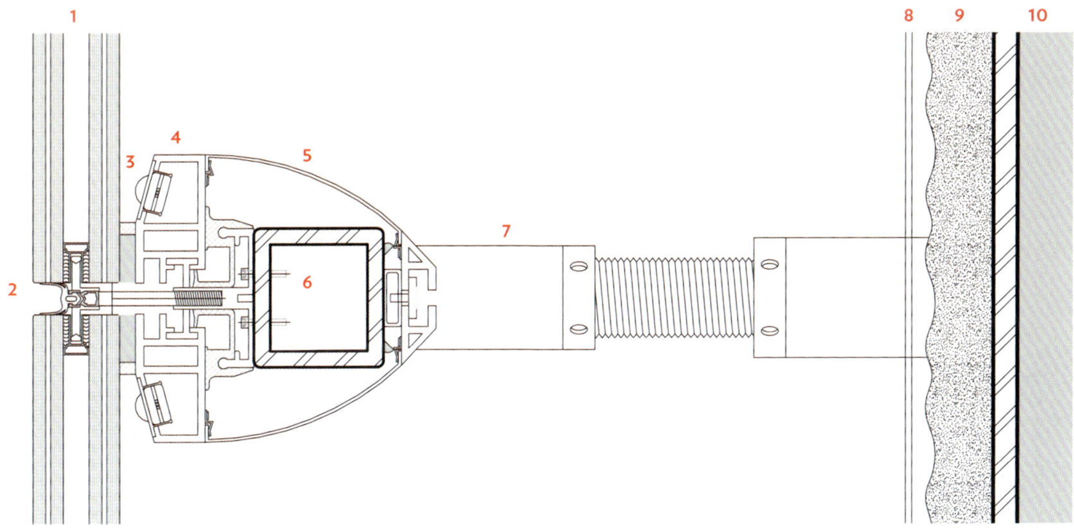

Integrated Glass

One of the building's design goals is to maximize its means of communicating with the local and international community. As a central piece of the expo event and the legacy district, its ability to engage with local and global audiences is a part of its success. When geometry is considered, the design relates to its context as a 360-degree platform. The glass facade becomes a programmable canvas, where digital content can be integrated to form a rich dynamic expression. Options ranging from LED meshes and other interior and exterior systems were considered.

In the final and built solution, LED strips were installed into the exterior wall panels, aligning with the organic and dynamic expression of the sphere cladding. The physical, static architectural elements that define the sphere during the day, come to life at night, saturating the building with various light displays, messages, and colors.

Details were developed to incorporate LED strips, which are integrated with the aluminum supports at each side of the joint and protected from the exterior environment. Maintenance and installation work are done from the interior of the structure. Even though the separation between the LED strips is significant, and the overall density of the LED points is low, therefore the vast size of the sphere and the movement of light at the panels, help make the system successful.

LED LIGHTING

Renewable Wind Energy

Wind power generation is another natural resource integrated into the design of the Sphere. Significant wind is available on the site and is directional, predictable, and consistent though the year. During the development of the design of the renewable energy component, several options were studied to incorporate wind energy, using CFD modeling.

The wind energy concepts were presented and discussed with the client, and the selected option was buildable, cost effective, and achieved a unique form that creates a space for a wind turbine. The top of the sphere was also the most effective place to locate the wind turbines, as wind velocity is increased with height.

This carved out spaces reinforces the Kazakhstan Pavilion as a symbol of "Future Energy." It was important for the overall performance of the building, but also as a physical expression and symbol of the Expo 2017 message. Given the scale and significance of the building, renewable energy generation is visible from a distance and from inside the building. At the top floor, visitors can see the turbines firsthand, installed and working.

WIND SCOOP GEOMETRY ITERATIONS

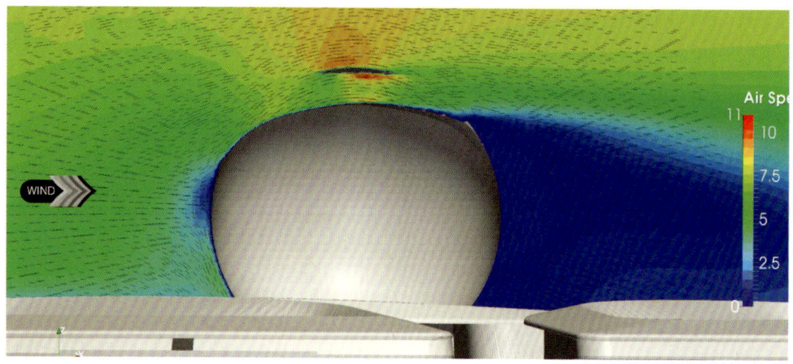

CFD SCOOP ANALYSIS

WIND CONCEPT DIAGRAM

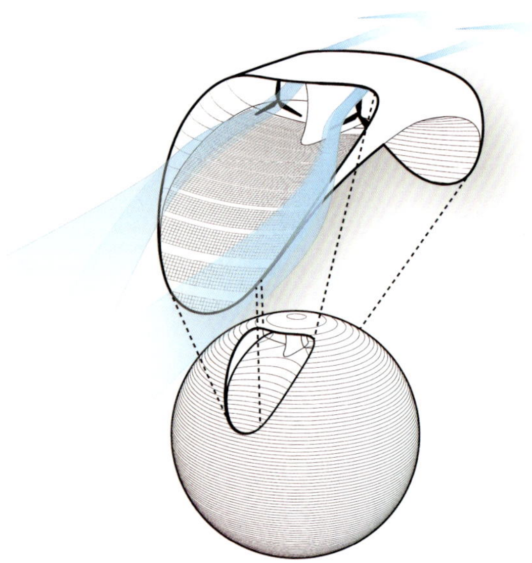

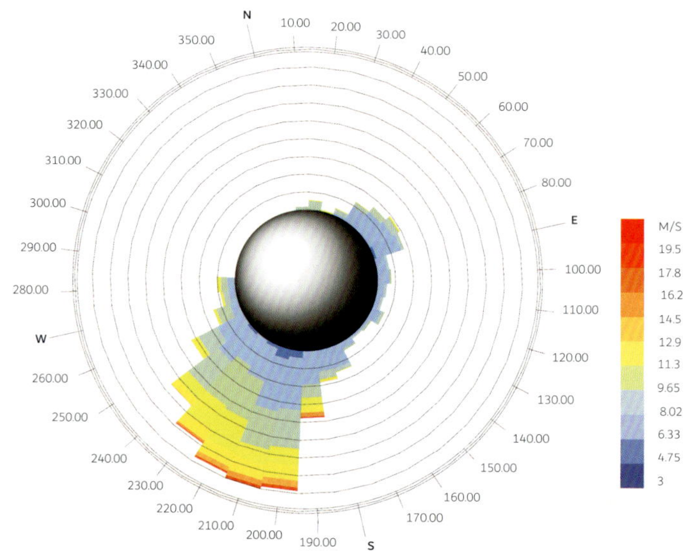

WIND ROSE
1 January - 31 December
Wind Speed > 3m/s - 74% of Total Hours

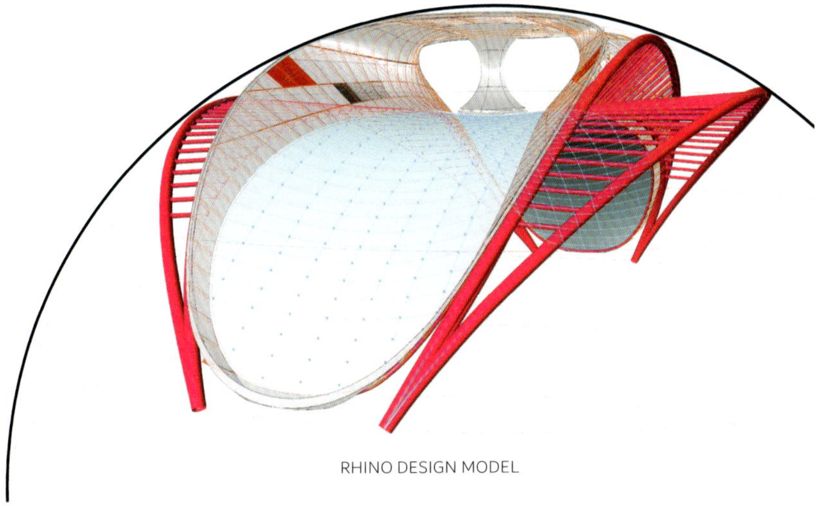

RHINO DESIGN MODEL

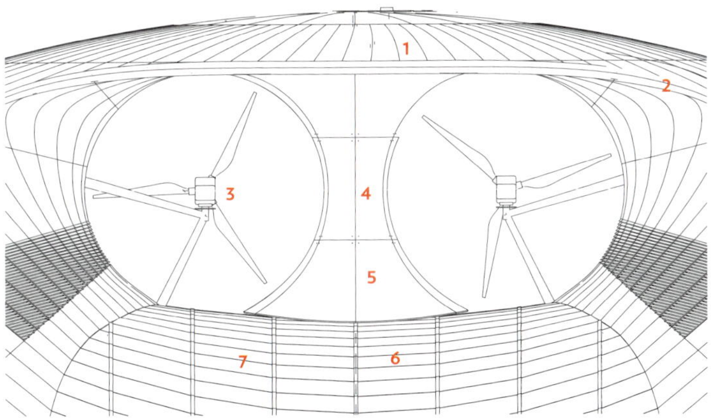

TURBINE ELEVATION

1. Double Vision Glazing
2. Metal Panel
3. Wind Turbine
4. Removable Accessible Panel
5. Glazing
6. Double BIPV Glazing
7. Stainless Steel Cap

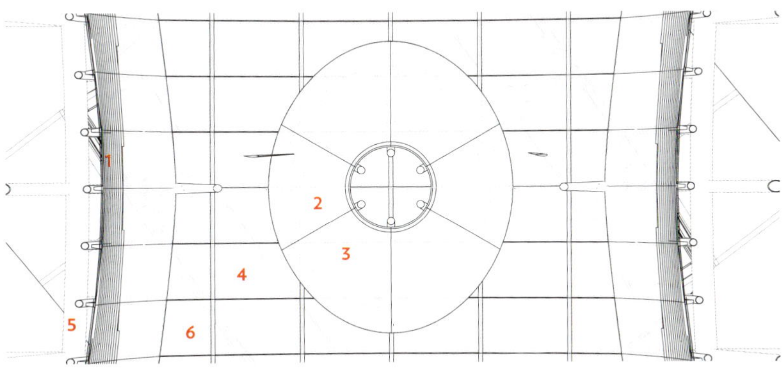

TURBINE DIVIDER PLAN

1. Double Vision Glazing
2. Glazing
3. Removable Accessible Panel
4. Stainless Steel Cap
5. Double BIPV Glazing
6. Sphere Primary Structure

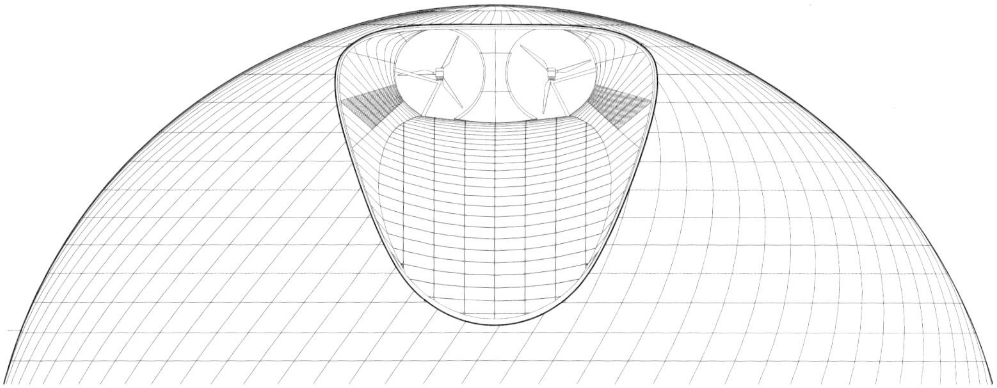

WIND SCOOP FRONT ELEVATION

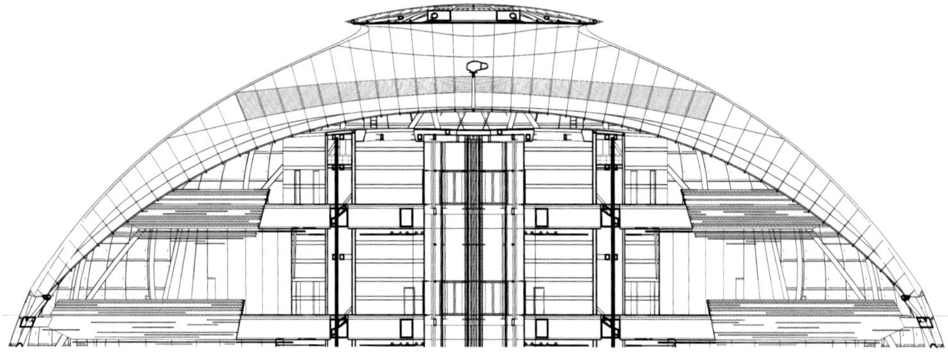

WIND SCOOP LONGITUDINAL SECTION

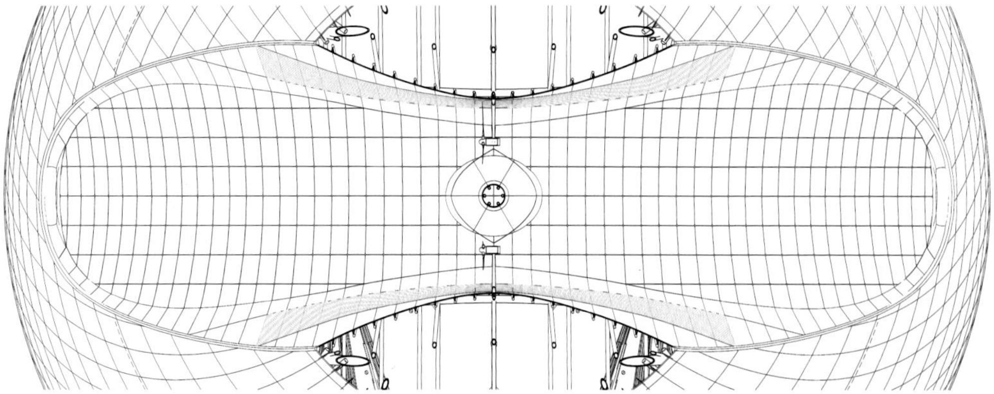

WIND SCOOP LONGITUDINAL ELEVATION

Solar Energy Generation

In addition to wind, the Sphere also includes solar photovoltaic technology. After studying several options, and due to the technical challenges with integrated photovoltaics into curved glass, it was agreed to focus on solar energy generation and PV installation in a smaller, more focused area at the top of the sphere.

The BIPV panels are integrated into a cable net glass skylight with flat panels in a zone at the base of the wind turbines. Their development required careful considerations to effectively incorporate them with the design of the wind scoop. In this area, 388 BIPV panels serve three purposes:

- Accommodate high velocity air to wind turbines
- Convert solar radiation into electrical energy
- Reduce direct solar radiation and glare at the top of the museum building and atrium spaces

Another intended goal of the BIPV was to communicate a "language of energy." The panels are a featured part of the exhibit space at the top floor and can be seen from all levels of the atrium.

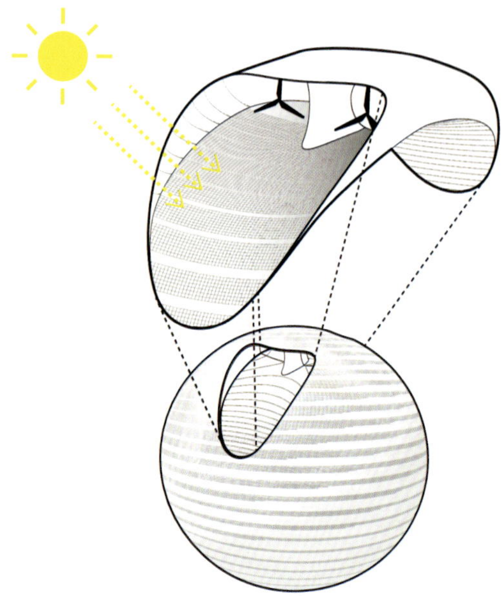

SOLAR CONCEPT DIAGRAM

SCOOP CONCEPT RENDERING

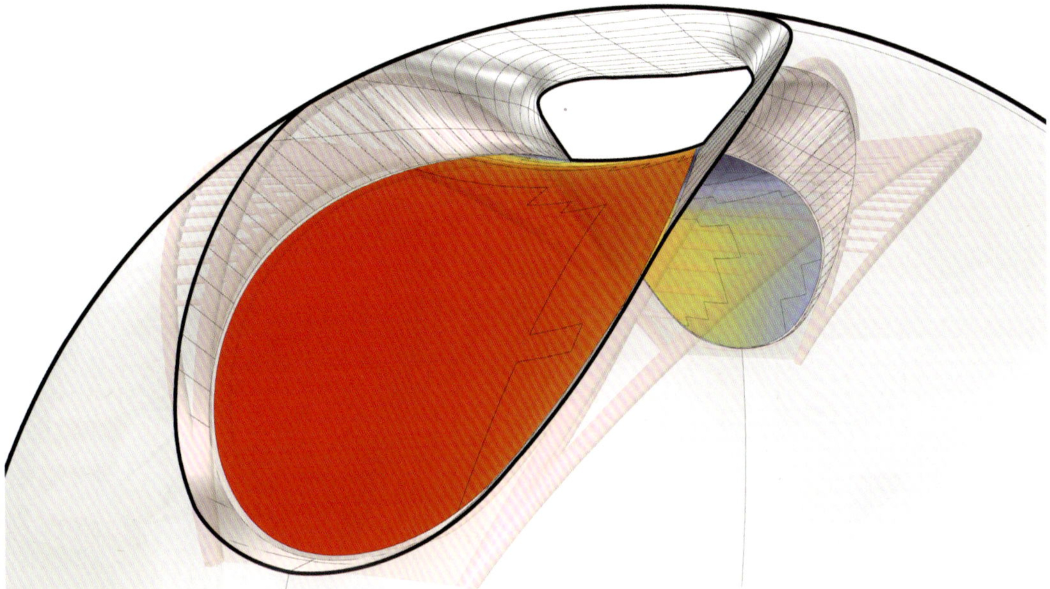

RHINO DESIGN MODEL

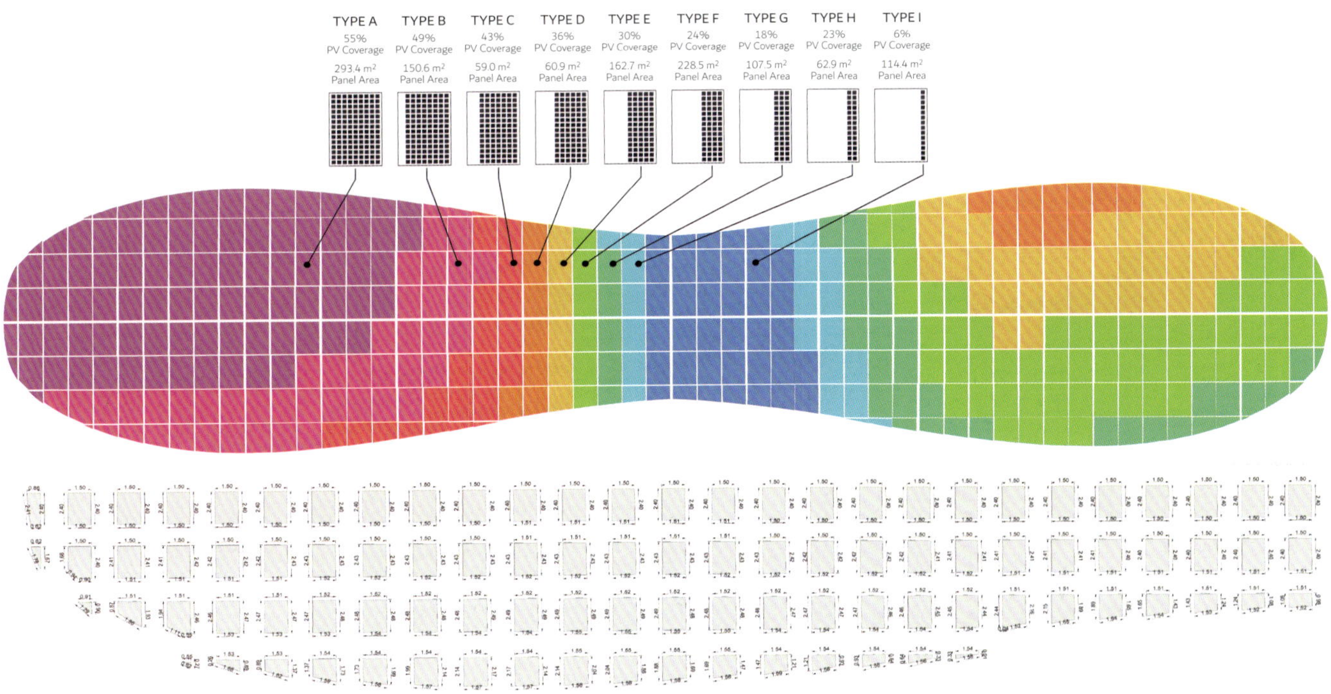

PANELIZATION STUDY

WIND SCOOP DETAILS

1. Stainless Steel Fitting
2. Low Iron Laminated Glass
3. Cablenet System
4. Steel Ring Beam
5. Insulation
6. Snow Melting Mat
7. Roof Drain
8. Composite Metal Panel
9. Sealant
10. Stainless Steel Cladding
11. Drainage Pipe with Insulation
12. Support Sub-Structure

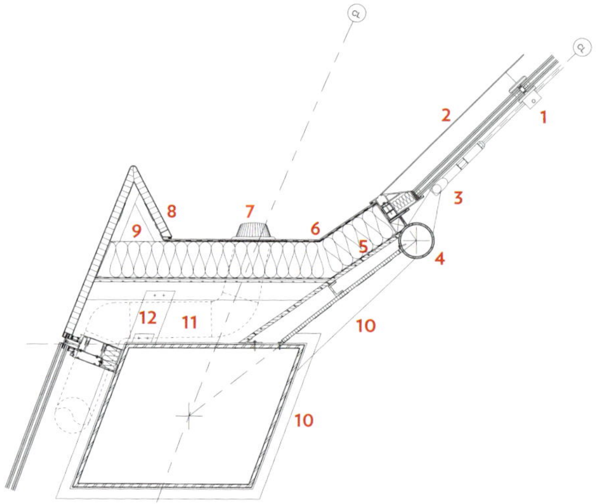

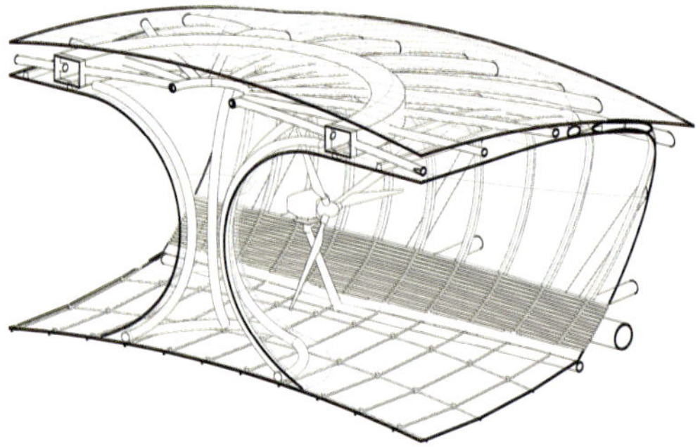

1. Double Vision Glazing
2. Metal Panel
3. Facade Structure
4. Glass
5. Stainless Steel Fitting

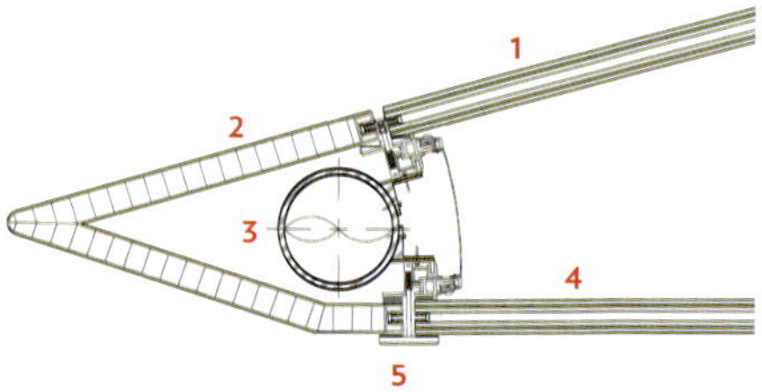

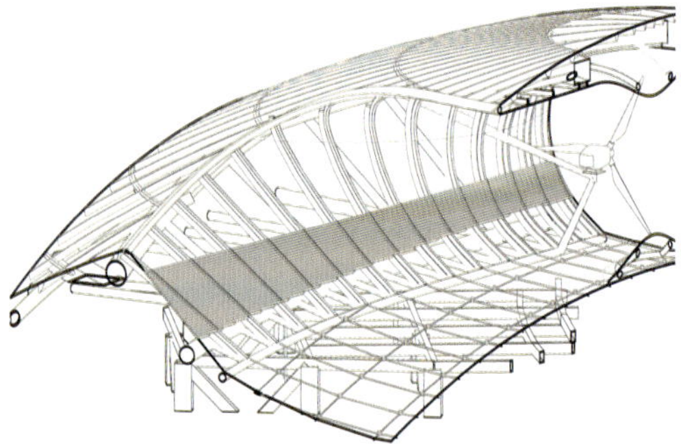

29 FRAME FACADE

Project:	Waldorf Astoria Beijing
Location:	Beijing, China
Climate Zone:	DWA - Continental, Dry Winter, Hot Summer
Program:	Hotel
Status:	Built
Client:	COFCO Hotel Group
Date:	2009-2014
Strategies:	Solar Control, Daylight, Ventilated, Luminous, Modular

The new exterior wall and 50-meter super-frame for the 176-room Waldorf Astoria in Beijing, China was designed to address the contemporary interpretation of the antiquities found in the local neighborhood adjacent to the Forbidden City, China's nation's most important historical treasure. The concept behind the exterior wall was to create a unique set of views for guests to experience the heritage neighborhood. The idea of a "compound eye" that optimized direct and peripheral views was developed and adapted for solar orientation, as well as city views.

The main design expression of the building is the bronze-clad exterior that articulates the character of the historic site. With the client's encouragement, the design team's intention was to subtly reflect traditional Chinese architecture using geometry and materials. Stylistically this influence can be seen in the hotel's symmetry, prominent eaves, and the use of bronze. Attention to detail was crucial to the design. The vertical and roof eave frames were purposefully shaped and are strongly connected at the corners, echoing the profile of a traditional Chinese roof soffit.

AS+GG joined the Waldorf Astoria Beijing project as designer of the exterior wall system during the interim schematic design stage, after the client had commissioned designs from other firms. Because of the project's strict program, high land value, and 50-meter height restriction, the design process proceeded under highly constrained conditions. AS+GG worked closely with the client, re-shaping the building massing, while advancing the program and re-establishing the building structure and its interior layout grid. The result is a modern building that reflects the contemporary luxury brand of Waldorf Astoria, while subtly responding to Chinese architectural tradition.

Views

The Forbidden City, Wang Fu Jing, Hutong courtyards, and the historical and modern urban fabric blend together to form a rich context, which is intentionally framed and presented through the "eyes" of the hotel. This unique facade system offers an unobstructed and private viewing experience for guests.

Solar Control

The orientation of the building and facade is important to the comfort of the building users and the environmental sensibility of the project. The shading frame system, created specifically for each room, provides the character of the hotel, while protecting the building and minimizing solar heat gain from all directions. The facade creates both an environmentally friendly and culturally specific building.

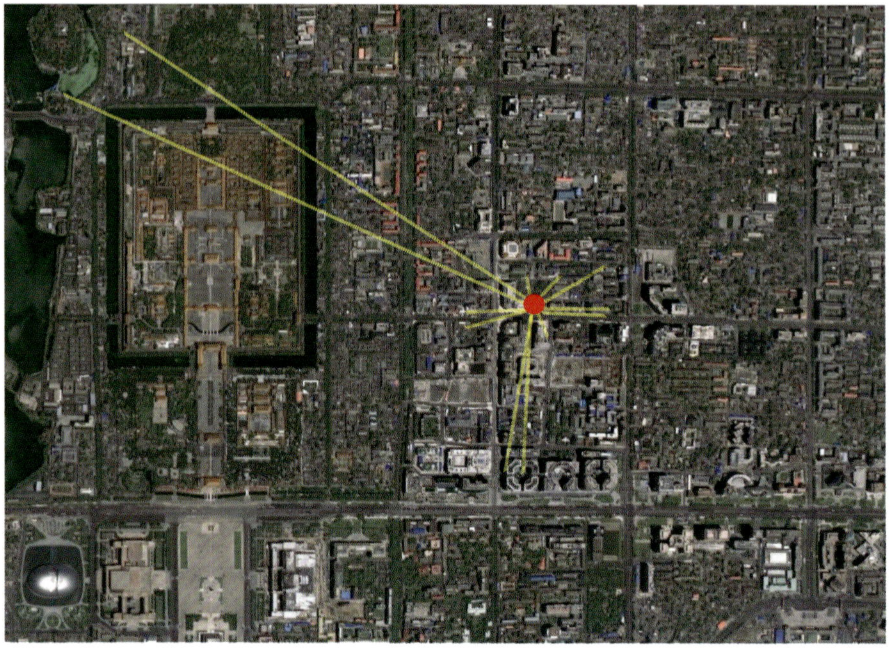

VIEW DIAGRAM

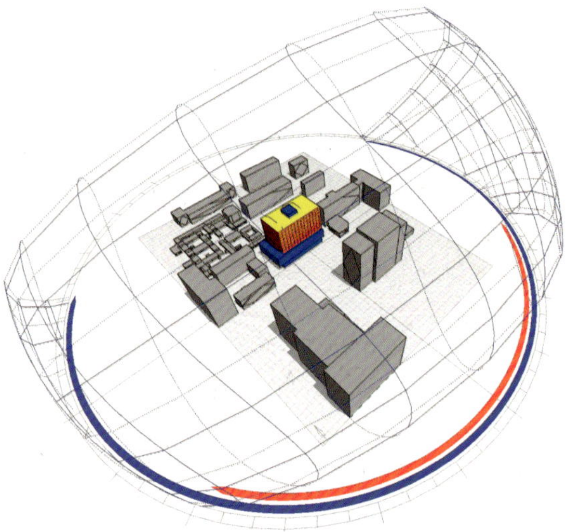

SOLAR RADIATION

THE FORBIDDEN CITY

Cultural Connection

The Forbidden City (c. 1406-1420), the Chinese imperial palace from the Ming to the Qing dynasties, is located three blocks from the Waldorf site. The palace is striking for its generous use of bronze on statues, water cauldrons, and door and window fixtures. Wooden roofs are recognized for their strong eaves and deep bronze color. The Waldorf design attempts not to directly evoke these Chinese architectural traditions but instead aims to subtly reflect them with the use of culturally sensitive materials and a strong attention to detail. The vertical frame and roof eaves are shaped, detailed, and strongly connected at the corners to echo the profile of a traditional Chinese roof soffit silhouette. Another connection is made by creating a 3D window system that frames the views and evokes memories of previous cultures.

South Facade

On the south facade awning extend from each window to shade the space within. Additionally, solar heat gain is minimized by using insulated laminated Low-E and low-Iron glass on the floor-to-ceiling windows that offer excellent city-wide views, improve user comfort levels, and provide daylighting to the interior spaces. Traditional geometric Chinese screen patterns are used on movable interior sunscreens. These ideas not only improve the building's performance but also enhance the guest room experience.

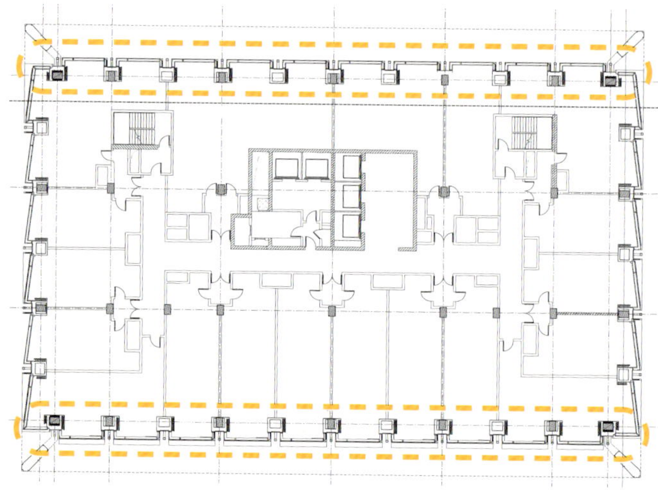

TYPICAL PLAN

Materials

Materials were chosen for their beauty and for their low-maintenance and highly durable qualities. Most materials used in the building have at least a 30-year lifespan. Bronze is used in large areas of the walls, as well as on window mullions, small clad sunshades, and perforated screens. Other high-end, traditional materials are used to the same effect: gray granite as a background material on the walls to recall the historic charcoal bricks of Beijing's traditional residential streets. Locally sourced materials are used whenever possible.

NORTH + SOUTH FACADE DIAGRAM

NORTH + SOUTH FACADE

EAST + WEST FACADE

PENTHOUSE BALCONIES

East + West Facades

On the east and west sides of the building, bronze-lined bay windows provide expansive views of the Beijing skyline, including some parts of the Forbidden City.

The stepped out and angled floor-to-ceiling window system creates a unique experience with a wider view, while protecting the guests' privacy at the same time. The shading frame system contributes to the character of the hotel and protects the building by minimizing solar heat gain from all directions, creating both an environmentally friendly and culturally specific building.

The superframe, which connects the roof and anchors the building corners, recalls the symmetry and steady character of Chinese traditional architecture. At the top of the frame, a trellis structure provides the penthouse balconies with shade and still allows access to desired sunlight.

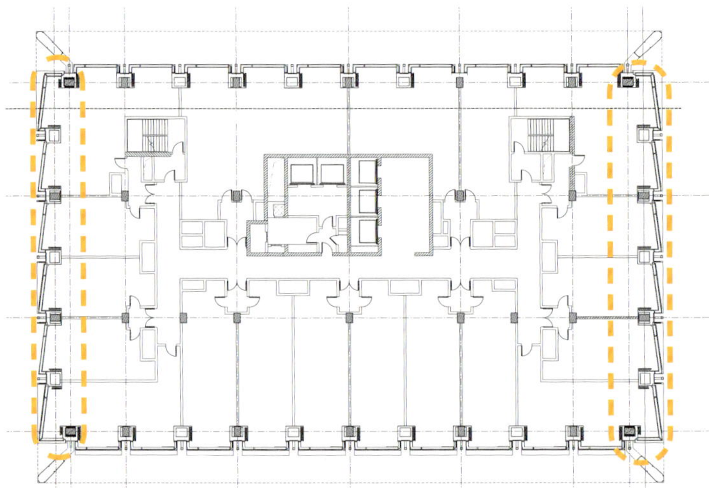

TYPICAL PLAN

Canopy Design

A bronze-clad canopy with special lighting creates a weather-protected outdoor environment at the hotel entrance. A series of lanterns are beautifully perforated—the patterns interpreted from Chinese traditional paintings—and covered with a fritted skylight.

Sunlight during the day and artificial light at night is filtered and diffused through this artistic bronze canvas to create a memorable experience for all guests from their rooms or and visitors passing by. The roof of the canopy is also treated accordingly, recognizing that this fifth elevation is critical to guest experience

CANOPY VIEW SECTION

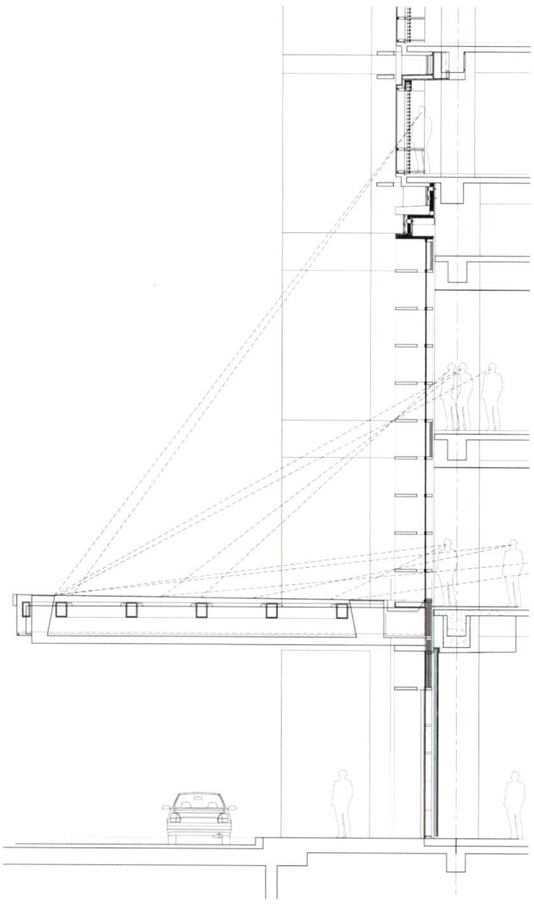

MAIN ENTRANCE (ABOVE + LEFT)

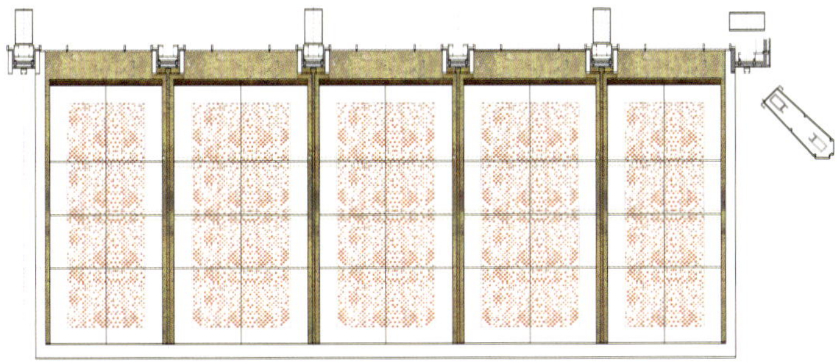

CANOPY ROOF PLAN

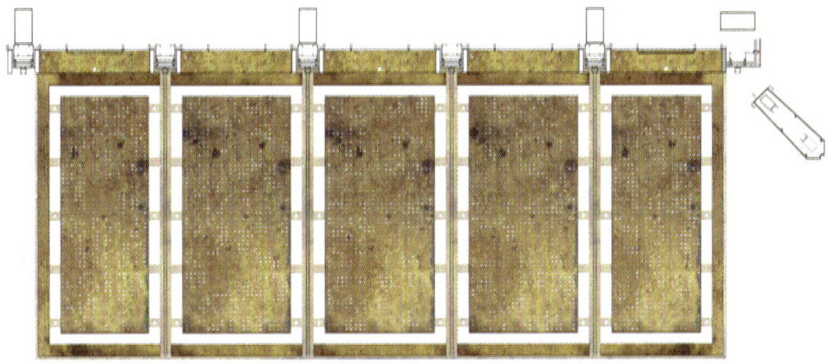

CANOPY REFLECTED CEILING PLAN

30 BRISE SOLEIL SHIELD FACADE

Project:	Wuhan Greenland Center
Location:	Wuhan, China
Climate Zone:	CFA - Temperate, Without Dry Season, Hot Summer
Program:	Mixed-Use
Status:	Construction
Client:	Wuhan Greenland Group
Date:	2010-present
Strategies:	Solar Control, Daylight, Ventilated, Modular

Wuhan, the capital city of Hubei Province in central China, is located on the Jianghan Plain, which joins the Hanjiang River and the Yangtze River. Divided by the Yangtze, Wuhan is known as the "Three Towns of Wuhan," with Hankou and Hanyang on the west bank and Wuchang on the east. The three tapered sides of Wuhan Greenland Center represent the three townships and two rivers that intersect to form one unified city.

The supertall mixed-use tower features a uniquely streamlined form that combines two key shaping concepts—a tapered body and top as well as softly rounded corners—to reduce wind resistance and vortex action that builds up around supertall towers. The building's efficient aerodynamic performance allows it to minimize the amount of structural material, and the associated embodied carbon, needed for construction. The tower's three corners rise from its tripod-shaped base and taper upward. The corners are smooth curved glass, contrasting markedly with the more textured curtain wall cladding of the tower's body. Apertures, or inlets, in the curtain wall at regular intervals assist in venting wind pressure against the tower; the apertures also house window-washing systems and air intake and exhaust systems on mechanical floors.

The tower is comprised of two main exterior wall types, which accentuate the formal expression: a shaded, textured main body and a reflective, smooth, curved shield. The exterior wall protects the interior from both strong mid-day and afternoon solar conditions. Glare is controlled by an exterior metal sunshade that also filters and diffuses sunlight. Integrated smart shading systems are incorporated into each unit giving the users and building owners control of the shades. By reducing incident solar radiation and therefore building cooling loads, daytime energy consumption is greatly reduced. Floor-to-ceiling glass windows also provide unobstructed views of the surrounding city.

Facade Components

The tower's massing is composed of two main exterior wall types. The body or main area has a heavy texture expression, made up of both vertical polished stainless-steel fins and perforated aluminum horizontal sun shading devices that will protect the interior from both strong mid-day and afternoon solar conditions. The corners of the tower, or "shields," are comprised of smooth reflective curved glass that functions as an anchor and as counterpoint to the body of the tower. The shields rise from the edges of the tower and join at the top to create holistic architecture expression.

PANELIZATION STRATEGIES

Total number of curtain glass wall panels				21,411 panels		129,430 m2
	total number of curtain wall panels - BODY			15,787 panels	73.7%	98,110 m2
	B1	body 1	sloped stepped	15,330 panels	71.6%	96,458 m2
	D1	dome 1	sloped stepped	333 panels	1.6%	952 m2
*	D2	dome 2	slumped	124 panels	2.4%	727 m2
	total number of curtain wall panels - SHIELD			5,624 panels	26.3%	31,320 m2
	S1	shield 1	horizontal bent	4,870 panels	22.7%	28,565 m2
	C1	crown 1	radial bent	244 panels	1.1%	1,230 m2
*	C2	crown 2	slumped	510 panels	2.4%	1,525 m2
*		shield	metal end panel	930 panels		2,585 m2
*		shield	metal return panel	930+ panels		7,711 m2

** indicates panels were not evaluated in panlization study*

OVERALL BUILDING DATA

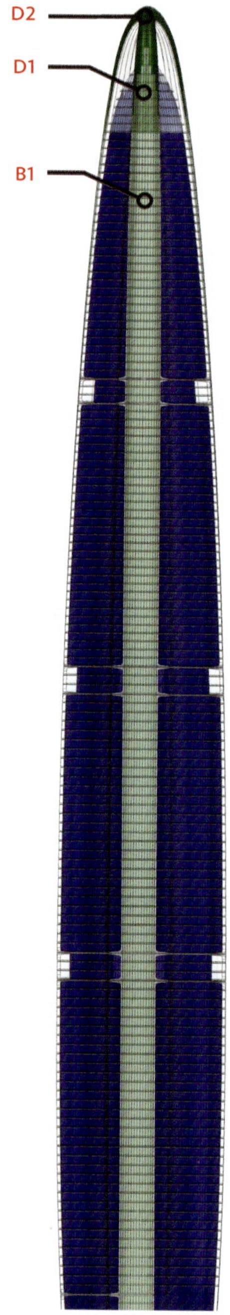

PANELIZATION STRATEGIES

Form Optimization + Parametric Modeling

The tower's form is a dynamic and fluid composition that is primarily driven by the client's programmatic requirements, the required structural efficiency, and the optimization of the facade geometry to reduce the number of panel types. Multidisciplinary inputs impacted the form of the tower and are best studied by integrating them into a parametric model that can be used to explores various solutions. The model was also used to coordinate with wind and structural engineers, consolidate the client program, and evaluate the design parameters in a continual feedback loop. Through multiple reiterations of this analyses, the form of the building was optimized.

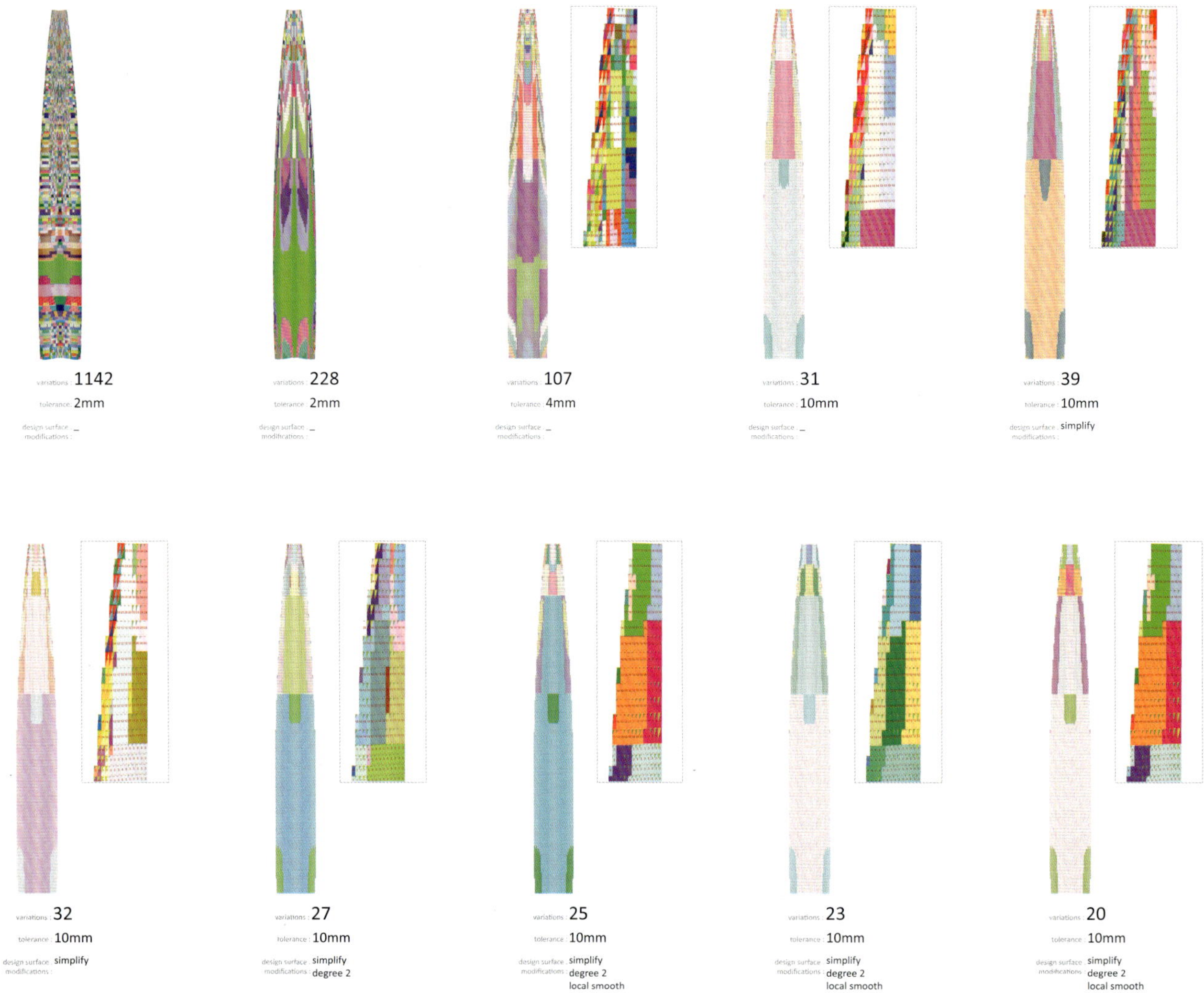

Geometry + Constructibility

Early in the design process, one of the main hurtles was the team's capability to prove that the tower's double-curved form was constructible within the client's budget. Various strategies were explored to rationalize the complex double curving geometry and to advise the client of alternatives that create a feasible and economical solution.

Solutions were derived that reduce the total number of unique panel types and use standard curtain wall detailing strategies. Solutions ranged from maintaining the complexity of the overall tower form, which would result in a high number of unique panel shapes, to an overall geometric rationalization that would compromise the design intent but create low numbers of unique panel types and consequently low cost.

As the depth of the design increased, various other detailed facade parameters were integrated into the parametric design model that allowed a greater depth of investigation and eventual coordination with the fabrication team. In addition to the panel geometry, critical parameters such as the alignment of vertical stack joints, vertical and horizontal pitch angle, and in the case of the shield panel's curvature radius. It was a balance of these factors that allowed the design to progress and adapt to the needs of the fabrication and construction teams, while maintaining a high alignment of the design intent, fabrication capabilities, and economic realities of supertall buildings.

As part of this rationalization process, the tower was separated into its basic geometric elements. In plan, the tower has a trilateral symmetry, meaning that each of the three sides of the tower is equal to the other two. Furthermore, each side can be broken down into two equal segments and each of these segments is made up of three simple curves. By breaking down the geometry into small components the design team was able prescribe and control the location of each panel floor by floor.

It was determine that the use of hot bent glass would not be feasible within the budget. For this reason, the team use d a variation of a step curtain system. Each panel is angled back toward the next floor instead of vertically. This small modification allowed the facade to closely follow the towers design surface, thereby using the more expensive and complex hot bend scheme.

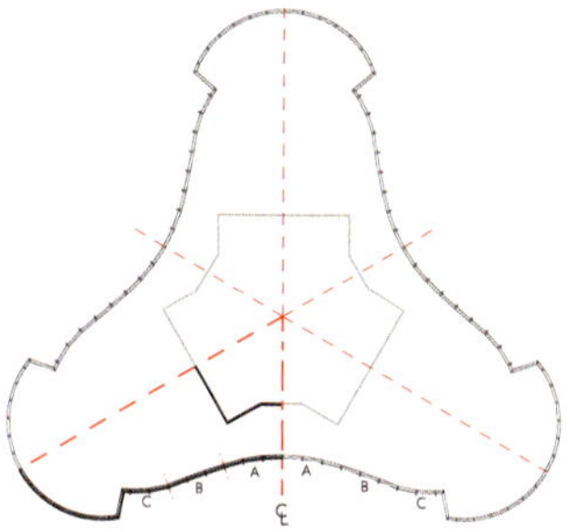

PANEL PLAN

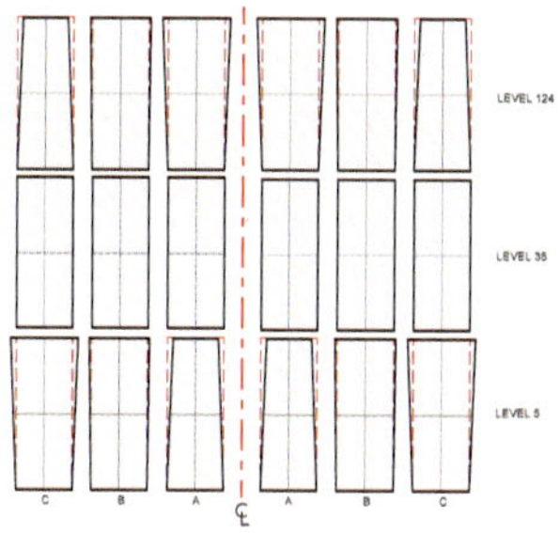

PANEL ELEVATION

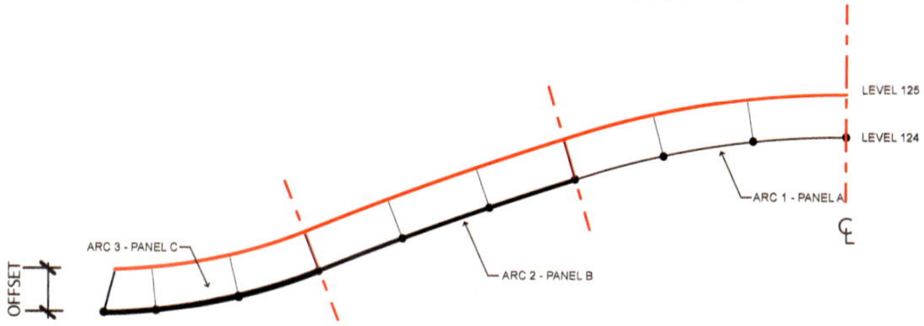

PANEL PLAN

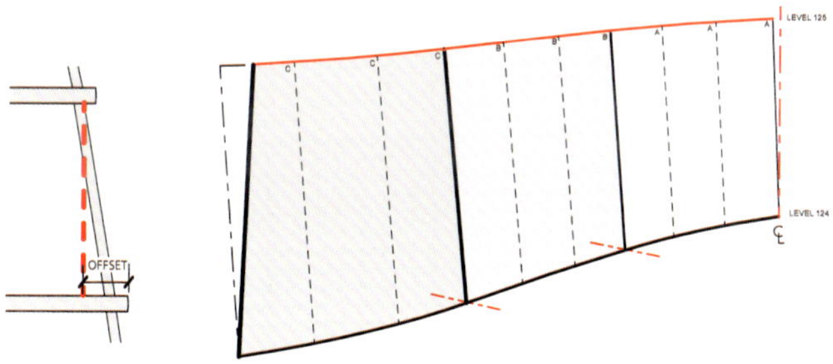

PANEL DIAGRAM

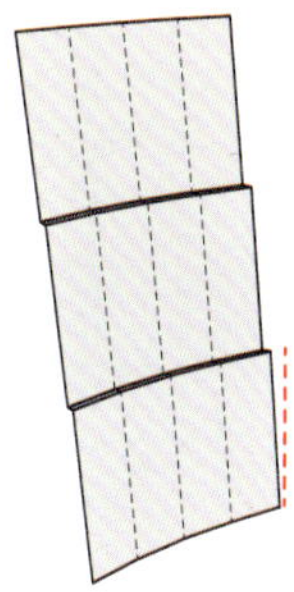

SLOPED STEP

STAGGER SLOPED STEP

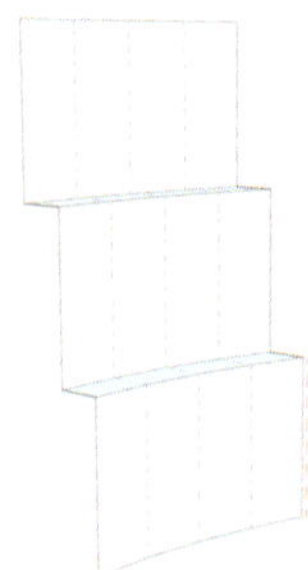

VERTICAL STEP

Body Panelization

To achieve the slope-step concept for the body of the tower, three primary variables are considered when developing the paneling system: the vertical step, the vertical angle, and the horizontal angle. For each variable, a set of parameters is developed to indicate the maximum division achieved. The vertical step is the maximum division that the panels can displace from one floor to the next. The vertical angle refers to the slope in which the glass needs to be placed for the panel to meet the requirements of the vertical step. The final variable is the horizontal angle, which refers to the angle in plan that the panels can be rotated from each other and still maintain the weather seal between the two panels.

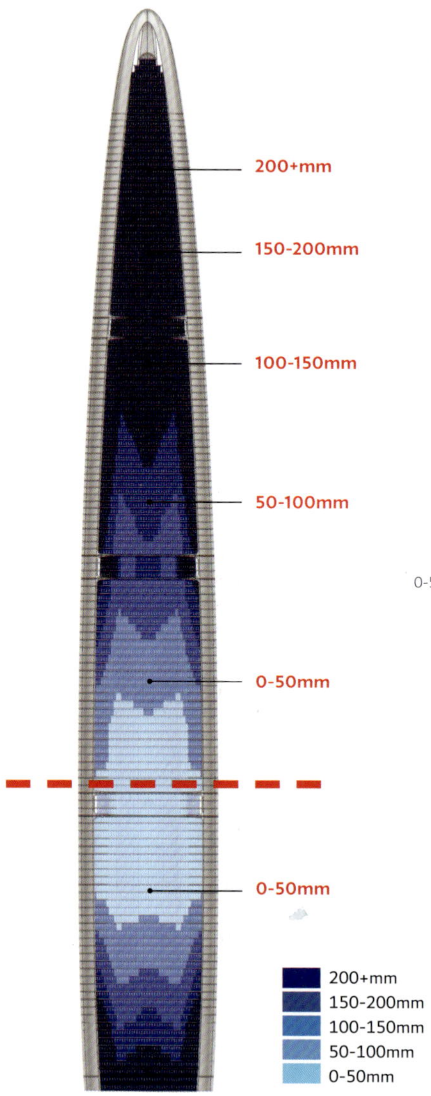

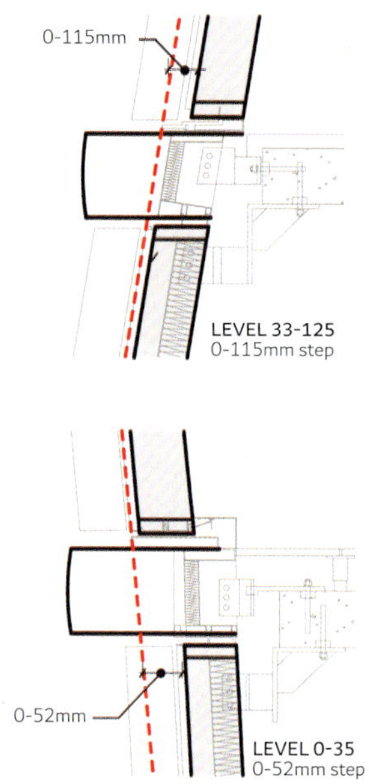

VERTICAL STEP

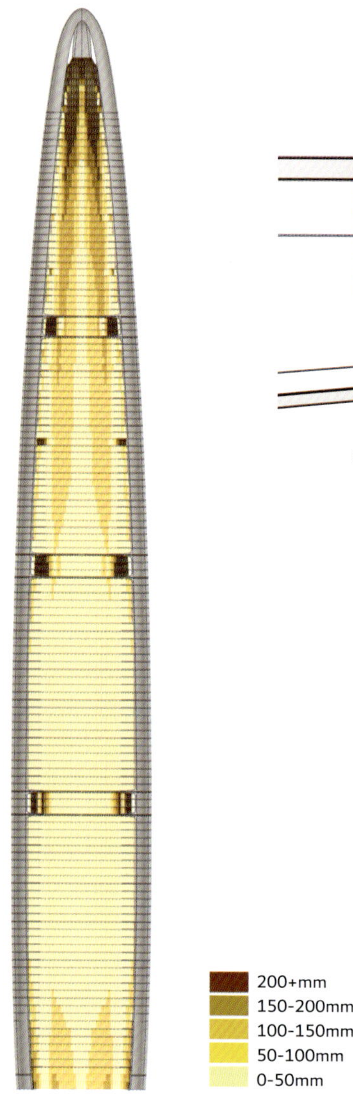

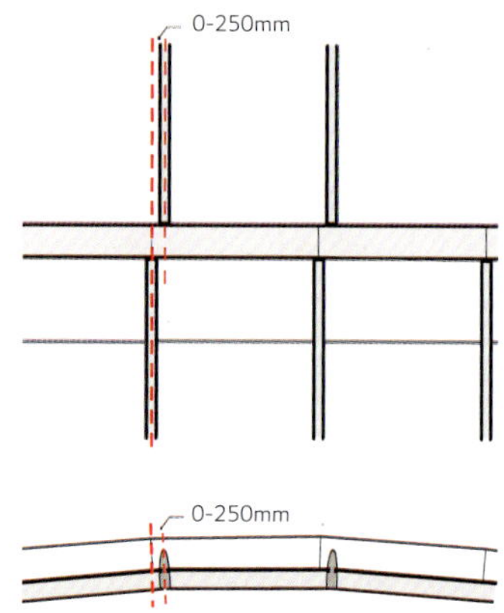

HORIZONTAL ANGLE

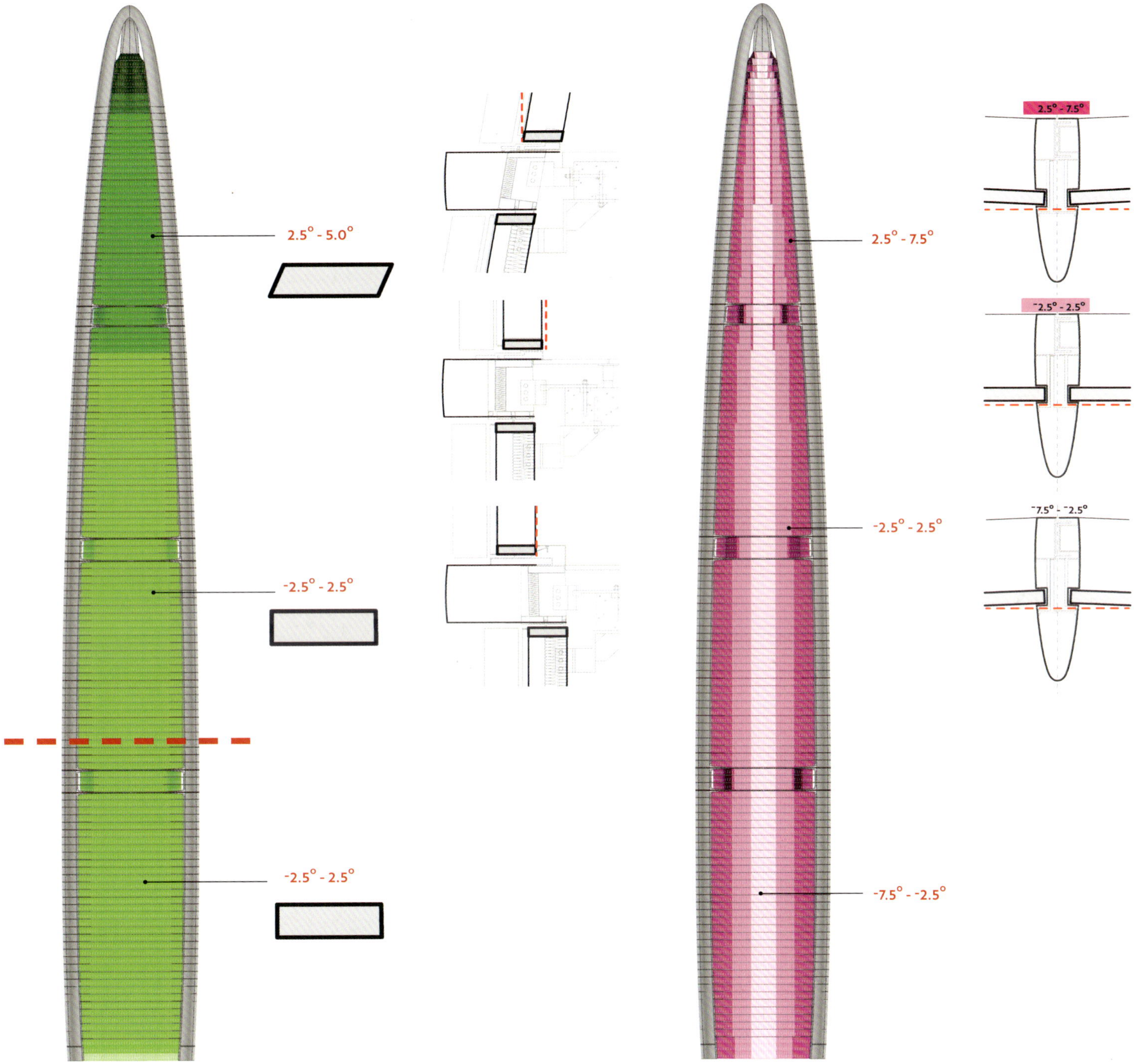

2.5° - 5.0°
-2.5° - 2.5°
-2.5° - 2.5°
2.5° - 7.5°
-2.5° - 2.5°
-7.5° - -2.5°
2.5° - 7.5°
-2.5° - 2.5°
-7.5° - -2.5°

Shield Panelization

The building's shields are tightly curved in plan view and gently curved in section, so that the general nature of the wall is a 3D convex surface. Similar to other portions of the building, this area is subdivided into unitized curtain wall panels, which are oriented in a portrait format, with a series of vertical glass joints (and mullions) that traverse the building surface as a group of parallel lines. Each horizontal joint is parallel to the ground plane. This geometric strategy for arranging the vertical joints is advantageous because it allows for panelization that is not warped or twisted. If desired, the glass lites can be curved in plan view—to follow the curve of the slab edges—but the panels are not curved in section. Therefore, the required glazing is classified as "bent" glass, which is more uniform and easier to fabricate than "slumped" glass.

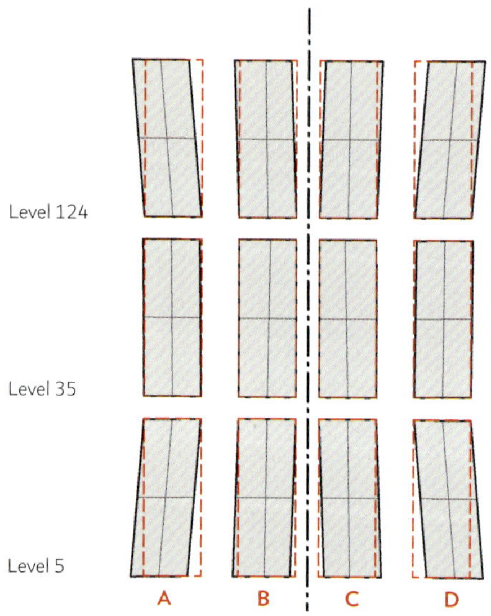

PANEL ELEVATION

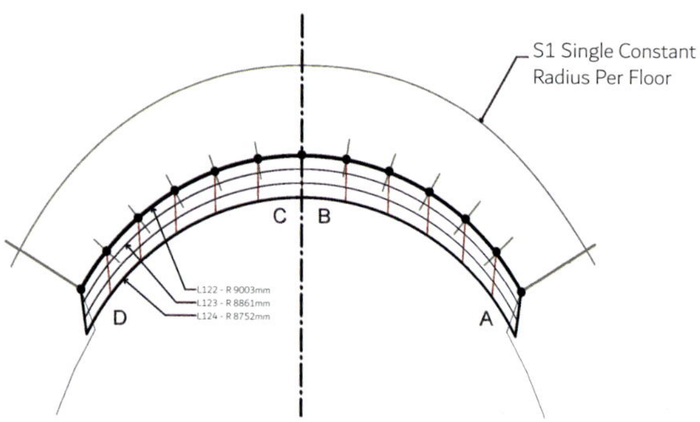

PANEL PLAN

SHIELD PANEL DIAGRAMS

Solar Shading

Horizontal solar shading devices are used in the body of tower to help reduce the incident solar radiation, and therefore building cooling loads, which in turn greatly reduce daytime energy consumption. To optimize the performance of the shades, an environmental analysis model was used to determine the ideal depth of the horizontal shades.

Due to the building's orientation, it was also determined that three three sides of the tower needed solar shading. The addition of solar shades allows the use of a less reflective glass, giving the building a softer appearance.

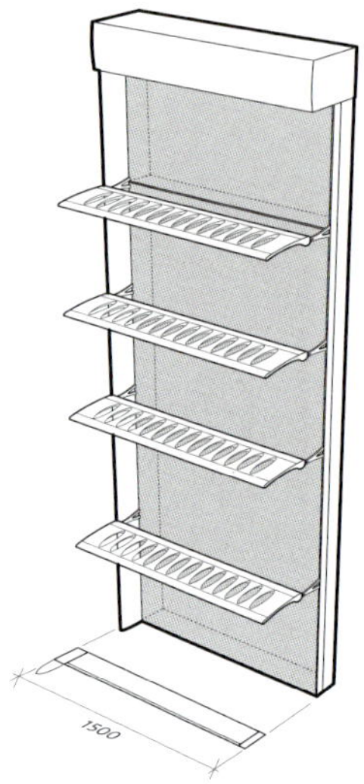

SOLAR SHADE PANEL DIAGRAM

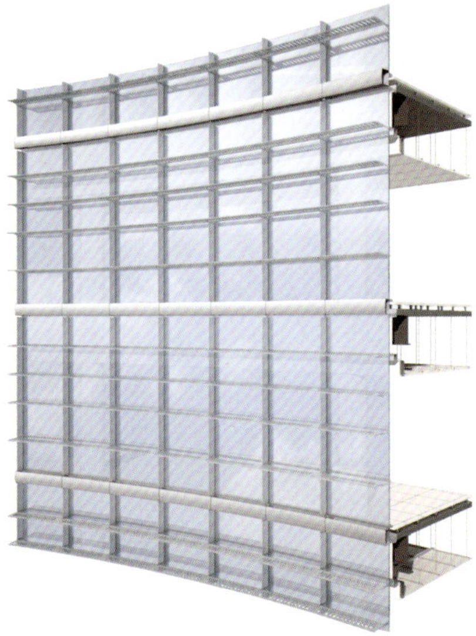

SECTION RENDERING

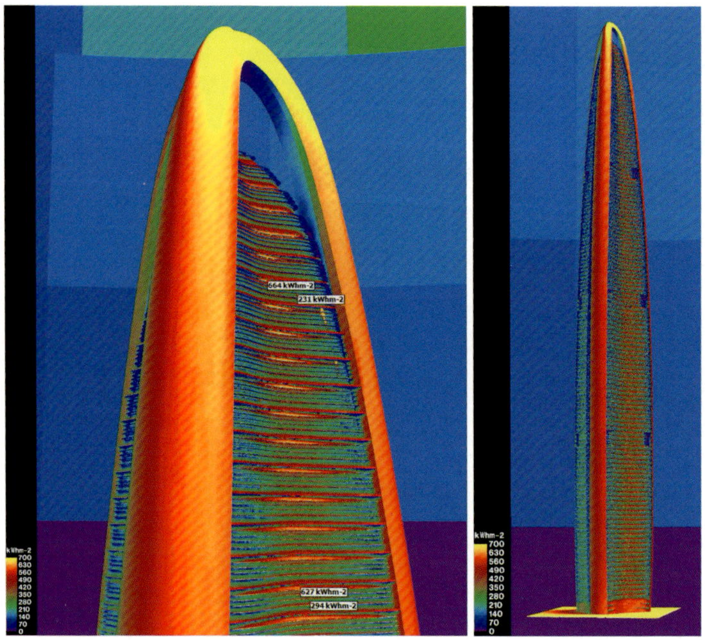

400MM - 800MM SUN SHADE ANALYSIS

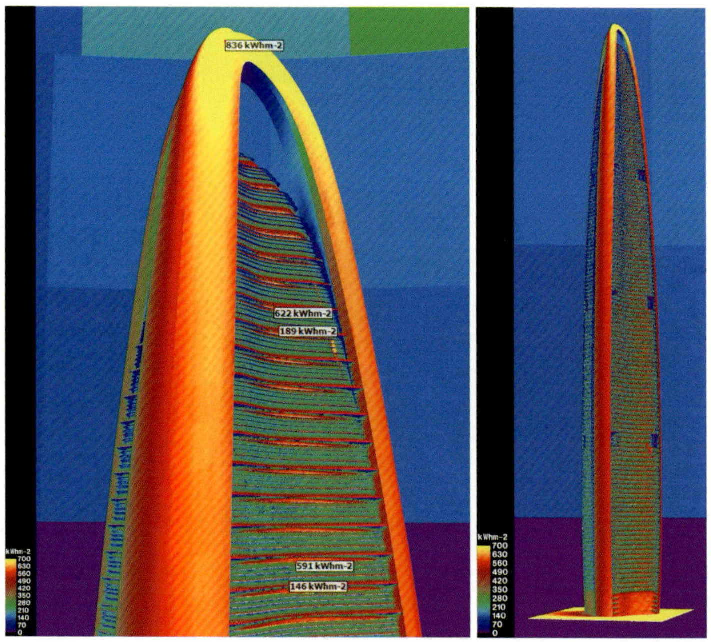

600MM SUN SHADE ANALYSIS

Louver Optimization

Openings, or slots, were incorporated into the body of the tower when designing the horizontal louver system. These slots were added to help maintain views, to allow a small amount of natural light to enter the space, and to soften the architecture expression of the tower. As with the other aspects of the tower, the size, location, and orientation of the slots were studied using a parametric model that helped determine which configuration strikes the best balance between the architecture and the environmental performance needs. The slots also give the building a tertiary architectural scale that can be experienced when looking up at the tower.

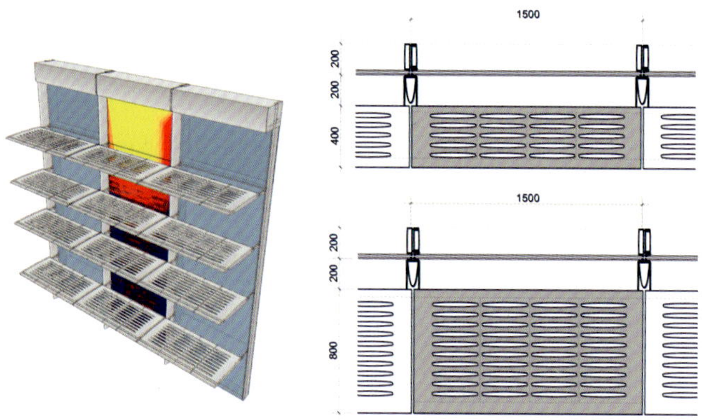

25% OPEN - PANEL DIAGRAM

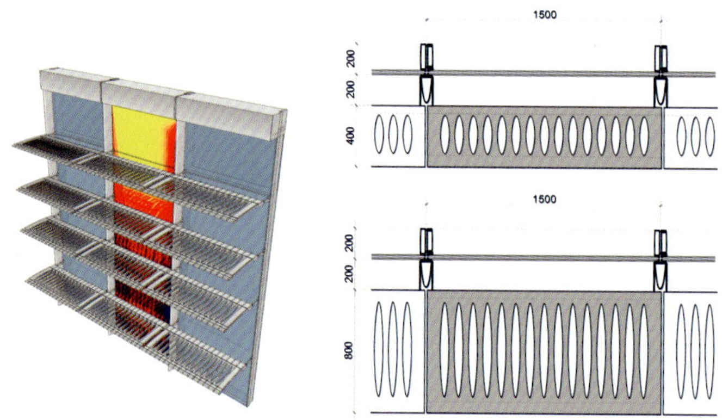

30% OPEN - PANEL DIAGRAM

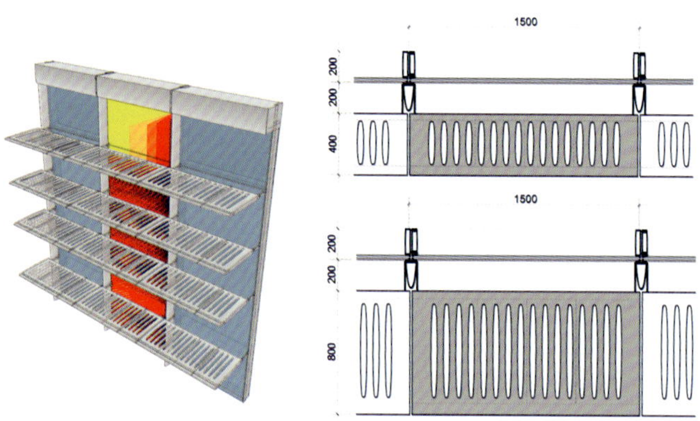

28% OPEN - PANEL DIAGRAM

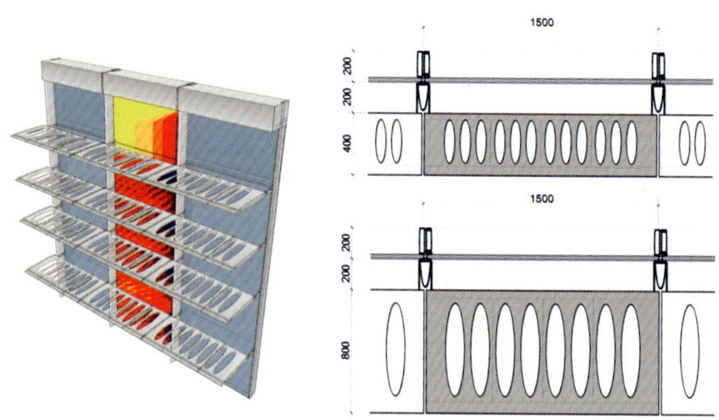

39% OPEN - PANEL DIAGRAM

Wind Relief Notches

To develop the building massing, the team used parametric modeling tools that evaluated the formal design of the tower along with program, wind performance, and structural optimization. This process determined the building's aerodynamic features, such as the overall tapering of the tower, the rounding of the corners, and a series of wind relief notches along the tower height.

The form of the tower was designed, and wind tunnel tested, so that the overall wind load, as well as the crosswind loading due to vortex shedding, was reduced. These large openings, located at vertical quarter sections, were tested and compared with strategies and a baseline tower with no openings.

A significant reduction in wind loading is achieved, which translates into substantial structural savings.

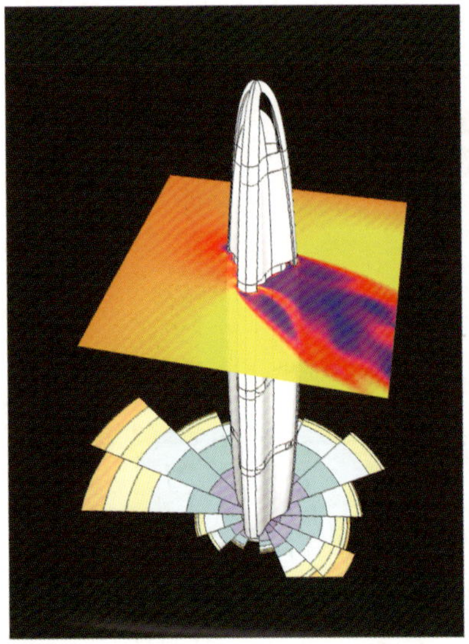

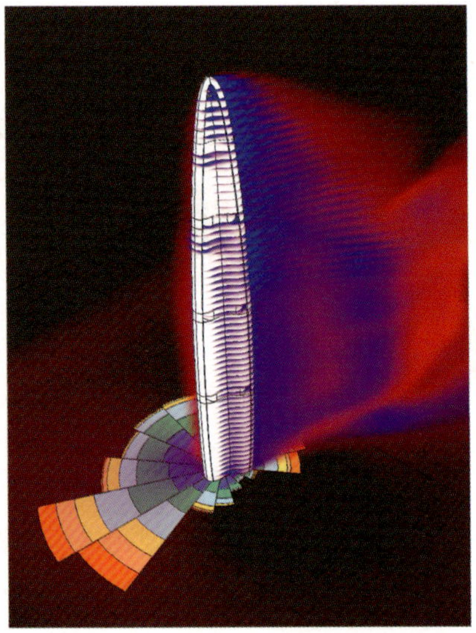

PARAMETRIC MODELING DIAGRAMS

appendix

team credits

FKI Tower Competition: Active Facade

Design Partners	Adrian Smith and Gordon Gill
Management Partner	Robert Forest
Project Manager	Brian M. Jack | Ben Johnson
Senior Designer	Juan Betancur
Senior Technical	Sae Hwang Oh

Project Team: Elyse Agnello, Miguel Alvarez, Olga Anaya, Sara Beardsley, Rachael Bennett, John Burcher, Alexis Burson, Marc Cerone, April Chen, Colin Craig, Rebecca Cryder, Michelle Dumont, Patrick Fitzpatrick, Danielle Gharst, Brendan Gibbons, Felix Griggs, Ryan Hayes, Gregg Herman, Kira Ho, Jessica Hogue, Brian Hubbard, Ben Johnson, Jeffrey Knapke, So Young Lee, Soeun Lee, David LeFevre, Michael Newton, Vanessa Newton, Tyler Noblin, Steven Pantazis, David Rariden, Dennis Rehill, Daniel Retzner, Beumhyeung Rhee, Sean Satterfield, Martin Salas, Corey Schnobrich, Daniel Seagraves, Joshua Smith, Eric Snow, Anthony Viola, Michael Waldo, Brent Watanabe, Peter Weismantle, Bradley Wilkins, Marc Woodcock

Energy Hall: Luminous Facade

Design Partners	Adrian Smith and Gordon Gill
Management Partner	Robert Forest
Project Manager	Brian M. Jack | Matthew Dumich
Design Director	Alejandro Stochetti
Senior Designer	Anthony Viola
Technical Director	Jorge Soler
Senior Technical	Alyson Hurd Sternquist

Project Team: Marc Cerone, Iliana Doytcheva, Christopher Drew, Natalya Ganyukova, Dimitra Gelagoti, Felix Griggs, Kira Ho, Liam Lowry, Jaclyn Marcus, Chris Miller, Miriam Neet, Natalia Quintanilla, Matt Simpson, Zilong Tan, Alex Valverde, Klarke Wang, Kirsten Weismantle

KAPSARC: Shell Facade

Design Partners	Adrian Smith and Gordon Gill
Management Partner	Robert Forest
Project Manager	Brian M. Jack
Senior Designer	Jeff Stafford
Senior Technical	Peter Weismantle

Project Team: Miguel Alvarez, Gabriel Ball, Rachel Banach, Juan Betancur, Jeff Boyer, Brett Bridgeland, Gabriel Bunea, John Burcher, Alexis Burson, Ashley Byers, Rebecca Cryder, Thomas Denney, Danielle Gharst, Brendan Gibbons, Gregg Herman, Jessica Hogue, Travis Howe, Christopher Hurst, Ben Johnson, David LeFevre, Vanessa Newton, Michael Newton, Matthew Nyweide, Benjamin Raines, David Rariden, Dennis Rehill, Sean Satterfield, David Schweim, Daniel Segraves, Jason Smith, Joshua Smith, Michael Waldo, Brent Watanabe, Marc Woodcock, Fei Xu

Dancing Dragons: Shingled Ventilated Facade

Design Partners	Adrian Smith and Gordon Gill
Management Partner	Robert Forest
Project Manager	Brian M. Jack
Senior Designer	Sara Beardsley
Senior Technical	Sae Hwang Oh

Project Team: Miguel Alvarez, James Bayless, Frederik Berte, Brett Bridgeland, John Burcher, Ashley Byers, Sally Cathcart, Marc Cerone, Raymond Coleman, Rebecca Cryder, Christopher Drew, Sobieslaw Fedyk, Katrina Fernandez Nova, Patrick Fitzpatrick, Masumeh Geranpayeh, Brendan Gibbons, Felix Griggs, Kira Ho, Brooke Ingram, Qi Jia, Laura Jimenez, Tamara Jimshitashvili, Hyungwoo Kim, Lin Kim, Soo Hye Kim, Hans Koesters, June Hae Lee, Soeun Lee, Randi Lesniewski, Takuya Mamada, Jonathan Orlove, Michelle Pak, Jongpil Park, Catherine Rogg, Mostapha Roudsari, David Schweim, Chen-Han Tu, Brent Watanabe, Margaret Yoo

Xi'an Greenland Tower: Passive Armored Facade

Design Partners	Adrian Smith and Gordon Gill
Management Partner	Robert Forest
Project Manager	Ben Johnson
Senior Designer	Juan Betancur
Senior Technical	Iris Gan

Project Team: Nora Ames, Jennie Tolfa, Anthony Viola, Jing Zhang

Tianjin Vantone Center: Self-Shading Facade

Design Partners	Adrian Smith and Gordon Gill
Management Partner	Robert Forest
Project Manager	Jonathan Orlove
Senior Designer	Fei Xu
Senior Technical	Iris Gan
China Director	Weiwei Luo

Project Team: John Burcher, Eric Cheng, Marc Cerone, Raymond Coleman, Colin Craig, Michelle Dumont, Iris Gan, Felix Griggs, Kira Ho, Jessica Hogue, Brooke Ingram, Tamara Jimshitashvili, Ben Johnson, Hyungwoo Kim, Lin Kim, Soeun Lee, Rebecca Lemaster, Christopher Miller, Tyler Noblin, Sae Hwang Oh, Carlo Parente, Jongpil Park, James Reisinger, Daniel Retzner, Catherine Rogg, Rachel Sears, Jason Smith, Joshua Smith, Jorge Soler, Anthony Trifiletti, Chen-Han Tu, Anthony Viola

Zhongzhou Holdings Finance Center: Brise Soleil Facade

Design Partners	Adrian Smith and Gordon Gill
Management Partner	Robert Forest
Project Manager	Brian M. Jack
Senior Designer	Jeff Stafford
Senior Technical	Peter Weismantle | Iris Gan
China Director	Weiwei Luo

Project Team: Fred Afshari, Mohamad Araji, Gabriel Bunea, April Chen, Gregg Herman, Travis Howe, Ben Johnson, Xiang Li, Weiwei Luo, Matthew Nyweide, Luis Palacio, Jason Smith, Joshua Smith, Renato Tonelli, Anthony Trifiletti, Anthony Viola, Brent Watanabe

Yixing Dongjiu Far East Development: Sail Screen Facade

Design Partners	Adrian Smith and Gordon Gill
Management Partner	Robert Forest
Project Manager	Brian M. Jack
Senior Designer	Fei Xu
China Director	Weiwei Luo

Project Team: Juan Betancur, John Burcher, Ashley Byers, Patrick Fitzpatrick, Brendan Gibbons, Brian Hubbard, Christopher Hurst, Michael Newton, Tyler Noblin, Matthew Nyweide, David Rariden, Sean Satterfield, David Schweim, Daniel Segraves, Jason Smith, Brent Watanabe

Clean Technology Tower: Clean-Tech Facade

Design Partners	Adrian Smith and Gordon Gill
Management Partner	Robert Forest
Senior Designer	Les Ventsch

Project Team: Ann Buckman, Jorge Soler, Brad Wilkins

Expo 2020 Mobility Theme Pavilion: Energy Facade

Design Partners	Adrian Smith and Gordon Gill
Management Partner	Robert Forest
Project Manager	Matthew Dumich
Senior Designer	Anthony Viola
Senior Technical	Jorge Soler

Project Team: Rafi Al-Alim, Christopher Drew, Laura Jimenez, Jaeho Jin, Patrick Keeney, Joel Kerner, Hyungwoo Kim, Ryan Kukuraitis, Seoun Lee, Luis Palacio, Andy Park, Natalia Quintanilla, Mario Romero, Alejandro Stochetti, Zilong Tan, Alex Valverde, Jiajing Xie, Shuonan Yang

1 Dubai: Diagrid Facade

Design Partners	Adrian Smith and Gordon Gill
Management Partner	Robert Forest
Project Manager	Brian M. Jack
Senior Designer	Jeff Stafford
Senior Technical	Peter Weismantle

Project Team: Nicholas Addison, Gabriel Ball, John Burcher, Charles Collett, Joshua Cooper, Reinaldo Correa, Thomas Denney, Robert Finigan, Iris Gan, Grendan Gibbons, Christina Halatsis, Christopher Harvey, Gregg Herman, Gregg Herman, Travis Howe, Brian Hubbard, Boyka Ivanova, Ben Johnson, Jeffrey Knapke, Phat Nguyen, Andrew Osvalds, Julia Robertson, Karen Rutherford, Kshitij Sawant, Mordecai Scheckter, Daniel Segraves, Siddant Sinha, Eric Snow, Brett Sterly, Rebecca Stewart, Anthony Trifiletti, Brent Watanabe

Masdar Headquarters: Aerodynamic Facade

Design Partners	Adrian Smith and Gordon Gill
Management Partner	Robert Forest
Project Manager	Jonathan Orlove
Senior Designer	Les Ventsch and Ying Liu
Senior Technical	Donald Stark

Project Team: Ahmed Abdeltam, Fred Afshari, Elyse Agnello, Fernando Alessandrini, Olga Anaya, Mohamad Araji, Gabriel Ball, Rachel Banach, Rachel Bennett, Emily Bernstein, Juan Betancur, Gail Borthwick, Nathan Bowman, Jeffrey Boyer, Hayes Brister, John Burcher, Alexis Burson, Ashley Byers, Marc Cerone, April Chen, Raymond Coleman, Charles Collett, Colin Craig, Rebecca Cryder, De Los Reyes, Sergio Dementrion, ThomasDrew, Christopher Dumont, Michelle Farmer, Mark Finigan, Patrick Fitzpatrick, Iris Gan, Danielle Gharst, Brendan Gibbons, Autumn Godwin, Felix Griggs, Christina Halatsis, Jon Hiatt, Kira Ho, Travis Howe, Christopher Hurst, Shahed Hydari, Laura Jimenez, Bethany Johnson, So Young Lee, David LeFevre, Thomas Loveless, Michael Newton, Tyler Noblin, Matthew Nyweide, Andrew Osvalds, Luis Palacio, Carlo Parente, Robert Perry, Silviu Petrea, James Pint, Darren Poon, James Reisinger, Daniel Retzner, Beumhyeung Rhee, Bradley Riemann, Mario Romero, Martin Salas, Corey Schnobrich, Brent Schuettpelz, David Schweim, Daniel Segraves, Siddant Sinha, Teddy Slowik, Jason Smith, Joshua Smith, Jorge Soler, Amy Sonbuchner, Quentin Stanton, Afaq Syed, Renato Tonelli, Tuan Tran, Anthony Trifiletti, Anthony Viola, Michael Waldo, Brent Watanabe, Eylul Wintermeyer, Julianna Wokurka, Marc Woodcock, Fei Xu

team credits

Masdar Headquarters: Sawtooth Facade

Design Partners	Adrian Smith and Gordon Gill
Management Partner	Robert Forest
Project Manager	Jonathan Orlove
Senior Designer	Les Ventsch and Ying Liu
Senior Technical	Donald Stark

Project Team: Ahmed Abdeltam, Fred Afshari, Elyse Agnello, Fernando Alessandrini, Olga Anaya, Mohamad Araji, Gabriel Ball, Rachel Banach, Rachel Bennett, Emily Bernstein, Juan Betancur, Gail Borthwick, Nathan Bowman, Jeffrey Boyer, Hayes Brister, John Burcher, Alexis Burson, Ashley Byers, Marc Cerone, April Chen, Raymond Coleman, Charles Collett, Colin Craig, Rebecca Cryder, De Los Reyes, Sergio Dementrion, ThomasDrew, Christopher Dumont, Michelle Farmer, Mark Finigan, Patrick Fitzpatrick, Iris Gan, Danielle Gharst, Brendan Gibbons, Autumn Godwin, Felix Griggs, Christina Halatsis, Jon Hiatt, Kira Ho, Travis Howe, Christopher Hurst, Shahed Hydari, Laura Jimenez, Bethany Johnson, So Young Lee, David LeFevre, Thomas Loveless, Michael Newton, Tyler Noblin, Matthew Nyweide, Andrew Osvalds, Luis Palacio, Carlo Parente, Robert Perry, Silviu Petrea, James Pint, Darren Poon, James Reisinger, Daniel Retzner, Beumhyeung Rhee, Bradley Riemann, Mario Romero, Martin Salas, Corey Schnobrich, Brent Schuettpelz, David Schweim, Daniel Segraves, Siddant Sinha, Teddy Slowik, Jason Smith, Joshua Smith, Jorge Soler, Amy Sonbuchner, Quentin Stanton, Afaq Syed, Renato Tonelli, Tuan Tran, Anthony Trifiletti, Anthony Viola, Michael Waldo, Brent Watanabe, Eylul Wintermeyer, Julianna Wokurka, Marc Woodcock, Fei Xu

Uptown Tower: Screen Facade

Design Partners	Adrian Smith and Gordon Gill
Management Partner	Robert Forest
Project Manager	Ben Johnson
Urban Designer	Richard Wilson
Senior Designer	Juan Betancur
Senior Technical	Peter Weismantle

Project Team: Rafi Al-Alim, Tyler Austin, George Baciu, Ryan Beemsterboer, Nicholas Berchtold, Ana Blomeier, Connor Borchardt, John Burcher, Marc Cerone, Wing Sum Cheng, Rebecca Cryder, Ryan Dalgaard, Stephen Dinnen, Christopher Drew, Elliot Eakin, Peter Eichberger, Rezvan Farahany, Kyle Faulkner, Sobieslaw Fedyk, Katrina Fernandez Nova, Natalya Ganyukova, Gail Goldstead, Felix Griggs, Travis Howe, Robert Jillson, Patrick Keeney, Joel Kerner, Changhoon Kim, Alexander Knowles, Sunghak Ko, Rebecca LeMaster, Mengxi Li, Liam Lowry, Jaclyn Marcus, Melissa Marrero, Christopher Miller, Mateusz Nosek, Michelle Pak, Andy Park, Jongpil Park, Shawn Phillips, Natalia Quintanilla, Daniel Ramos, Seychelle Reed, Yi Ren, Alyson Reuter, Jonathan Reyes, Lauren Sajek, Thomas Schneider, Myongki Seong, Jeff Snodgrass, Christopher Strasser, James Struthers, Maria Sturchio, Michelle Swanson, Zilong Tan, Jennie Tolfa, Anthony Viola, Ning Wang, Zhaochen Wang, Xueting Wei, Preston Welker, Jonathan Wilkinson, Timothy Winstanley, Jiajing Xie, Tianyu Xu, Jing Zhang, Ruoqi Zhong

Al Wasl Plaza: Trellis Facade

Design Partners	Adrian Smith and Gordon Gill
Management Partner	Robert Forest
Senior Designer	Alejandro Stochetti
Senior Technical	Peter Weismantle

Project Team: Narjes Abbasabadi, Tyler Austin, Alexander Bahr, Gregory Barber, Sara Beardsley, Nicholas Berchtold, Aaron Berman, Marc Cerone, Alison Conley, Jennifer Cooper, Rebecca Cryder, Stephen Dinnen, Tobias Dold, Christopher Drew, Matthew Dumich, Kiel Fahnstrom, Kyle Faulkner, Sobieslaw Fedyk, Katrina Fernandez Nova, Gail Goldstead, Felix Griggs, Victoriano Hernandez, Theodore Hogan, Brian Jack, Lizhi Jiang, Joel Kerner, Changhoon Kim, Sunghak Ko, Ryan Kukuraitis, Inyong Lee, Soeun Lee, Yifei Li, Miaoqi Liu, Yuchen Liu, Yue Liu, Alvaro Luna, Melissa Marrero, Jose Marti, Cory Mollet, Dilip Muralidharan, Christian Newman, Loran Newman, Sae Hwang Oh, Hazem Owais, Luis Palacio, Griffin Pemberton, Jessica Pfeiffer, Natalia Quintanilla, Daniel Ramos, Hiram Rodriguez, Mario Romero, Michael Sandrzyk, Thomas Schneider, Michaela Singson, Jeff Snodgrass, Donald Stark, Alyson Hurd Sternquist, James Struthers, Michelle Swanson, Jennie Tolfa, Eric Tomich, Pablo Velazquez, Ning Wang, Amber Watkins, Richard Wilson, Timothy Winstanley, Xi Yi, Yuxin Zheng, Ruoqi Zhong

Kuwait University Master Plan: Thermal Mass Facade

Design Partners	Adrian Smith and Gordon Gill
Management Partner	Robert Forest
Project Manager	Brian M. Jack
Senior Designer	Christopher Hurst

Project Team: Miguel Alvarez, Rebecca Cryder, Brendan Gibbons, Michael Newton, Matthew Nyweide, David Rariden, Dennis Rehill, Bradley Riemann, Sean Satterfield, David Schweim, David Siegel, Siddant Sinha, Tuan Tran, Michael Waldo, Marc Woodcock, Fei Xu

Gang Xia: Louvered Facade

Design Partners	Adrian Smith and Gordon Gill
Management Partner	Robert Forest
Project Manager	Ben Johnson
Senior Designer	Jeff Stafford
Senior Technical	Peter Weismantle

Project Team: Olga Anaya, Rachel Banach, Brett Bridgeland, Gabriel Bunea, John Burcher, Sarah Cathcart, Marc Cerone, April Chen, Raymond Coleman, Rebecca Cryder, Sobieslaw Fedyk, Iris Gan, Felix Griggs, Jessica Hogue, Travis Howe, Brian Hubbard, Robert Jillson, Laura Jimenez, Bethany Johnson, Randi Lesniewski, Xiang Li, Liu Liu, Weiwei Luo, Emily McGuire, Luis Palacio, Daniel Ramos, Katie Rariden, Daniel Retzner, Beumhyeung Rhee, Mostapha Sadeghipour Roudsari, Rachel Sears, Daniel Segraves, Matthew Simpson, Jason Smith, Joshua Smith, Afaq Syed, Renato Tonelli, Anthony Trifiletti, Anthony Viola, Michael Waldo, Brent Watanabe, Siyuan Zhang

Chengdu Greenland Tower: Facet Facade

Design Partners	Adrian Smith and Gordon Gill
Management Partner	Robert Forest
Project Manager	Ben Johnson
Senior Designer	Fei Xu
Senior Technical	Peter Weismantle

Project Team: Tyler Austin, Rustem Baishev, Mariela Bayer, Sara Beardsley, Rachael Bennett, Nicholas Berchtold, John Burcher, Jessica Butler, Ashley Byers, Sally Cathcart, Daniel Caven, Marc Cerone, Rebecca Cryder, Katherine Dailey, Michelle Dumont, Elliot Eakin, David Emmons, Keara Fanning, Sobieslaw Fedyk, Dian Feng, Patrick Fitzpatrick, Joshua Frank, Iris Gan, Natalya Ganyukova, Dimitra Gelagoti, Brendan Gibbons, Gail Goldstead, Felix Griggs, Kira Ho, DongSoo Jang, Tamara Jimshitashvili, Joel Kerner, Angela Khermouch, Changhoon Kim, Hyungwoo Kim, Alexander Knowles, Alison Lampier, Rebecca LeMaster, Randi Lesniewski, Mengxi Li, Yuchen Liu, Weiwei Luo, Jaclyn Marcus, Tashio Martinez, Christopher Miller, Jongpil Park, Benjamin Raines, Daniel Ramos, Yi Ren, Catherine Rogg, Matthew Simpson, Chad Smith, Jeff Snodgrass, Jiatuo Song, James Struthers, Anthony Trifiletti, Luis Villafane, Anthony Viola, Brent Watanabe

Central Park Tower: Fin Facade

Design Partners	Adrian Smith and Gordon Gill
Management Partner	Robert Forest
Project Manager	Brian M. Jack
Senior Designer	David Schweim
Senior Technical	Donald Stark

Miguel Alvarez, George Baciu, Nicholas Berchtold, Frederik Berte, Jae Yun Cho, Allison Conley, Nathan Diestelkamp, Patrick Fitzpatrick, Marshall Ford, Brendan Gibbons, Richard Gnat, Gail Goldstead, Heng Gu, Charles Harris, Kira Ho, Robert Jillson, Changhoon Kim, Hyungwoo Kim, Paul Kim, Todd Mackinson, Jennie Matusova, Michelle Pak, Viorica Pisau, David Rariden, Yi Ren, Thomas Schneider, Myongki Seong, Jeff Snodgrass, Alex Valverde, Les Ventsch, Timothy Winstanley, Jing Zhang

Shenzhen Bayview Tower: Actuated Facade

Design Partners	Adrian Smith and Gordon Gill
Management Partner	Robert Forest
Project Manager	Ben Johnson
Senior Designer	Juan Betancur
Senior Technical	Iris Gan

Project Team: Nicholas Berchtold, Marc Cerone, Rebecca Cryder, Christopher Drew, Kiel Fahnstrom, Sobieslaw Fedyk, Taylor Hess, Nash Kennedy, Ryan Kukuraitis, Miaoqi Liu, Weiwei Luo, Loran Newman, Joseph Peltier, Natalia Quintanilla, Mario Romero, Jeff Snodgrass, Anthony Viola, Richard Wilson, Yueming Zhou

team credits

Runmao Tower: Undulating Fin Facade

Design Partners	Adrian Smith and Gordon Gill
Management Partner	Robert Forest
Project Manager	Ben Johnson
Senior Designer (Tower)	Fei Xu
Senior Designer (Portal)	Luis Palacio
Senior Technical	Iris Gan

Project Team: Nora Ames, Tyler Austin, Alexander Bahr, Nicholas Berchtold, Jennifer Cooper, Rebecca Cryder, Caitlin Dashiell, Sobieslaw Fedyk, Iris Gan, Gail Goldstead, Rebecca Greenberg, Wilson Harkhono, Yongsan Huang, Nash Kennedy, Ryan Kukuraitis, Miaoqi Liu, Yuchen Liu, Weiwei Luo, Melissa Marrero, Joseph Peltier, Natalia Quintanilla, Jonathan Reyes, Thomas Schneider, Zilong Tan, Anthony Viola, Perry Wreaks, Tianyu Xu, Dong Yan, Ailing Zhang, Jing Zhang, Meng Zhang, Ruoqi Zhong, Yeuming Zhou

Ahlamana: Glass Fin Facade

Design Partners	Adrian Smith and Gordon Gill
Management Partner	Robert Forest
Project Manager	Ben Johnson and Jonathan Orlove
Senior Designer	Matt Snoap
Senior Technical	Donald Stark

Project Team: Fred Afshari, Miguel Alvarez, George Baciu, Rachel Banach, Rachel Bennett, Brett Bridgeland, Hayes Brister, Gabriel Bunea, John Burcher, Ashley Byers, Marc Cerone, Raymond Coleman, Colin Craig, Rebecca Cryder, Thomas Demetrion, Michelle Dumont, Keara Fanning, Robert Finigan, Patrick Fitzpatrick, Iris Gan, Danielle Gharst, Felix Griggs, Christopher Harvey, Kira Ho, Jessica Hogue, Brian Hubbard, Christopher Hurst, Shahed Hydari, Brendan Gibbons, Bethany Johnson, Brian M. Jack, Trudie Kahler, Lin Kim, Peter Kindel, So Young Lee, Soeun Lee, Ying Liu, Michael Newton, Matthew Nyweide, Robert Perry, Benjamin Raines, David Rariden, Beumhyeung Rhee, James Reisinger, Daniel Retzner, Alyson Reuter, Catherine Rogg, Daniel Ruberg, Martin Salas, Sean Satterfield, Corey Schnobrich, David Schweim, Rachel Sears, Jorge Soler, Amy Sonbuchner, Corey Thomas, Anthony Trifiletti, Angel Valtierra, Brent Watanabe, Bradley Wilkins

KLIFD Iconic Tower: Transformative Facade

Design Partners	Adrian Smith and Gordon Gill
Management Partner	Robert Forest
Senior Designer	Dennis Rehill

Project Team: Nathan Bowman, Brian Hubbard, Joshua Smith

Jeddah Tower: Solar Shield Facade

Design Partners	Adrian Smith and Gordon Gill
Management Partner	Robert Forest
Project Manager	Brian M. Jack
Senior Designer	Alejandro Stochetti
Senior Technical	Peter Weismantle

Project Team: Miguel Alvarez, Mohamad Araji, George Baciu, Ryan Bakke, Rachel Banach, Sara Beardsley, Frederik Berte, Juan Betancur, Jillian Blakey, Ana Blomeier, Gail Borthwick, Nathan Bowman, Brett Bridgeland, Hayes Brister, Sydney Brown, John Burcher, Alexis Burson, Jessica Butler, Ashley Byers, Sally Cathcart, Marc Cerone, Raymond Coleman, Charles Collett, Colin Craig, Rebecca Cryder, Katherine Dailey, Ryan Dalgaard, Thomas Demetrion, Christopher Drew, Michelle Dumont, Elliot Eakin, Kyle Faulkner, Sobieslaw Fedyk, Robert Finigan, Patrick Fitzpatrick, Robert Forest, Joshua Frank, Natalya Ganyukova, Krystian Gardula, Dimitra Gelagoti, Danielle Gharst, Brendan Gibbons, Gordon Gill, Gail Goldstead, Felix Griggs, Christopher Harvey, Zachary Heaps, Jessica Hogue, Travis Howe, Stephen Hsueh, Brian Hubbard, London Huenefeld, Christopher Hurst, Brooke Ingram, Brian Jack, DongSoo Jang, Matthias Janikowski, Robert Jillson, Laura Jimenez, Tamara Jimshitashvili, Ben Johnson, Changhoon Kim, Lin Kim, Soo Hye Kim, Peter Kindel, Alexander Knowles, Hans Koesters, So Young Lee, Soeun Lee, David LeFevre, Rebecca Lemaster, Randi Lesniewski, Todd Mackinson, John Maher, Takuya Mamada, Jaclyn Marcus, Tashio Martinez, Rucha Mehendale, Olia Miho, Christopher Miller, Michael Newton, Vanessa Newton, Tyler Noblin, Matthew Nyweide, David Osmond, Luis Palacio, Griffin Pemberton, Michael Perez, Robert Perry, Benjamin Raines, David Rariden, Katie Rariden, Dennis Rehill, Yi Ren, Albert Rhee, Beumhyeung Rhee, Catherine Rogg, Mostapha Roudsari, Sean Satterfield, Thomas Schneider, David Schweim, Rachel Sears, Myongki Seong, Mohamed Sheriff, Matthew Simpson, Jason Smith, Donald Stark, Andrew Suszko, Michelle Swanson, Afaq Syed, Anthony Trifiletti, Chen-Han Tu, Les Ventsch, Anthony Viola, Michael Waldo, Christopher Walker, Brent Watanabe, Kirsten Weismantle, Preston Welker, Marc Woodcock, Margaret Yoo

Biophilic Tower: Biophilic Facade

Design Partners	Adrian Smith and Gordon Gill
Management Partner	Robert Forest
Project Manager	Ben Johnson
Senior Designer	Juan Betancur

Project Team: Rachael Bennett, Charles Harris, Travis Howe, Brooke Ingram, Hyungwoo Kim, Michelle Pak, Jongpil Park, Robert Perry, James Reisinger, Yi Ren, Anthony Viola

FKI Tower: Multifaceted Facade

Design Partners	Adrian Smith and Gordon Gill
Management Partner	Robert Forest
Project Manager	Brian M. Jack | Ben Johnson
Senior Designer	Juan Betancur
Senior Technical	Sae Hwang Oh

Project Team: Elyse Agnello, Miguel Alvarez, Olga Anaya, Sara Beardsley, Rachael Bennett, John Burcher, Alexis Burson, Marc Cerone, April Chen, Colin Craig, Rebecca Cryder, Michelle Dumont, Patrick Fitzpatrick, Danielle Gharst, Brendan Gibbons, Felix Griggs, Ryan Hayes, Gregg Herman, Kira Ho, Jessica Hogue, Brian Hubbard, Ben Johnson, Jeffrey Knapke, So Young Lee, Soeun Lee, David LeFevre, Michael Newton, Vanessa Newton, Tyler Noblin, Steven Pantazis, David Rariden, Dennis Rehill, Daniel Retzner, Beumhyeung Rhee, Sean Satterfield, Martin Salas, Corey Schnobrich, Daniel Seagraves, Joshua Smith, Eric Snow, Anthony Viola, Michael Waldo, Brent Watanabe, Peter Weismantle, Bradley Wilkins, Marc Woodcock

Burj Vista: Vista Facade

Design Partners	Adrian Smith and Gordon Gill
Management Partner	Robert Forest
Project Manager	Brian M. Jack
Senior Designer	Alejandro Stochetti
Senior Technical	Sae Hwang Oh

Project Team: Fernando Alessandrini, Olga Anaya, Nathan Bowman, Brett Bridgeland, Ann Buckman, Joshua Cooper, Colin Craig, Rebecca Cryder, Barbara Di Gregorio, David Ellis, Patrick Fitzpatrick, Brendan Gibbons, Simon Gore, Ryan Hanlon, Ryan Hayes, Jessica Hogue, Matthew Kidd, David LeFevre, Hrishikesh Madane, Ian Mills, Vanessa Newton, Matthew Nyweide, Steven Pantazis, Carlo Parente, Jean Reibel, Mario Romero, Sean Satterfield, Brent Schuettpelz, Siddant Sinha, Jorge Soler, Jeff Stafford, Matthew Stewart, Les Ventsch, Bradley Wilkin

Kazakhstan Pavilion: Compound Curve Facade

Design Partners	Adrian Smith and Gordon Gill
Management Partner	Robert Forest
Project Manager	Brian M. Jack and Matthew Dumich
Design Director	Alejandro Stochetti
Senior Designer	Anthony Viola
Technical Director	Jorge Soler
Senior Technical	Lin Kim and Sae Hwang Oh

Project Team: Marc Cerone, Iliana Doytcheva, Christopher Drew, Misha Efremov, Peter Eichberger, Rezvan Farahany, Kyle Faulkner, Natalya Ganyukova, Dimitra Gelagoti, Felix Griggs, Jaclyn Marcus, Melissa Marrero, Chris Miller, Natalia Quintanilla, Katherine Seaver, Matt Simpson, Zilong Tan, Kirsten Weismantle

Waldorf Astoria Beijing: Frame Facade

Design Partners	Adrian Smith and Gordon Gill
Management Partner	Robert Forest
Project Manager	Weiwei Luo
Senior Designer	Fei Xu
Senior Technical	Donald Stark

Project Team: Mohamad Araji, Rustem Baishev, Raymond Coleman, Michelle Dumont, Patrick Fitzpatrick, Joshua Frank, Brendan Gibbons, Shahed Hydari, Hyungwoo Kim, Michael Newton, Mengxi Li, Silviu Petrea, Sean Satterfield, Brent Schuettpelz, David Schweim, Afaq Syed, Michael Waldo

Wuhan Greenland Center: Brise Soleil Shield Facade

Design Partners	Adrian Smith and Gordon Gill
Management Partner	Robert Forest
Project Manager	Ben Johnson
Senior Designer	Juan Betancur
Senior Technical	Peter Weismantle

Project Team: Rachael Bennett, Jillian Blakey, Ana Blomeier, Nathan Bowman, John Burcher, Sally Cathcart, Marc Cerone, Raymond Coleman, Colin Craig, Rebecca Cryder, Emily Dones, Patrick Fitzpatrick, Joshua Frank, Iris Gan, Brendan Gibbons, Felix Griggs, Kira Ho, Brian Hubbard, Brooke Ingram, DongSoo Jang, Qi Jia, Robert Jillson, Laura Jimenez, Tamara Jimshitashvili, Trudie Kahler, Joshua Kuffner, Ryan Kukuraitis, Soeun Lee, David LeFevre, Rebecca Lemaster, Randi Lesniewski, Miaoqi Liu, Weiwei Luo, Takuya Mamada, Christopher Miller, Suncica Milosevic, Luis Palacio, Robert Perry, James Reisinger, Yi Ren, Catherine Rogg, Mario Romero, Rachel Sears, Daniel Segraves, Mohamed Sheriff, Matthew Simpson, Jason Smith, Joshua Smith, Matt Snoap, Jorge Soler, Michelle Swanson, Corey Thomas, Anthony Trifiletti, Chen-Han Tu, Anthony Viola, Perry Wreaks, Si Wu, Dong Yan, Margaret Yoo, Andrew Zell, Jing Zhang, Yueming Zho

awards + publications

FKI Tower Competition: Active Facade
FKI Tower: Multifaceted Facade

Bavarian Association for the Promotion of Solar Energy Building Integrated Solar Technology, Architectural Award, Shortlist, 2017

The American Architecture Prize, Architectural Design | Tall Buildings, Winner, FKI Tower, 2017

Re-Thinking the Future, Sustainability Award, First Award, Commercial, 2016

AIA Chicago, Divine Detail Award, FKI Tower BIPV, 2016

The Chicago Athenaeum, International Architecture Award, 2016

The Chicago Athenaeum, Green Good Design Award, Green Architecture, 2015

Civic Trust Awards, Civic Trust Award, 2015

Korean Architecture Award, Excellence Award, 2014

Korea Presidential Commission on Architecture Policy, Korea Green Building Award, 2014

Re-Thinking the Future, Sustainability Award, Honorable Mention, 2014

Chicago AIA, Distinguished Building Award, Citation of Merit, 2014

CTBUH, Best Tall Building Asia and Australasia, Finalist, 2014

SEAOI, Excellence in Structural Engineering Award, Winner, Best Project $150 million and over, 2014

Architizer A+ Award, Office Building High Rise, Finalist, 2014

Civil Engineering, "Angled Facade Boosts Energy Efficiency," Februay 25, 2014

Architect Magazine, "The New Seoul Skyscraper," January 28, 2014

World Architecture News, "Unique facade for FKI headquarters," January 24, 2014

Concept Magazine, "New Head Office of the Federation of Korean Industries," May 2010

The Architect's Newspaper, "Unveiled: Federation of Korean Industries Tower," February 11, 2010

Energy Hall: Luminous Facade

ArchDaily, "EXPO 2017 Legacy: What is Venue's Future?" October 16, 2017

AIA National Tap/CCA Innovation Awards, Stellar Design, Astana Expo City, 2016

Business Insider, "A multi-billion-dollar futuristic city will host the 2017 World's Expo — take a look inside," October 18, 2016

KAPSARC: Shell Facade

The Chicago Athenaeum, American Architecture Award, 2012

AIA Chicago, Unbuilt Design, Honor Award, 2011

Dancing Dragons: Shingled Ventilated Facade

The Chicago Athenaeum, Green Good Design Award, Green Architecture, 2015

The Chicago Athenaeum, International Architecture Award, 2014

The Chicago Athenaeum, American Architecture Award, 2013

Civil Engineering, "Ancient Architecture Inspires Contemporary Tower Complex," September 2012

Architecture Source, "Breathing Life into Korean Architecture Feat," May 17, 2012

World Architecture News, "Year of the Dragon: AS+GG unveils design for supertall mixed use towers for Seoul, South Korea," May 11, 2012

inhabitat, "Adrian Smith + Gordon Gill Unveil Dancing Dragons Towers with Scaly, Breathable Skin," May 11, 2012

Zhongzhou Holdings Finance Center: Brise Soleil Facade

The Chicago Athenaeum, Green Good Design, Green Architectural Design, 2018

Clean Technology Tower: Clean-Tech Facade

Riscaldamento Climatizzazione Idronica, "Biomimicry in building design," February 2009

Space, "Clean technology building," January 2009

Modern Design, "The 11th hour...and the carbon-conflict: smooth operator," May 2008

1 Dubai: Diagrid Facade

L'espresso, "The new design is born," J. Caracciolo Falck, January 15, 2009

Identity Magazine, "The future is now," Dorothy Waldman, November 2008

Cityscape Magazine, "New look for old," Clair Malcolm, November 2008

Building, "The tallest building in the world: the contenders," Dan Stewart, October 14, 2008

World Architecture News, "Meraas Development taps Adrian Smith + Gordon Gill for megaproject," Sharon McHugh

Chicago Sun-Times, "Looking Up..." David Roeder, October 8, 2008

Chicago Tribune, "Chicago architects plan more towers in Dubai," Blair Kamin, October 7, 2008

The National, "Dubai sees no reason to stop scraping skies," Bradley Hope, October 6, 2008

Masdar Headquarters: Aerodynamic Facade

Masdar Headquarters: Sawtooth Facade

International Property Awards, Arabian Property Award for Architecture, Mideast Region, 2010

Cityscape Architectural Awards, Environmental Award, 2008

Middle East Architect Awards, Green Project of the Year, 2008

Construction Week Awards, Sustainable Design Award, 2008

One, "(Re)Conceiving Cities," Spring/Summer 2011

Men's Book Chicago, "Mr. Positive," Spring 2011

The New York Times, "Planning a Sustainable City in the Desert," September 25, 2010

Engineering News-Record, "Design Team Held to Competition Promises," December 9, 2009

Fortune, "A green city blooms in the desert," December 2008

Architectural Record, "Model Behavior: Anticipating Great Design," December 2008

Green Source, "Urban Harvest," November/December 2008

Globe and Mail, "A building with an energy all its own," November 11, 2008

identity, "Green Giants," November 2008

Metropolis Magazine, "Innovation from the innovators," October 2008

domain-b, "GE focuses on Middle East with $8-billion carbon-neutral city," July 24, 2008

Sustainable Design Update, "Masdar building brings positive energy," June 24, 2008

Architect Magazine, "Positive Energy," June 8, 2008

BPM, "Masdar," Summer 2008

Architectural Record, "Smith + Gill tapped for ultra-green Abu Dhabi project," May 7, 2008

Building, "The Middle East green building challenge," February 29, 2008

Al Wasl Plaza: Trellis Facade

The Chicago Athenaeum, International Architecture Award, 2021

The Chicago Athenaeum, Green Good Design Award, 2021

Architectural Record, "Dubai Expo's Fantastical National Pavilions," Ilana Herzig, October 29, 2021

Khaleej Times, "Expo 2020 Dubai: Al Wasl Plaza is my best work ever, says designer," SM Ayaz Zakir, October 28, 2021

The New York Times, "A World-Class World Expo," Sam Lubell, October 24, 2021

Architect's Newspaper, "Expo 2020 Dubai teases blossoming pavilions ahead of rescheduled festival," October 14, 2020, Matt Hickman, October 14, 2020

Designboom, "Expo 2020 Dubai Reveals Pavilions," Philip Stevens, October 6, 2020

Arch Daily, "One Year to Go: Expo 2020 Reveals Latest Pavilions as the Event Moves Forward," Christele Harrouk, October 5, 2020

Dezeen, "Dubai Expo reveals main pavilions ahead of rescheduled event," Tom Ravenscroft, October 1, 2020

Dezeen, "Nine examples of spherical architecture from around the globe," Tom Ravenscroft, August 29, 2020

Wallpaper*, "Exploring The Dubai Expo's architecture in progress," Harriet Thorpe, May 28, 2020

Construction Week Online, "Expo 2020 Dubai video features HE Reem Al Hashimy praising Al Wasl Plaza; says 'she carries the original name of Dubai'," Neha Bhatia, September 19, 2019

Construction Business News, "Expo2020 Dubai lifts final piece of Al Wasl Plaza's dome into place," September 9, 2019

MEED, "Al-Wasl Plaza dome adorned with steel crown," September 18, 2019

Gulf News, "Al Wasl Plaza at Expo 2020 site to offer a variety of experiences," April 17, 2017

Forbes Middle East, "A New Breathtaking Hall Is In The Making For Expo 2020 Dubai," Amro Elserty, April 5, 2017

awards + publications

Uptown Dubai: Screen Facade

Arabian Business, "Uptown Tower, Dubai's new supertall skyscraper set for Q3 completion," January 29, 2022

The National News, "Dubai's latest skyscraper Uptown Tower peaks at 329 metres," January 25, 2022

Middle East Construction, "Dubai's latest super-tall rises dramatically," January 1, 2021

Khaleej Times, "Five iconic buildings that are set to change Dubai's skyline," December 22, 2020

Time Out Dubai, "Construction starts on the first supertall tower at Uptown Dubai," August 27, 2018

Central Park Tower: Fin Facade

The Chicago Athenaeum, American Architecture Award, 2021

CTBUH, Best Tall Building +400 Meters, Winner, 2020

Surface, "Inside Central Park Tower, the World's Tallest Residential Building," Ryan Waddoups, August 16, 2021

Architectural Digest, "Exclusive Look Inside the World's Tallest Residential Skyscraper," Nadja Sayej, August 12, 2021

The New York Times, "Buildings With Sections That Seem to Hover in Midair," Tim McKeough, June 4, 2021

Architectural Digest, "The 11 Most Anticipated Buildings of 2020," January 14, 2020

Wall Street Journal, "The Decade in Architecture: Strutting Structures Soaring in Triumph," December 17, 2019

The Architect's Newspaper, "Central Park Tower tops out to become the world's tallest residential building," September 19, 2019

Architectural Digest, "New York City's Central Park Tower Just Became the World's Tallest Residential Building," September 25, 2019

New York Magazine, "The Challenges of Constructing New York's Tallest Apartment Building," September 16, 2019

Architectural Digest, "An Architecture Lover's Guide to Manhattan's 57th Street," August 29, 2019

Metropolis Magazine, "Take a Closer Look at the Design of the World's Tallest Residential Tower," October 18, 2018

Design Boom, "New York's 'Central Park Tower' Will Be The Tallest Residential Building In The World," October 16, 2018

Dezeen, "Central Park Tower to become world's tallest residential skyscraper," August 16, 2017

Chengdu Greenland Tower: Facet Facade

The Chicago Athenaeum, International Architecture Award, 2016

Architizer A+ Award, Unbuilt Category, Architecture + Technology, Finalist, 2014

Curbed, "Supertalls and Sustainable Skyscrapers: Architect Adrian Smith on the Mile-High Building," April 12, 2016

Wired, "How to Keep a 1,500-Foot Skyscraper From Falling Over," July 27, 2015

Forbes, "7 Record-Breaking Skyscrapers in the Works Around the World," April 17, 2015

Dezeen, "Construction starts on Smith and Gill's ice-inspired skyscraper for Chengdu," November 20, 2014

Runmao Tower: Undulating Fin Facade

Architectural Record, "On the Boards: a Museum, Towers, and New Urban Waterfronts," January 2020

World Architecture News, "500 meter tower to achieve LEED-Gold," November 26, 2019

ArchDaily, "New Financial District in China," November 13, 2019

Architect Magazine, "A Tower in China that Repurposes Rainwater," November 15, 2019

Architect Magazine, "South HeXi Yuzui Financial District and Tower," November 6, 2019

BD+C, "AS+GG's design scheme for the South HeXi Yuzui Financial District and Tower," November 6, 2019

Jeddah Tower: Solar Shield Facade

AIA Middle East, Non-Built Category, Merit Award, 2014

Forbes, "7 Supertall Buildings in the Works Around the Globe," July 26, 2018

The Architect's Newspaper, "Saudi Arabia is building a future for its millennial population," June 25, 2018

Curbed, "10 tallest buildings under construction or in development around the world," June 25, 2017

Civil Engineering Surveyor, "Learnings from the Jeddah Tower," September 2016

Structure, "Rising to the Clouds with Confidence," June 2016

Wall Street Journal, "Rising to the Clouds with Confidence," February 3, 2016

City Lab, "Can a Skyscraper Soar Above the Clouds?" December 31, 2015

The Telegraph, "Onwards and upwards for the skyscraper," December 6, 2015

Jeddah Tower: Solar Shield Facade (con't)

Chicago Tribune, "Saudi Arabia plans to build the world's tallest skyscraper," December 2, 2015

Architectural Record, "Big Bigger Biggest," March 2014

Popular Science, "Rise of the Supertalls," March 2014

Discovery Channel Magazine, "Reach for the Sky," April 2012

Arabian Business, "Kingdom Tower architect grapples the wind at 3,000 ft," August 30, 2011

New York Magazine, "Higher," August 14, 2011

Chicago Tribune, "Chicago firm's design towers over the rest," August 3, 2011

The Wall Street Journal, "Saudis Plan World's Tallest Tower," August 3, 2011

Biophilic Tower: Biophilic Facade

Architectural Review, MIPIM Future Project Award, Tall Buildings, Commendation, 2015

The Chicago Athenaeum, American Architecture Award, 2013

Burj Vista: Vista Facade

AIA Chicago, Divine Detail Award, Burj Vista Self-Shading Balconies, 2021

Kazakhstan Pavilion: Compound Curve Facade

AIA Tap/CCA Innovation Awards, Stellar Design, Astana Expo City, 2016

Dezeen, "Nine examples of spherical architecture from around the globe," Tom Ravenscroft, August 29, 2020

New York Times, "Can a Giant Science Fair Transform Kazakhstan's Economy?" David Segal, September 9, 2017

Dezeen, "Architects unveil energy-themed pavilions at Astana Expo 2017," Jessica Mairs, June 20, 2017

Architect's Newspaper, "Adrian Smith + Gordon Gill's ambitious glass sphere pavilion," Heather Corcoran, August 11, 2017

Departures Magazine, "Expo 2017: Astana Unveiled," Nathan Turner, April 20, 2017

Building Design + Construction, "How to make a 'pure' glass sphere," Robert Cassidy, February 18, 2016

Dezeen, "Adrian Smith + Gordon Gill Architecture to design Astana Expo 2017," October 23, 2013

Waldorf Astoria Beijing: Frame Facade

WAN Awards, Facade Award, Finalist, 2017

AIA Chicago, Divine Detail Award, Waldorf Astoria Beijing Bronze Facade, 2017

LEAF Awards, Hospitality Building of the Year, 2016

The Chicago Athenaeum, International Architecture Award, 2016

Architizer A+ Awards, Plus Categories, Details: Architecture +Metal, Finalist, 2016

Chicago AIA, Distinguished Building Award, Citation of Merit, 2015

The Chicago Athenaeum, American Architecture Award, 2015

HD Awards, Winner, Hotel Luxury/Upscale, 2015

Civic Trust Awards, Civic Trust Award, 2015

Rhapsody, "Beijing's New Bronze Age," May 2014

The Architect's Newspaper, "Adrian Smith + Gordon Gill Bronze the Waldorf Astoria Beijing," June 19, 2015

Wuhan Greenland Center: Brise Soleil Shield Facade

The Chicago Athenaeum, Green Good Design Award, Green Architecture, 2017

Re-Thinking the Future, Sustainability Award, First Award, Mixed-Use, 2016

Curbed, "10 tallest buildings under construction or in development around the world," February 21, 2017

Popular Science, "Rise of the Supertalls," March 13, 2016

Perspective, "High up in the wind," September 2011

The Big Project, "The Big Players," August 2011

Architectural Record, "On the Boards: Wuhan Greenland Center," August 2011

Chicago Tribune, "Smith and Gill win competition for supertall tower in China," June 21, 2011

inhabitat, "AS+GG's Aerodynamic Wuhan Greenland Center to be World's 4th Tallest Building," June 21, 2011

photography credits

FKI Tower Competition: Active Facade pages 12-15

All drawings and images ©Adrian Smith + Gordon Gill Architecture

Energy Hall: Luminous Facade pages 16-19

All drawings and images ©Adrian Smith + Gordon Gill Architecture

KAPSARC: Shell Facade pages 20-23

All drawings and images ©Adrian Smith + Gordon Gill Architecture

Dancing Dragons: Shingled Ventilated Facade pages 24-27

All drawings and images ©Adrian Smith + Gordon Gill Architecture

Xi'an Greenland Tower: Passive Armored Facade pages 28-31

All drawings and images ©Adrian Smith + Gordon Gill Architecture

Tianjin Vantone Center: Self-shading Facade pages 32-35

All drawings and images ©Adrian Smith + Gordon Gill Architecture

Zhongzhou Holdings Finance Center: Brise Soleil Facade pages 36-39

Photographs by ShuHe Architectural Photography Studio pages, 36, 37, 38

All other drawings and images ©Adrian Smith + Gordon Gill Architecture

Yixing Dongjiu Far East Development: Sail Screen Facade pages 40-43

All drawings and images ©Adrian Smith + Gordon Gill Architecture

Clean Technology Tower: Clean-Tech Facade pages 44-47

All drawings and images ©Adrian Smith + Gordon Gill Architecture

Expo 2020 Mobility Theme Pavilion: Energy Facade pages 48-51

All drawings and images ©Adrian Smith + Gordon Gill Architecture

1 Dubai: Diagrid Facade pages 52-55

All drawings and images ©Adrian Smith + Gordon Gill Architecture

Masdar Headquarters: Aerodynamic Facade pages 56-59

All drawings and images ©Adrian Smith + Gordon Gill Architecture

Masdar Headquarters: Sawtooth Facade pages 60-63

All drawings and images ©Adrian Smith + Gordon Gill Architecture

Al Wasl Plaza: Trellis Facade pages 64-67

All drawings and images ©Adrian Smith + Gordon Gill Architecture

Uptown Dubai: Screen Facade pages 68-71

All drawings and images ©Adrian Smith + Gordon Gill Architecture

Kuwait University Master Plan: Thermal Mass Facade [ages 72-75

All drawings and images ©Adrian Smith + Gordon Gill Architecture

Gang Xia: Louvered Facade pages 76-79

All drawings and images ©Adrian Smith + Gordon Gill Architecture

Central Park Tower: Fin Facade pages 80-83

Photograph ©Paul Clemence pages 80, 82

All other drawings and images ©Adrian Smith + Gordon Gill Architecture

Chengdu Greenland Tower: Facet Facade pages 84-87

Photograph ©Greenland Holding page 87

All other drawings and images ©Adrian Smith + Gordon Gill Architecture

Shenzhen Bayview Tower: Actuated Facade pages 88-91

All drawings and images ©Adrian Smith + Gordon Gill Architecture

Runmao Tower: Undulating Fin Facade pages 92-95

All drawings and images ©Adrian Smith + Gordon Gill Architecture

Ahlamana: Glass Fin Facade pages 96-99

All drawings and images ©Adrian Smith + Gordon Gill Architecture

KLIFD Iconic Tower: Transformative Facade pages 100-103

All drawings and images ©Adrian Smith + Gordon Gill Architecture

Jeddah Tower: Solar Shield Facade pages 104-109

All drawings and images ©Adrian Smith + Gordon Gill Architecture

Biophilic Tower: Biophilic Facade pages 110-115

All drawings and images ©Adrian Smith + Gordon Gill Architecture

FKI Tower: Multifaceted Facade pages 118-129

Photographs by Namgoong Sun pages 118, 125, 126, 128

All other drawings and images ©Adrian Smith + Gordon Gill Architecture

Burj Vista: Vista Facade pages 130-139

All drawings and images ©Adrian Smith + Gordon Gill Architecture

Kazakhstan Pavilion: Compound Curve Facade pages 140-157

Photographs by Leyla Kabdi pages 140, 156

Photograph by Nick Melnichenko page 141

Photographs by National Company Astana EXPO 2017 page 153, 157

All other drawings and images ©Adrian Smith + Gordon Gill Architecture

Waldorf Astoria Beijing: Frame Facade pages 158-169

Photographs by ShuHe Architectural Photography Studio page 158, 159, 161, 163, 166, 167, 168, 169

Photograph ©Hilton Brands Global Hospitality Company page 165

All other drawings and images ©Adrian Smith + Gordon Gill Architecture

Wuhan Greenland Center: Brise Soleil Shield Facade pages 170-185

Photograph by ©whhb123 page 171, 178, 185

Photograph by ©Keitma/shutterstock page 173

All other drawings and images ©Adrian Smith + Gordon Gill Architecture